dear elia

LETTERS FROM THE
ASIAN AMERICAN ABYSS

Duke University Press
Durham and London   2024

dear elia

mimi khúc

Printed in China on acid-free paper ∞
Project Editor: Liz Smith | Designed by Aimee C. Harrison
Typeset in Portrait Text and Helvetica Neue LT Std
by Copperline Book Services

Library of Congress Cataloging-in-Publication Data
Names: Khúc, Mimi, author.
Title: Dear Elia : letters from the Asian American abyss /
Mimi Khúc.
Description: Durham : Duke University Press, 2024. |
Includes bibliographical references and index.
Identifiers: LCCN 2023018777 (print)
LCCN 2023018778 (ebook)
ISBN 9781478025672 (paperback)
ISBN 9781478020936 (hardcover)
ISBN 9781478027799 (ebook)
Subjects: LCSH: Asian Americans—Mental health. | Asian
American students—Mental health. | Asian Americans—
Psychology. | COVID-19 Pandemic, 2020—United States. | Asian
Americans—Social conditions. | BISAC: SOCIAL SCIENCE /
Ethnic Studies / American / Asian American & Pacific Islander
Studies | SOCIAL SCIENCE / People with Disabilities
Classification: LCC RC451.5.A75 K483 2024 (print) | LCC
RC451.5.A75 (ebook) | DDC 362.1089/95073—dc23/eng/20230912
LC record available at https://lccn.loc.gov/2023018777
LC ebook record available at https://lccn.loc.gov/2023018778

Bird illustrations throughout by Matt Huynh.
Cover art: Vietnam, 2018. Photo by the author.

Publication of this book is supported by Duke University Press's
Scholars of Color First Book Fund.

Duke University Press gratefully acknowledges the Ford Foundation
U.S. Disability Rights Program, which provided funds toward the
publication of this book.

for elia

for students

for adjuncts

contents

Dear Elia,

Six years ago I made a box and told you to open in emergency. I told you it was an emergency already, because I had come to learn, as a daughter of refugees, as Vietnamese American, as Asian American, as a woman of color, as queer, as disabled, that the world makes us sick and we were not meant to survive it. I made that box for you as inheritance: an archive of Asian American unwellness and our attempts to move through that unwellness. I and your stepfather dreamed that box into being, filling it with hope and knowledge and tools, along with those of a whole community trying to make sense of this world so that you and others like you might learn how to save your own lives. To my greatest delight, that box went into the world and indeed began saving lives: magic.

In your hands now is a book. The goal remains the same: hope, knowledge, and tools to make sense of this world—everything I've learned in the years since making the box, everything the life of that box has taught me about the shape of our collective unwellnesses and what it means to hurt and build care and go on living while it hurts in these times, in this world. A central lesson of the box is that wellness is a lie; this book explores the breadth and depth of that lie as I've traveled across its vast domain, and then shows us that the only way to survive is to be unwell together.

I hope this book, like its predecessor, goes out into the world and saves lives. This too is your inheritance, my love. A box and a book, the kind of magic your mother has figured out how to make. May this magic help you understand all the ways the world will break your heart, and may it help you find joy and meaning and care throughout that journey. May it help you make your own magic, in all your glorious unwellness.

From my heart to yours, always,
mama

October 2022

Elia is pronounced EH-lee-uh.

1 a pedagogy of unwellness

Dear reader,

I don't write books. I make cool shit: unclassifiable hybrids that break genre and form to give us something we didn't know we need: tarot cards, curse-casting advent calendars, hacked DSMs, mental health pop-ups.[1] What I make is as much about play as reading and thinking, as much about feeling as understanding, imbued with the too-many feelings I have and know that others share. Theorize pain, but make it fun, and healing.

Academic books are not fun or healing.

This is a book that pretends to be an academic book. It's not an academic book in that it doesn't do what academic books do. It's unconnected to tenure or other forms of academic advancement. As a permanently contingent scholar, I don't have to write a tenure book. I have no way of getting tenure, a forever foothold in the academy, nor do I want to. Tenure books are the mechanism by which new scholars demonstrate their worthiness to be accepted into the academy writ small and large. Tenure books follow rules that uphold academic hierarchies and value systems. There are entire industries teaching new scholars these rules. This book doesn't follow those rules.

But this book *is* an academic book in that it does what an academic book *should* do: intervene in academic discourse, evaluate received knowledges, critically assess knowledge production, revolutionize higher ed pedagogy. It does these things with the further step of examining the academy itself as a central site of that knowledge production—and the work of decolonizing mental health. It just does all of this academic labor in weird ways.

Its genesis was Duke University Press editor Elizabeth Ault asking me if I was working on a book. "Why, yes!" I answered. *Now I am*, I thought to myself. As an adjunct, and because I found academic books a whole lot of not-fun, and because I couldn't imagine a scholarly press being capacious enough to value my work, which is artsy and irreverent, I had never considered writing a scholarly book. Until Elizabeth asked. Which made me ask myself: Do I *want* to write a scholarly book?

The answer was yes. Sort of.

In your hands is the only kind of scholarly book I would want to write. It is a work on mental health that draws on and intervenes in Asian American studies, a work of critical university studies from the vantage point of a disabled, unwell Asian American adjunct. It is a pedagogical treatise that reframes teaching and knowledge making as transformative care projects, a disability studies and disability justice grappling with our collective unwellness. It is also a book full of stories and feelings, both mine and yours, as you'll see. Theory in the flesh, mine and yours, so that we find our way through this thing called Life. We plumb what we know and feel, together. This book is a plea and a prayer that we all survive. It is a letter—to you, and my partner, and my daughter, whose name graces the cover. It is a letter to Asian American students, Asian American studies, Asian American community. It is a letter to help us imagine a future worth living in. It is a call to feeling. It is grief and hope together. It is an exit strategy.

This book can only do all these things by opting out of the academic book as genre and the tenure book as initiation and the university as good-faith project.

So here is a scholarly book that is an extension of my hybrid arts project on Asian American mental health, *Open in Emergency*, a sustained engagement with the same crucial questions that animated that first project: *What hurts? And how do we go on living while it hurts?* Through my conversations on mental health with students, scholars, artists, organizers, and community since *Open in Emergency*'s publication in 2016, I've realized that we all needed more time and space to ask and answer these questions. Elizabeth asked me, "Why a book now?" The honest answer is that *I* needed more time and space to dwell in these questions as well. An academic book that is not an academic book is the right form for this dwelling: time and space to directly engage questions of how we know what we think we know, while forcing us to face why we feel what we feel.[2]

Open in Emergency has its own thrilling life in the world now, beyond me, but I start with the story of its making here so you and I can build a foundation together of what it means to do mental health work. You may think you know what mental health is, but I'm here to tell you that what we've thought mental health is all along is actually killing us. It is part of what hurts. This book's central intervention is quite simple: the existing industry and scholarly understandings of mental health are part of the problem, and we need new frameworks to better identify and tend to our unwellness, together. To say it another way: we need to move away from the medical model of individual pathology toward a model focusing on larger structures of unwellness. Another way: psychology, psychiatry, clinical psychotherapy, university counseling centers, and popular discourses of wellness and self-care are all failing us, and their chief failures are along the axes of *race* and *ableism*. Or yet another way: this book offers something I call a *pedagogy of unwellness*, the understanding that we are all differentially unwell. By this I mean that we are unwell in different ways at different times, in relation to differentially disabling and enabling structures, and so we need differential care at all times. This is a disability studies, disability justice, and ethnic studies approach I developed while thinking specifically about Asian American mental health, but one that has grown outward to encompass an entire way of being in the world. A pedagogy of unwellness tells us that being unwell is not a failure, that our unwellness is not our fault, that we live in a world that differentially abandons us, that because of these things we deserve all the care imaginable.[3]

This chapter walks through the making of *Open in Emergency*, as well as its theoretical and formal interventions, in order to lay out this pedagogy of unwellness and begin exploring what that approach makes possible. The book goes on to trace the trajectory of my mental health work since *OiE*'s emergence. Chapter 2 reflects on what students have told me during my speaking tour across the country about their experiences at their respective universities—about what hurts, what they need, what they dream of. I would venture to say that I have visited more universities and listened to more students—in mental health workshops, discussions, meetings—than anyone else in Asian American studies or mental health over the last six years. This chapter is a dispatch from the field, a travelogue reporting on the state of student mental health, and Asian American student mental health in particular. It is also a close reading of the university as structure, revealing the cruel irony that university "wellness" makes students unwell. Chapter 3 examines the particular shape of Asian American suffering crafted in the Asian immigrant family. Here I reflect on what it has looked like for me over the past decade to try to teach thousands of Asian Americans about this shape, best learned through erin Khuê Ninh's work on the cost of raising model minorities, and how to imagine our way out of it. erin's work and my students' engagement with it over the years make clear there is a kind of Asian American parental love crafted and enacted in the merciless confines of model minoritization—and it kills.[4] Chapter 4 takes a closer look at the academy itself, locating unwellness in the story of meritocracy that we as professors have all imbibed and inflicted upon ourselves and each other—a story of racialized ableism that I argue is best told from the academic margins. Adjuncts are both the gears and waste product of the academic machinery, and we are all unwell because of it. The final chapter reflects on how my teaching has had to transform during the COVID-19 pandemic, responding to what I felt was an ethical mandate to deepen access and care in the classroom in times of crisis. Here I apply a pedagogy of unwellness to the classroom itself, examining my, our, attachments to particular forms of teaching and locating those forms in ideologies of merit and rigor and, yes, ableism. What we were all doing in the before-times was not all that accessible—or humane. Creating true access and care in the classroom requires some drastic upending.

In between the chapters you will find short interludes engaging you in reflection and writing and making. These interludes draw on the materials and insights of *Open in Emergency* to guide you in nurturing the kind of mental health we all need. This book itself is an expression of a pedagogy of unwellness, enacting for you, reader, the kind of care it describes. Its form invites you to explore your own unwellness alongside Asian Americans' and engage in new forms of care. You can approach the interludes as a separate set of activities to do at any time, but they are also meant to help move you from one chapter to the next, preparing you for the ideas and feeling work to come. Together the chapters and interludes ask you to sit with the question of what hurts, dwell as deeply as possible in Asian American unwellness, turn your gaze to structures shaping that unwellness—race, ableism, the university—and generate new understandings of what it means to care for ourselves and each other in a world that makes, and keeps, us unwell. I write letters, to you and others, in the hopes that we can figure out how to move through this world together in all of our unwellness and not feel alone.

Open in Emergency, published through The Asian American Literary Review (AALR), an arts antiprofit cofounded and directed by my partner, Lawrence-Minh Bùi Davis, is grounded in a pedagogy of unwellness.[5] It is a hybrid book arts project that engages the arts and humanities to generate new approaches to understanding wellness and unwellness in Asian American communities. It pushes us to move beyond the medical model of individual pathology, to reconceive mental health in the context of historical and structural violence—and in the context of community meaning making and practices of survival. It asks us to shift away from traditional models of wellness and unwellness that have historically been structured by whiteness, capitalism, and empire—and it engages critical arts practices while drawing on ethnic studies, critical disability studies, and queer of color feminist critique. We needed new tools, new knowledges. We needed to decolonize mental health. What might an antiracist and anti-ableist arts project on mental health look like? I gathered over seventy-five contributors across scholarly, arts, and organizing communities to answer this question, together.

Apparently, the answer is a box. A box containing six components: an editor's note from me in the form of a letter to my daughter; a hacked mock DSM: Asian American Edition exploring alternate modes of "diagnosis"; an original deck of tarot cards, created from Asian American knowledge production to reveal the structural forces shaping our lives; handwritten daughter-to-mother letters tracing both intimacies and violences in our families; a redacted, rewritten pamphlet on postpartum depression to intervene in medical knowledge dissemination; and a tapestry poster of collective wounds gathered from across the Asian American community. Together these pieces form a love letter, from my partner to me, from me to my daughter, from our family to the larger Asian American community, from Asian Americans to each other. A letter to make visible and care for wounds. A letter to collectively imagine how to dwell in unwellness and care together, for all our sakes.

The response to the project was shocking. Our summer 2016 Kickstarter generated $10,000 in two days and $23,000 by the end of the month-long campaign. We were bombarded by inquiries and orders on a daily basis. Since its publication, the issue has been taught in so many classrooms I've lost count. I've talked to thousands of students, scholars, artists, and organizers about its interventions. Our initial print run sold out in a year, and the requests continued to pour in afterward, so in 2019, we worked to create an expanded second edition, paying attention to community responses to identify gaps and then curating over a dozen new pieces. After many a pandemic delay, we finally launched the second edition in late 2020. By that time, pandemic stress and trauma and stark anti-Asian violence made it all the more urgent and necessary.

But I am getting ahead of myself. Let me try to start at the beginning.

Dear anh,

Do you remember the exact moment we conceived of *Open in Emergency*? I don't. I remember the energy and excitement of what felt like never-ending conversation, near-constant exploration of ideas, across dinner tables, on the couch, on the phone, in writing, in bed. The journey of this project is intertwined with the journey of us, too easily forgotten now. Summer 2013 we fell in love in letters. That first month we wrote forty-page journals for each other; the six months after, we exchanged weekly ten-page journals. I did not know I could dream like this. I did not know this kind of becoming was possible.

You've said that *Open in Emergency* was your love letter to me. You trusted me with an entire special issue, the most ambitious and wildly expensive in the journal's history; I had never edited a project before. What in the world made you think I could create a whole gigantic new thing? As a mentor once said, sometimes you have to have faith in others' faith in you. I did not know if I could do this thing, but you did, and so I trusted you and leaned into your rock-steady faith.

Open in Emergency has changed the face of Asian American mental health, of critical disability studies, even of Asian American literary arts. It has changed our lives, too.

Dear reader,

Let me remember back to an even earlier beginning, before *Open in Emergency*, before my partner.

In 2011, I became a mother. And I became deeply unwell.

At the time I still believed in aspirational wellness, that we are supposed to strive toward something we're told is "normal" and "healthy," and that deviations from those are pathological, to be fixed.[6] And so when I spiraled into postpartum depression in my daughter's fourth month, ninth month, tenth month, I thought: *Something is wrong with me. I want to die; something must be wrong with me.*

Time felt like quicksand, a trap that held me in place, slowly, inevitably, dragging me under. Life with a new baby was a never-ending routine of tedium and exhaustion. Where was the joy that was promised, expected? Failure to be a good mother, to have the correct experience of motherhood, is not something that one experiences once but unendingly—every moment of every day, waking and sleeping. The time of failed personhood, as erin Khuê Ninh has taught me in her work on daughterly failure in Asian immigrant families, does not end.

It is not once that you are the wrong kind of person but every day. This kind of failure is all-encompassing, endless, forever: a kind of crip time that I had no name for then.[7] An endless suspension in failure, even as every day you are trying to "do" your way out. There is no way out.

Unless you realize the game is rigged.

As I began to build structures to make life feel more livable for myself, through the help of my then-partner/coparent and family members, as I read books on postpartum depression, and, most importantly, as I began applying my training in Asian American studies and queer women of color feminism to my own personal experience, I stepped outside of what I would later name "the imperative of wellness" and "compulsory wellness," and began to examine it. I began to see the structures that shape well-being—both how we experience it and how we think about it.

Because the stories I had been told—that mothers are supposed to sacrifice, that they do not and should not need, that Asian Americans can belong in the United States only through assimilation and respectability and model minoritization, that Vietnamese Americans are resilient survivors of the worst kinds of war and refugee trauma—were not only wrong but also the very structures that shaped why life felt unlivable for me. And so I turned my eye to these stories and asked where they came from, and how they harm. I asked, what else is hurting us, invisibly, that we internalize as individual pathology to be individually overcome? I asked, what alternative stories might we tell about ourselves, about our suffering and our healing, and what new languages would we need to do so?

⸻

Dear anh,

I always say falling in love with you was like being struck by lightning. Sudden, all-consuming. Almost painful in its intensity. We called it "drunk love" that summer. Intoxication not simply with each other but with the magic that emerged from us being together.

We make magic. Asian American tarot cards and a new kind of tarot practice for mental health that cultivates alternative ways of knowing and being. We also make magic in that we do what often seems impossible or unimaginable to others. We generate ideas outside of existing channels, and we bring those ideas to life in unexpected ways. And the things we put out into the world often seem mysteriously magical to others—creations puffed into being from nothing. I remember asking erin to reflect in an interview on the making of *Open in Emergency* as one of its guest curators, and she said, "All I remember is that one day we were all crying in a tiny room at AAAS, and then next there was this box full of treats on my doorstep."

But *Open in Emergency* wasn't made in one poof of magic. That afternoon of crying at the Association for Asian American Studies conference and the box arriving on erin's doorstep are both distinct moments in the three-year process of *Open in Emergency*'s creation, each marking an important part of what it means to do intellectual and artistic work through a process of community curation.

Dear reader,

I began teaching at the University of Maryland in 2009 as a PhD candidate, returning to my undergrad alma mater and the program that first introduced me to Asian American studies.[8] I remember walking into the office and meeting two fellow grad students, one dressed very seriously in shirt and tie who quietly and shyly said hi to me. *Who is this white guy teaching Asian American studies?* I thought. I learned very quickly that this person, who would later become my partner, was not white, though I would continue to think of him as quiet and shy for many years. (He is neither quiet nor shy, reader.)

In 2013, after finishing the dissertation, I began teaching more in the program. I developed a new course that quickly became popular: Growing Up Asian American: The Asian Immigrant Family and the Second Generation. I opened the course, as I now do with almost all my courses, with Eliza Noh's "A Letter to My Sister," written under the pseudonym Lisa Park: a letter to her sister who killed herself that names structural violence as culprit. This course opened with Asian American suicide, because those are the stakes, and Eliza's letter reveals not only the fact of unlivability for second-generation Asian Americans but the racialized and gendered conditions that create that unlivability. This gave my students permission to admit out loud that their lives felt unlivable sometimes, all the time, too. I told my students the point of a college course is to transform you—you should grow and have more tools for making sense of your life, or else that course has failed you. They agreed to embark on a journey with me, examining immigrant family power dynamics, racialized narratives of conditional belonging, normative gender and sexuality. Students' final projects were to create workshops that applied course concepts to their own lives and to the lives of those around them; they were to choose what mattered most to them and then create a public program that would help others engage those issues. Some would go on to stage these programs outside the course. We were figuring out, together, how to make life more livable, for all of us.[9]

My students were the first community to whom I felt an urgent need to be accountable. Their lives were at stake. Any work to address suffering among Asian Americans would need to look directly at student life and student death and not flinch. Asian Americans have the highest rates of suicidal ideation among college students by race.[10] The idea for *Open in Emergency* was first conceived in my classrooms because my students were dying, and they needed me, us, to see.

And we need to see more than just the suicide attempts, more than the breakdowns, the institutionalizations, the medical leaves, the dropping out. We need to see the slow dying that precedes these moments of acute crisis. The slow violence of model minoritization, the strangling of personhood, the endless time of constant failure.[11] The slow death of not being enough. What kind of project could capture and address this?

I asked my students.

And after I asked my students, we asked our Asian American studies colleagues. And then we asked Asian American writers and artists and community organizers. And then we all dreamed together.

The crying session erin reminisced about was at the 2015 conference of the Association for Asian American Studies, the second AAAS dreaming session we organized. There were forty-plus people crammed in a tiny room, probably no more than 12 × 12, designed for intimate conversation for fifteen or twenty. We moved the chairs to the outer edges. The audience mostly sat on the floor in the center, covering every inch of the dingy carpet (including Lawrence, who proclaimed his pants were too tight). As the panelists began sharing their stories, there was a domino effect of tears. I remember Eliza weeping, talking about her updated letter to her sister, twenty years after her sister's suicide. erin wept, talking about how Eliza's work has so powerfully impacted her own. Jim Lee was solemn, as he usually is.[12] I cried silently, on and off. Audience members shared stories as well, the conversation, and tears, moving seamlessly throughout the room. Everyone remembers this session. They don't remember what exactly was said, but they remember how it felt. Countless folks have invariably brought it up to me over the years.

Chad Shomura's work in *Open in Emergency*, "ChadCat's Corner of Heart-to-Hearts," helps me rethink this moment in terms of public feelings. What kinds of feeling are allowed in what kinds of spaces? What is appropriate feeling (and expression of feeling)? There is not supposed to be crying at academic conferences, at least not in the formal sessions. (Grad students on the job market can cry but only in the privacy of their shared hotel rooms!) What does it look like to inject feeling, to give permission for feeling, in a space like an academic conference? What stakes reveal themselves? And what people begin to matter, differently? Whose feelings get to matter? And what modes of inquiry are suddenly opened up? This session, and others that we hosted afterward, were not simply theoretical or disciplinary interventions—they were affective, too.[13]

We held more dreaming sessions, some with students, some with writers and artists, some formal as at AAAS, some more informal over dinners. The dreaming sessions were an important part of community curation: creating structures to have community engage the process of knowledge making and cultural production. These sessions enabled a kind of listening to discover the shape and scope of community pain and community needs. This takes time. But it also needs structures that interrupt the kind of usual time people move in. Public feeling is an interruption of not only public space but also the kinds of time we allot ourselves for feeling—and what kinds of feeling are appropriate and not appropriate at particular times. Dreaming sessions, the prompts that we designed, the kinds of conversation we stewarded, asked people to disrupt compulsory wellness—the need to pretend we are all okay and functioning and being productive—to *stop* being productive and to *dwell* in our unwellness. To take time to hurt.

What we learned:

- We are all differentially unwell. We are all unwell in relation to the various structures that shape our lives. Unwellness must be understood in relation to structures of violence. Wellness—that universal ideal we are all striving for, or think we already have and can keep—is a lie.
- Asian American suffering is tied to Asian American racialization, and any project that wants to capture the scope and shape of our suffering must investigate the kinds of personhood we are being forced to become.
- When given permission, when structurally enabled, people will tell you what hurts. People are already dreaming different ways of being, are already working to care for themselves and others. Psychology and psychiatry have led us to think they are the only authorities on

something called mental health, but our communities have existed long before those inventions, have struggled with the worst that humanity does to itself, have developed knowledge (ways of knowing and ways of being) and temporalities (time for feeling and time for care) in response.

- Psychology and psychiatry have failed, are failing, our communities spectacularly. These fields dominate our understandings of and approaches to mental health, but they are medical models of individual pathology, relying on and reifying social constructions of "disorders," and fueling industries structured by disparity and injustice. There is knowledge to be had and help to be found in these fields, but they cannot be the only way, or even the primary way, to name and tend to what hurts. They miss so much and do so much harm. If we already know that our subjectivities are intersectional, our personhoods complex, then why wouldn't our hurts—and the care we need—be too?
- We need new, different languages for what hurts.

So we made a box.

<hr>

CONTENT WARNING: mentions of suicidal ideation

Dear Elia,

Sometimes I think of killing myself. I can remember two moments clearly. One, lying in bed next to your tiny always-needing body, exhausted, sleep-deprived for months, seeing no way out, there was no way out. Two, sitting on the edge of the bed as your father walked out of the room, out of my life, a disembowelment, my dreams of love, partnership, family, spilling out onto the floor from somewhere in my middle.

I still have flashes. Moments when I imagine slicing my wrist, the acute burn of the cut, the relief of not feeling anymore.

You have always kept me here. Resentfully so at first. And now, a life preserver. An anchor. A mission.

This thing called Life is no fucking joke. The world is built on our backs, our wombs, our tears, but it was not made for us. And yet I claim it for us.

Auntie Eliza writes, "The Asian model minority is not doing well." I am not doing well. I'm writing you this letter because I need you to see the crisis that is Asian American life. The civilizing terror that is model minoritization, the neoliberal American Dream.

Madness as the psychic life of living under siege. I'm writing you to tell you the lie of the thing called wellness.

My child, the world makes us sick. And then tells us it is our fault. Sickness as individual pathology, a lack of ability or will to "achieve" wellness. The world tells us what wellness looks like, marks it as normal. Moral. Like whiteness, wellness as an ideal to strive for, a state of being in constant performance. Invisibilized structures holding up bodies and persons—certain bodies, certain persons. Invisibilized structures tearing apart other bodies, other persons.

Your worth is not tied to how "well" you can perform racialized capitalist productivity or gendered constructions of the self-made/martyring/sacrificing woman-mother or what Auntie erin calls the debt-bound daughter, parental sacrifice exchanged for daughterly personhood. People are not to be measured by their usefulness, their ability to perform "health," their proximity to racialized gendered ideals, their fulfillment of neoliberal dreams. I need you to understand that we are all differentially unwell, that people are vulnerable, made vulnerable, kept vulnerable. That our vulnerabilities are both our death and our life. That our vulnerabilities link us, connect us, in a web of death and survival.

This thing called Life is no joke, my sweet child. It is okay to hurt. We must allow ourselves to hurt, to trace the losses, the heartbreak, the death. We must allow ourselves to be whole people, in all our brokenness. Our lives as always negotiating violence, trauma, crises of meaning. Our lives as always finding new ways of making meaning, making community. I tell you this to free you, but also to show you how to allow others to be free.

In your hands is a project I dreamed, for me and for you. For the brokenness we all share, so different and so similar. I dreamed this project to save my own life. To help others save their own lives. To help you save yours.

Open in emergency, my darling child.

It's an emergency. Right now.[14]

Dear anh,

I remember that we came up with the pieces first. We knew there were going to be multiple parts. We knew that we needed different forms to address different aspects of Asian American mental health.

Different forms. Thinking with you helped me to reflect on the role of form in intellectual and cultural production. Not everything has to be an academic book. In fact, the academic book may be the *least* generative form for some of the issues we wanted to address. Received, calcified, tradition-bound forms limit knowledge and meaning making; they silo and encourage individual labor, neoliberal conceptions of the self, and ideologies of merit.

And within these conceptions and ideologies lie normative bounds of time: the academic book stands not only as the pinnacle of knowledge production, it is also how we measure our professional trajectories, our careers—what "real" scholarship looks like and how long it takes, what a real scholar must go through and achieve to be legitimate (and tenured). The correct amount (and kind) of productivity over the correct amount of time. *How's the book coming along?* we ask each other. *Which presses and editors are you talking to? Do you have a contract?* And most important: *Will the book come out in time for when you go up for tenure?* To reject existing forms is to recognize their constraints and limitations in and of themselves but also their naturalization as process.

The first form we decided on was the tarot cards. Our friend, Long Bùi, a force unto himself, was doing spectacular tarot readings during "downtime" at AAAS in 2014 in San Francisco. They were deeply uncanny and meaningful. Long is not fucking around when he does divination! Fortune-telling, a practice familiar to both of us through our viet families, is also a practice that my inner religious studies scholar has an analytical eye for. Here was Long, a trained scholar himself, doing magic, something the academy allows us to study but does not recognize as a legitimate form of knowledge making. Tarot did not happen in the official AAAS program; it happened in the cracks of the conference, giving us something the official conference could not. A way of being vulnerable, making alternative sense of our lives, connecting to our colleagues beyond intellectual work and academic rank and professional development—to be more fully human. To understand our wellness and unwellness in new ways. This was care and knowledge, wrapped into one, with all the makings of critical cultural work. And so I said to myself and to you, how much more powerful would this be if the cards being used were not Italian medieval playing cards that had been repurposed as divination tools—that is, white as fuck—but cards made by Asian Americans, for Asian Americans, drawing on Asian American knowledge production, especially Asian American studies? How much more useful would they be if they could provide not "universal" (again, i.e., white as fuck) frameworks of analysis but ones grounded in the kinds of critical knowledges that ethnic studies has developed? And how much more useful would the critical knowledges of ethnic studies be if crafted into this new form? How might an Asian Americanist tarot project open up how Asian Americanist "theory" is generated and deployed—where, when, and for whom? How might we be able to broaden access to Asian American studies, circulating its work through new channels to new recipients?

Dear reader,

I have many favorites from the tarot deck, but perhaps the ones that surprise the most demonstrate the project of mutual faith between writer, artist, and editor best. Jim Lee's card, The Hangman, surprised him, I think, which is how our editorial magic works. When I first told Jim about this tarot idea, he was wary. Maybe too whimsical, he warned. But I asked him to trust me, and then I tasked him with writing The Hangman, a play on an archetype from the original tarot. I gave him the prompt we developed for all our tarot writers, a kind of Mad Libs that asked them to generate meaning and interpretive tools for their archetype. He promptly ignored the Mad Libs and wrote a stunning theoretical and affective intervention in what it means to suffer and die in relation to structural violence in community.

The Hangman: Art by Camille Chew, Text by James Kyung-Jin Lee

See plates 1 and 2 for full card

The Hangman is the twenty-first card in the major arcana. The Hangman is the body rent asunder by the violence of empire, racism, patriarchy, and ableism. As people pass him hanging there, they thank God that they are not him, until they are. Then, they begin to think differently about this hanged body, because theirs is being hoisted and harnessed to their own suffering borne of empire, racism, patriarchy, age, everyday violence, bodily failure. Then they realize that she who seemed so alone as she hangs there was in fact not so, but instead hung there as witness to the violence but not fully consumed by it. Because even here, in the cataclysm of her hanging, another witnesses her in her suffering and thus liberates her suffering for an altogether different—dare we say—utopian impulse. And so now, they, who are also being hanged, can join in a community of sufferers, a brotherhood and sisterhood who bear the marks of pain, and invite others into such solidarity, so that when they, when we, meet our ends, we will know that we are surely not alone. Receiving this card may feel like the worst fate imaginable, but take heart! The very cosmos weeps with you.

I chose Jim, an Asian American studies and disability studies scholar and an Episcopal priest, for this card because of its Christian origins and my faith in Jim to reclaim this Christian image and its related theologies for the social justice needs of today. I trusted in Jim's theological and scholarly dexterity to make us rethink what a hanged man means for us now, in complex and ethical ways. And so here we have hanging as manifestation of structural violence, of "empire, racism, patriarchy, ableism." And we have witness as first a process of distancing oneself from victimhood but then recognizing oneself in another's suffering, recognizing one's own suffering as intimately connected to another's, and then building community through this connection. This card asks us to take the time to witness each other's suffering, and our own, because that is the only way to not be alone.

Open in Emergency would find several other interventional forms. Reader, we made our own DSM. We were brainstorming how to hold together all the essays, stories, and visual work that we wanted, trying to think of a form that was and wasn't a book. A regular anthology wouldn't do any theoretical or interventional work on the level of form. Unless it was our own DSM.

The *Diagnostic and Statistical Manual of Mental Disorders* is the psychiatric "bible," the book that is supposed to tell us everything about what mental illness is. The book to diagnose, evaluate, treat. A repository for all things mental health. What would it look like to make our own? By, for, about Asian Americans. What would it look like to allow our community to diagnose our own suffering and develop our own healing?

We decided to make ours a *hacked* DSM — a DSM in which we had torn out all the pages and inserted our own. Because even if the American Psychiatric Association actually made an Asian American Edition of the DSM (this obviously does not actually exist), it would be absolutely terrible. Not to say there aren't individual psychologists and psychiatrists and therapists who do the work of developing their individual practice in terms of understanding race — but as field and industry, psychology and psychiatry remain not only uninterested in but actually disdainful of the knowledge produced in the arts and humanities, which is where much of the most complex and important work on racialization happens.[15] And they hold tightly to their dominance of the territory called mental health.

Hacking disrupts this dominance. It asserts that power must be interrogated and intervened in. It takes back authority, places it in the hands of those not normally allowed to access it. It is unauthorized authoring. It does not reform but revolutionizes. We hacked the DSM to discover and offer new languages for our suffering and new models for care. In more academic terms: we hacked the DSM to enable marginalized epistemologies and ontologies, marginalized ways of knowing and ways of being in the world, and marginalized temporalities, nonnormative time.

But this would of course be deeply threatening to the psychological and psychiatric establishment. A *DSM* out of the hands of those who claim not only the highest expertise on mental health but often the *only* expertise—and in the hands of those intentionally kept outside the bounds of expertise. In late 2016, as we were finishing up production of *Open in Emergency* and readying for its launch, we sent out an excited announcement to our networks: it's finished, and it's coming soon! We immediately received the following email from an Asian American psychiatrist—who had not yet read the issue, only our announcement:

Dear Editors:

As someone who has devoted my life to bettering mental health, who also shares great concerns for the Asian-American community, and a writer myself, I was initially very excited to see your special issue-project on Asian-American Mental Health. However, I'm somewhat concerned about the otherwise impressive list of contributors and sponsors in that, except for one Mental Health organization, **I don't think I see anyone who seems formally/directly involved in mental health care itself: like a department of psychiatry or psychology or a licensed professional** in that regard. I could be wrong; I haven't looked through everyone named on that list, but if that's actually the case, **it seems like a huge missed opportunity for direct outreach and collaboration with providers who could actually bridge the well-known gap and stigma between Asians and mental health care**. I realize the project was mainly literary-artistic in intention, and probably a gathering of first-person stories, and as a literary writer myself, I love and respect that idea, and have written several pieces in that vein myself. But when I see a rewritten *DSM* as one topic, even if tongue-in-cheek or as a cultural critique, **I really hope that the information you're disseminating has some basis in actual psychiatric/psychological research and science.** There is so much misinformation and stigma out there about mental health as it is, particularly among the Asian community, that **I would hope this project involved some discussion and collaboration with those who have actual scientific expertise** on a complex and rigorous subject.

My questions/concerns might be moot since I admit I have not read the issue itself yet; I'm just asking ahead of time for any future initiatives you may be pursuing for mental health, that you make sure to include/reach out to the extensive mental health provider and academic community (and although there aren't enough, there are Asian ones out there!), which will ensure Asian-Americans whose mental health needs are so often ignored/ neglected get the appropriate resources they need.

Best wishes,
Clinical Assistant Professor of Psychiatry[16]

I've shared this email in talks I've given about *Open in Emergency*, and as I like to say in my talks: as good humanities scholars, *let's close-read this together*. What are the assumptions and assertions? That psychologists and psychiatrists and "licensed professionals" are the only experts, the only people who can "actually" address the gap between Asian Americans and mental health care. That science is the foundation of knowledge, and information should only come from those engaged in scientific research. That a collaborative work cannot be responsible or valuable without engaging the true experts of mental health, the scientists. That art and literature are reducible to "a gathering of first-person stories"—which of course doesn't have the value of "actual research." Audiences love noting how many times "actual" appears in the email. And they enjoy seeing the power of the humanities in action—we use our close-reading skills to unpack what exactly is being said about mental health and who is and isn't allowed to do work on it.

And then my partner's magnificent response, which I've also shared in talks, to audiences' (and his) extreme satisfaction:

We hear and understand and admire—and share—your concern about how responsibly any project that tackles Asian American mental health takes its work. We're happy to engage in a conversation about what constitutes responsibility—it's a question the special issue means to address directly. Some of the language in your message—and please correct me if I'm wrong on any of the assumptions I'm making here—suggests we hold pretty different notions. AALR is not of the mind that psychological research is the only or even best form of knowledge production when it comes to mental health; so much space has been given to that form of production, and our aim is precisely to make more space for other forms, work by visual artists, literary writers, practitioners, survivors, and non-psychiatry/psychology scholars. We also want to draw attention to the limitations and failures of psychology as field and industry—when it comes to its incomplete and sometimes violent lenses on race, and queer and trans experience, for instance.

"Checking our credentials" to make sure we are including psychologists/psychiatrists and materials based in actual psychiatric/psychological research is pretty clearly privileging one form of knowledge production over others, and it feels like an invalidation of other forms, as well as the people and communities for whom those forms are important. There is a difference between asking for accountability and policing what counts as valid/who gets to speak.[17]

The psychiatrist was very unhappy with this response, claiming she approached us in good faith and we responded with defensiveness. Indeed, she doubled down on her fragility, attacking us for so-called hostility. What audiences have found so satisfying is the process of making this fragility visible, of demonstrating psychiatry's grasp for power—and calling it out. They especially enjoy taking authority back from this psychiatrist—this so-called expert does not understand the basic workings of discourse, of the politics of knowledge that she was engaging, something a humanities training would possibly have enabled her to do. I'm sure this psychiatrist, whom we never heard from again and who requested that we never write to her again, would be even more unhappy if she knew I was close-reading her email in public talks and now here in this book. But this email exchange is so wonderfully demonstrative of how so-called experts dominate mental health discourse and why an arts and humanities intervention is challenging, in both senses: it challenges the singular dominance of psychiatry, and it is incredibly difficult to do because of that. And this exchange is suggestive of why this kind of intervention is so necessary.

Had this psychiatrist actually read our DSM, she likely would not have been reassured—she would probably have been even more disturbed. Because within the pages of what we call our DSM are essays and stories and visual art and interactive care activities that directly challenge what we've been told mental health is and how one is to achieve it. Most threatening is a critical disability studies and disability justice critique of ableism that destabilizes psychology and psychiatry's definition of mental health and its (racialized) imperative of wellness.

Kai Cheng Thom in her essay "The Myth of Mental Health" examines the World Health Organization's definition of mental health, interrogating its focus on productivity as measure or marker of mental well-being. For WHO, the point of wellness, and how one measures it, is the ability to work.[18] This conflation of mental health and productivity is deeply troubling, requiring that we reflect intentionally on what we actually mean when we say mental health. I've asked thousands of people over the last few years what mental health means to them. Almost none have said "the ability to work." Then I've shown these thousands of people the WHO definition, and while there is collective disapproval and rejection, there is also recognition. This idea of mental health is familiar to everyone; we are always being measured by our ability to work, our ability to appear "normal" and acceptable in a culture that conflates wellness, idealness, and productivity.[19]

So, if mental health is measured by the ability to be productive and "contribute" to society (in correct ways), then failures of mind (and body) lead to failures of labor lead to failures of contribution lead to failures of personhood.

The failure of personhood, as we've already learned, is endless.

But if unwellness were not failure, if it were not measured by productivity and societal contribution but simply by how unlivable life feels, then perhaps we would be allowed to be as unwell as we need to be—and then ask for as much care as we need to make life feel more livable. In *Open in Emergency*, Johanna Hedva asks us to identify as sick, as a sick woman, because if we think wellness is the norm and requires nothing to sustain itself, then we think sickness is temporary—and so then must be care. The imperative of wellness produces the lack of care; it pathologizes unwellness and thus structures of care as well. We should need care only intermittently; we should fail only sometimes, and only for the right reasons, and even then, perhaps we should be sorry for how we need, how we burden.

A pedagogy of unwellness asks that we all dwell in an unwell temporality, a crip time, together. It requires a commitment to doing intellectual, artistic community work from a recognition of our differential unwellness. To look at what hurts, and to understand that hurt within both structures of violence and structures of care. To continually gauge capacity and need for each community member and respond by creating shifting structures to address those capacities and needs. What does continually holding space for our mental unwellness look like? What would continual mental health care look like? What if instead of parsing out "appropriate" amounts of time for care—and clearly demarcating those periods from the rest of "normal" life—we thought of care as a continuous, unending communal and individual responsibility?

What if we were all personhoods in the endless time of failure?

And what does healing look like in this endless moment of care? Surely not teleological, a trajectory toward some elusive wholeness we're supposed to be able to achieve and then effortlessly maintain to be recognized as human. Surely the time of healing is not linear, nor is it circular. Because if we are always differentially unwell, and always deserving of care, then healing is the endless process of care by which we try to make life feel more livable, in all the ways we need, whenever we need.

––––––––––––

Open in Emergency sold out by the beginning of 2018—but requests came unabated throughout that year. We began dreaming of a second edition: a chance not only to reach more people but also to expand the work itself, taking into account all the conversations I had had on the road with students, colleagues, survivors, community organizers.

For what we affectionately call "*OiE* 2.0," we curated six new DSM entries and seven new tarot cards. Two new DSM entries engage the official fifth edition of the American Psychiatric Association's DSM, hacking several of its entries through poetry. We hadn't felt the need to address the actual text of the APA's DSM in the first edition, but after hearing from folks about its power over their lives, we decided it was important to write into its contents directly. We generated new archetypes for the tarot deck, two through an open contest, The Village and The Mongrel. Another new card, The Student, we created through a student curation process, soliciting ideas, concepts, and language from students while on my speaking tour, then having a student editorial team at AALR synthesize the material. Lawrence and I would finalize the card, agonizing over each word. I share it in chapter 2; perhaps it will do justice to your pain as well.

May *OiE* continue to grow to meet the needs of those whose hands, and hearts, it reaches.

––––––––––––

Reader,

We had no idea what we were getting ourselves into when we started this journey of making *Open in Emergency*, a journey of making mental health. We had no idea of the thing we would produce and the way people would respond to it. We had no idea it would propel me to become a leading voice in mental health, in Asian American studies, in disability studies. We had no idea it would save so many lives. We just knew we had to do it.

This book chronicles the life of *Open in Emergency* and, since its publication, my mental health work to track unwellness and map the changing landscape of mental health discourse. The language of wellness now suffuses almost every space I encounter. *Everyone* is talking about mental health. It has become a buzzword to signal an institution's care for its members, a corporation's commitment to its workers. But beyond that, mental health is going through a profound transformation on the ground. People in organizing spaces, in community spaces, in student spaces, and yes even in workplaces want to directly engage issues of mental health. They are openly looking for resources, openly creating spaces of conversation, openly exploring new ways of supporting each other. They are *doing* mental health, and they are doing it differently than ever before. This is a quiet revolution we should be paying attention to, and nurturing. This book is part of that revolution, and it invites you into that same terrifying and brave work of changing how you do mental health.

The last decade has been punctuated by several acute crises of care at the national (and global) level: anti-Black police violence and the birth of Black Lives Matter; right-wing fascism in the Trump presidency and its followers; sudden widespread awareness of sexual violence through the #MeToo movement; and the onset of a global pandemic, which has led to its own spiral of crises, including the pandemic's differential burden on BIPOC and disabled communities, increased anti-Asian violence, political battles over mitigation strategies and testing and vaccines, and of course infrastructural collapses in health care, education, and the economy. What is mental health in the context of the lack of structural care? In the context of structural *un*caring? Some may argue we have created more structures of care in response to these crises, and they would not be wrong. But are we actually in a time of greater care now? We are definitely in a time of greater death. At the time of this writing in early 2022, COVID deaths in the United States total well over 900,000. That count will easily be over one million by the time this book is out. The mortality numbers alone should tell us there is not enough care, for the dead and dying or their loved ones. In the context of all of these crises, I want to reflect on what we are saying about care, what we think about it, how we are building and accessing it—and where institutional care is continuing to fail us. I want to track how we have been unwell, how we continue to be unwell, how we make each other unwell, so that we can carefully and responsibly build the kinds of care we need. All of this is the work that is left out of but must be made central to what we call mental health.

It's work that's not as hard as it used to be. Students today are well versed in the languages of self-care and wellness, impressively and alarmingly so. The popular idea that Asian Americans don't talk about mental health isn't true. I'm not sure if it ever was, but it definitely is not true of the millennial and Z generations. They are talking; many of us just aren't listening. That is partly because we don't know how. Here the academy is actually behind. Academic work on mental health has been the strict purview of the social sciences and medicine, of psychology and psychiatry—and those tools as they have been crafted historically are just too limited to capture and theorize what is happening on the ground. This book comes out of a project of listening, first and foremost, to the unwellness of students. I have continued over the years to keep an eye (ear?) on what students are saying and feeling and doing, because I have learned that students are both the canaries in the coal mine and the revolutionaries calling for the mine to be shut down. But I am not simply an observer in this story; I'm also an agent, actively nurturing new languages of mental health wherever I go, supporting and catalyzing student movements. *Open in Emergency* was an intervention. My work since its publication is fundamentally interventional. This book is another intervention, a deep theorization of Asian American unwellness at the intersections of ableism and model minoritization. In the book you will find a steady through line of what it looks like to approach mental health through a pedagogy of unwellness and disability studies/justice, but also critical university studies through the lens of mental health, mental health through the lens of critical university studies, and both mental health and critical university studies through the lens of racialization. I chronicle unwellness and care as I've engaged them over the last decade at the meeting place of these frameworks in the hopes of illuminating a way forward for all of us.

My partner and I made *Open in Emergency* to dwell in the oft-obscured collective unwellness of our communities, the invisible and invisibilized crisis of Asian American mental health, to dwell with each other in that unwellness, so that we could be fully human, so that we could know we are not alone. So that our beloveds could know they are not alone. I've written this book to keep dwelling, with you.

Reader: you are not alone.

interlude 1
the corner

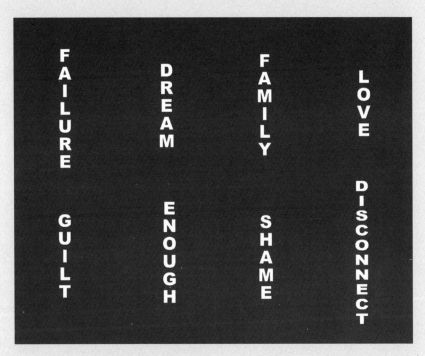

FAILURE
GUILT

DREAM
ENOUGH

FAMILY
SHAME

LOVE
DISCONNECT

[Inter1.1] From "ChadCat's Corner of Heart-to-Hearts" in the DSM: Asian American Edition of Open in Emergency.

Welcome to the Corner of Heart-to-Hearts.

Choose one word and discuss whatever that word brings to mind with a friend or loved one or stranger, taking turns talking for two minutes each while the other person just listens. Or do one with me. Read my reflection below, and pen one of your own for two to five minutes, on the same word or a different one, and send it to me.

On failure. I'm setting my timer for five minutes, now.

I've always been so afraid of failure. To fail, to be bad at something. Growing up, I would do only things I excelled at, only if I was sure I would succeed. My partner says praise is my love language, and that's because I need heaps of it. I need constant reminders that I am not a failure, that I did something good, am something good.

But praise is double edged. Sometimes I worry I don't deserve the praise. I worry I'm a fraud and those praising me will discover that I'm not who they think I am. *Open in Emergency*'s immediate success actually made me even more afraid of failure at first. What if everyone realizes I'm not actually as smart and amazing as they keep saying I am?

Praise that focuses on my achievements is both salve and poison. *Accomplish something—something remarkable—and you are worth something.* The model minority runs deep. It sometimes feels inescapable.

I tell others to embrace failure, embrace being "bad," to reject these racist and ableist and capitalist systems of (de)valuation—and, truth is, I'm still working on this myself. Every day.

———

Now you go.

———

Chad Shomura designed the Corner of Heart-to-Hearts as a public feelings project, an activity nurturing intentional vulnerability to reclaim the public space as one for intimacy and to disrupt the everyday experience (and rules) of feelings—what kinds of feelings we're allowed to have and when and where. He published the Corner with AALR in *Open in Emergency* in our hacked DSM: *Asian American Edition*, and I first experienced it in real time when he staged a Corner in CTRL+ALT: *A Culture Lab on Imagined Futures*, a pop-up exhibition hosted by the Smithsonian Asian Pacific American Center in downtown Manhattan in late 2016. Small tables were scattered with prompts, Corner cards, notepaper, and pens. Visitors perused, sitting down for a few minutes or an hour, in twos and threes and fours. I sat down with my then-five-year-old daughter, mostly to rest during the bustle of the event, and she picked up cards curiously. "What does 'shame' mean, mama?"

Uhh—how the fuck do I explain shame to a five-year-old?! But then I emerged from my initial panic, realizing that she already knows what shame is. She's already felt shame, been shamed. Because kindergarteners are assholes. She has seen, heard, felt the terrible things kids say to each other as they test out their growing sociality. This was not an introduction to the feeling of shame; this was an introduction to the concept and name. It was the beginning of what I realized would need to be a lifelong conversation, perhaps one of the most important of her life, so that she might know the forces that attempt to make her smaller, make her doubt herself, and find ways to live despite them.

Next she asked about *family*. Then *loss*. There were several more I can no longer remember, each unlocking a conversation that I should've already been having with her as a parent but hadn't been, a conversation that no structures in our lives had enabled. Until the Corner.

Right now you're likely doing the Corner in the private space of your home, not somewhere public. Does it still break open something new? How does it feel to try to form intimacy over whatever platform you are using—phone, Zoom, text, email, in person? Was there a reason you chose the word you did, or did you choose at random? What was it like to be intentionally vulnerable with your Heart-to-Hearts partner, to talk and be listened to, to listen without interrupting? What did you learn? What surprised you?

Now try the activity with someone different. Another friend or loved one or stranger. Try with new words. See what opens, or deepens. Think about what has kept you from having these kinds of inquiries and exchanges and intimacies before. Think about what you need to be able to keep having them.

2 touring the abyss

Dear reader,

The places, the hosts, the students have all started to blur together, I have to admit. I want to remember, but that has become increasingly difficult, especially during the pandemic when talks all went virtual. All the Zooms look the same. Sometimes, I'm not even staring at an array of black boxes and unmoving profile pics; sometimes I'm just staring at myself as I talk while interacting with participants through the chat. I've wondered what is lost, who is lost, during this particular juncture of crisis. I tour unwellness and pain, you see, and when that tour moved to the virtual, I worried those screens would obscure the evolving shapes of that unwellness. I should have trusted in what I had already learned in the beforetimes: when you make it safe, people will tell you what hurts.

I've been on a national speaking tour for the last six years, launched into an entirely new kind of orbit with the publication of *Open in Emergency* in late 2016. Some of my speaking invitations come from professional and community organizations, but most come from universities, from academic units, student services, and student orgs. I've now met with thousands of students, teachers, scholars, writers, artists, mental health professionals, community organizers, and university administrators, all wanting to figure out together why and how life feels unlivable, especially for BIPOC students, particularly Asian American ones. I urge them all to think about what the responsibility of our institutions might be—in contributing to our unwellness and being accountable to our health. University faculty, counseling staff, and administrators have been relatively enthusiastic, recognizing the desperate need for resources but not knowing how (or not being willing or able) to do things differently. But students, students have been electrified by these conversations, by the sudden insistence that they matter, that they are allowed to name and address their suffering.

Vanderbilt, Colgate, University of Minnesota, UC Santa Barbara, UC San Diego, UC Berkeley, UC Irvine, UCLA, Ohio State University, Princeton, Yale, University of Pennsylvania, Georgetown, Harvard, University of Michigan, CSU Fullerton, United States Naval Academy, Gustavus Adolphus College, Tufts, Amherst College, University of Kansas, Williams College, University of Virginia, Smith College, University of Illinois Chicago, University of Chicago, University of Connecticut, Garrett Theological Seminary, Washington University at St. Louis, Pomona, Connecticut College, Northwestern, NYU, Brooklyn College, Barnard, Hiram, University of Southern California, Yonsei University, Colorado College, St. Olaf, University of Toronto. The hunger for conversations on mental health, and disability, and on Asian American experiences in particular, has been overwhelming—but not surprising.

Students in my own courses at the University of Maryland, where I taught from 2009 until 2017, had expressed this deep hunger.[1] When I opened my courses with Eliza's "A Letter to My Sister," which I mentioned in chapter 1— her haunting, gut-wrenching indictment of processes of model minoritization in American society for their part in causing her sister's suicide, her recounting of what it looks like for Asian immigrant families to be both victim and accomplice to the death trap of racialization in the United States—students said *yes, this, more, please*. On suicide, immigrant family dynamics, and gendered racialization. On Asian American studies through mental health and mental health through Asian American studies. Students wanted a language to bridge Asian American studies and Asian American everyday experience, their academic and home lives, their immigrant parents' version of the American Dream and their own. Day one, this discussion cracked something open for them. The stakes were laid bare, the needed language began to form. Together we began the work of grappling with why their—our—lives have felt unlivable. And they wanted to know: *How do we live?*

Fast forward to my speaking tour, where I took these questions on the road. I've met students at every university I've visited, some organizing my visit themselves. And while there are historical and geographical and structural specifics for each place, student experience has been eerily, horrifically, similar across my visits.

One through line is that students are ubiquitously encouraged to "seek help at the counseling center," especially after large-scale trauma. A mass shooting, a peer's death, a pandemic—certain kinds of crises are legible, and when those occur, universities remind students that counseling centers exist and that they exist to help. Students are told, "You are not alone."

They feel incredibly, irrevocably alone.

Even surrounded by thousands upon thousands of other students who feel the same.

———

I'd like you to answer this question for me: *What does unwellness look and feel like for you?* Indulge me, and write it down below: a list, some phrases, some descriptions.

_____

_____

_____

_____

_____

_____

_____

_____

_____

_____

_____

_____

_____

_____

_____

_____

_____

_____

I've made it a practice to ask students this question in my workshops. Exhaustion, they say. Not enough time. Feeling like a failure. An impostor. Feeling overwhelmed. Isolation. No support. Pretending to be well. Pressure to maintain "normal." Hopelessness. Not doing enough, not being enough. Guilt. Feeling like a burden. Feeling lost. Feeling ashamed. Something is wrong with me.

Did any of your answers resemble these?

Helplessness. So many students talked about feeling like they had no control, no choices, no agency in anything in their lives—their families, their classes, their futures, the pandemic, the increasing anti-Asian violence. In the context of college life, they reported about pressures to succeed, to not fail, from their families, from their professors, from their jobs, even from the very spaces that are supposedly created to provide support: counseling centers. All the different responsibilities they've faced, all the choices they didn't feel they had, the tunneling of their future that felt like suffocation, like drowning. Be well, do well, at all costs. No wonder "seek help at the counseling center" rings hollow.

Just asking them this question of what unwellness looks and feels like is stunningly transformative. I'm not sure they've ever been asked before. Asking them, and affirming their answers as real, opens a door they didn't even know existed. Students respond powerfully when they are given permission to hurt. They want to know that their pain is real, that it matters—and that it is shared. They want to know they are not alone, that others who look like them feel like them. There is something incredibly powerful about being in a space with dozens, hundreds, of other Asian Americans and discovering that others feel the same fears and longings as you. That others also want something different than what they've been given.

Students want to know that shame belongs to people and structures inflicting the pain, not to those trying to survive its crushing weight. They want to know that failure is not what they've been told it is. They want their humanity, their complex personhood, seen. Something changes for them when their suffering is no longer an individual pathology to be measured and then cured but a collective trauma that is both normal and completely unjust—and deserving of care.

And then I do something even more unfamiliar to them: I ask them what they need.

What does wellness look and feel like to you? What does "mental health" mean to you? Hazard a list yourself. Ask a friend to do it with you. Really take a moment to do this before you go on reading. It'll be worth it, I swear.

_____

_____

_____

_____

_____

_____

_____

_____

_____

_____

_____

_____

I ask students what *mental health* means to them, and I write their collective answers on a whiteboard. Across my dozens of workshops, there's some of what we might expect: the ability to cope and bounce back from setbacks, not being depressed, not being "mentally ill"—whatever the fuck that means. But also, some richer, perhaps unexpected, answers. Feeling safe. Belonging. Having community that you trust. Liking yourself. Experiencing a full range of feelings, not numbness. Feeling fulfilled. Having a purpose. Healthy boundaries. A supportive community. Feeling valued. Feeling understood. The ability to "be yourself." Hope. Feeling like you have a future. Being happy. Laughing. Being able to be vulnerable with others. Holding loved ones. Agency—feeling like you have control and can make choices. (As I list these here, I find myself once again in wonderment. Students know what's up. They have a vision for themselves so rich, so full of deep longing, my heart aches and is healed all at once. Their yearning, and hope, is fucking breathtaking.)

Then, inspired by Kai Cheng's essay, I show them the World Health Organization's definition of mental health:

Mental health is defined as the state of well-being in which every individual realizes his or her own potential, can cope with the normal stresses of life, can work productively and fruitfully, and is able to make a contribution to her or his community.[2]

Students stare in horror at this definition. Their eyes flit back and forth between the two lists. The WHO definition feels both familiar and foreign: its focus on productivity, individual coping and functionality, and the ability to "contribute" to society is what they've been implicitly told their whole lives; simultaneously it looks absurd now sitting next to the definition we just collectively generated. The dissonance hums in the air.

Then I give them humanities tools to examine this dissonance. We close-read the WHO definition together, identify its assumptions and assertions, reflect on its consequences. What is "potential" and who gets to tell you it's been "realized"? What are "normal stresses"? (Is racism a "normal stress"? I ask them. Is student life "normal stress"?) What counts as "productive" work and valuable "contributions" to society? Then we compare the two definitions, side by side. Students easily point out the differences. They easily see the limitations of the WHO definition even as they recognize its dominance in their lives. They recognize they have already been dreaming much bigger than the WHO definition, even if not consciously or intentionally before. They feel affirmed—and affirm each other—in their collective desire for something more than what WHO promises.

Then I ask the question that usually feels like a gut punch: *Which definition does your university align with?*

At my visit to Amherst College, a counseling center therapist sat among the participants. The therapist slowly raised their hand, still looking at the two lists side by side in horror: "I want to do this," they said, pointing to the side that we collectively generated. "But I'm pretty sure I do this," pointing to the WHO side. They then admitted to not knowing how to do the first within the constraints of the university counseling center. Everything put in place is to help students go back to being productive students—no more, no less.

Every single student at every single place I've visited over the last six years has said that their university aligns much more closely with the WHO definition.

There is something simultaneously banal and awful about the way mental health is done on college campuses. Mental health "happens" almost exclusively at the counseling center—mental health is the strict purview of the counseling center and a few other units or spaces. There might be a wellness center to complement the counseling center (Does this mean the counseling center is the illness center?) that offers a variety of classes on stress management, alcohol consumption, nutrition, sleep, time management. Or wellness programming that includes public talks on "tolerating distress" or "regulating emotion" by counseling center psychiatrists.[3] But by and large, universities imbue counseling centers with the sole authority to "do" mental health, and they turn to their counseling centers as the solution to all crises deemed mental health related. No one seems to question this authority, this strict delineation.

Let's back up for a second: even if we don't question this authority, we don't seem to even notice the very simple contradiction of capacity. Universities keep saying they want more students to go to the counseling center; counseling centers try to invent new ways of doing outreach, including promotional videos meant to demystify counseling center processes.[4] But it is already nearly impossible for counseling centers to see the students that *do* come—students from nearly every place I've visited report long waits, limits on number of sessions, rotating clinicians, and inevitable referrals to private off-campus services, not to mention an array of clinicians with little to no training in working with Asian Americans and other students of color (or queer, trans, nonbinary, and/or disabled students). And it is definitely impossible for counseling centers to see every single student on their campus—because, let's be real, every single student, every person, needs and deserves mental health care. Counseling centers as they are do not have the capacity to serve all their students—numerically or intersectionally.

But beyond the capacity issue, why is it that counseling centers are the official "center" of mental health on college campuses? And why do they get carte blanche decision-making power to determine what that mental health care looks like? No one (in authority) questions what kind of care is being given at counseling centers, the purpose of it, the shape of it, the implications of it.

Remember that all the students I've met have said that their universities align with the WHO definition of mental health.

An example: in 2017, I was invited to an elite liberal arts college in the northeastern United States to do mental health workshops for students—and, surprisingly, counseling center staff and academic deans as well.[5] One therapist, a queer Latina intimately familiar with ethnic studies and community organizing and one of the only people of color (maybe *the* only) on staff at the counseling center, saw a need for more—and different—mental health resources for students of color at this predominantly white school. She also saw a need for more and different mental health resources for her fellow colleagues so that they could better meet the needs of students. "They need help," she said to me when I got there. I think she might have meant the counseling center staff even more than the students.

So I asked the counselors and the deans what they thought mental health is. Some similar answers to students: having a range and balance of feelings, the ability to be present and to self-soothe. Some wildly different:

- "self awareness of baseline" especially "cognitive"
- "ability to learn, think, problem-solve, self-direct"
- "free of debilitating symptoms" especially "psychosis"
- "awareness and engagement of social rules"

These professionals were defining mental health in terms of students' ability to meet their responsibilities. Students need to understand their cognitive baseline, need to be able to learn, need to not be debilitated by psychosis, need to follow social rules. The focus here was very individual, very psychological, with a heavy emphasis on coping skills and behaviors. Disturbingly, psychosis, or a debilitating state of being unable to reality test, was the bar of mental illness—and mental health was simply to be free of this. This was so unimaginative in terms of both highs and lows—that being out of touch with reality is the only way to imagine deep suffering and that being free of that debilitation is the only way to imagine wellness. But also disturbing was how these answers reflected institutional expectations. These answers were deeply colored by the counselors' and deans' sense of responsibility to the institution, the need to direct students to meet the expectations of the university. Wellness is being able to follow the rules. To be a good student.

I wonder: Would they have answered this way if they were thinking about themselves and not students? Maybe, maybe not. I wonder if they would recognize their own human needs in a different context—or if this ability has been trained, institutionalized, out of them completely.

I've already shared what students across the country in aggregate have said about their unwellness and wellness. But I'd like to take a moment to look at what students at this college said in particular, to directly compare with their counselors and deans (see fig. 2.1).

Students there want to know themselves, to be safe, to have community, to feel, to heal. They want an environment that is enriching and encouraging, one that supports them, does not judge them, gives them hope. They want a reckoning with their individual and communal histories. They want so much more than what their college is giving them—more than even what their college, in its counselors and academic deans, dreams for them.

Mental Health

- resiliency - healing
- historical reckoning

- sense of who you are - identity

- safety - physical
          - emotional
          - spiritual

- biology - physical wellness

- environment
        - safe
        - enriching - process, reciprocal
        - encouraging

- hopeful - coping with trauma / challenges

- adaptive / adjusting

- regulating emotions

- having a support system
        - awareness of needs - asking - community
        - interdependence

- listen + process emotions

- embrace emotion - range of feeling
        - free of judgment

[2.1] Student definition of mental health.

Even more striking was the vast difference between how these two groups defined *unwellness*.

First on the list for the counseling center and deans was "sleep deprivation." Because of too many "extracurriculars." Second was "procrastination." Then "substance abuse." From there, they were willing to expand to "academic pressures," "uncertainty about future," "impostor syndrome," "social pressures," "social life/interpersonal conflict," and "sense of belonging."

Now let's look at what their students said (figs. 2.2 and 2.3 on next pages).

Looking at this list again now, I am first struck by how long it was. Two pages. And this was already condensed, me the notetaker writing in shorthand. Second: holy shit, this list perfectly diagnosed how the institution, their college, makes them sick. Unwellness is feeling like you have to do it all alone, like you have to always be productive, independent, high achieving, positive. Unwellness is martyring yourself, not being able to be vulnerable or admit your limits. Unwellness is denying your own feelings, not having language for your suffering, devaluing your own experiences—to be gaslighted, to gaslight yourself. Unwellness is normalizing and romanticizing stress, glorifying busyness. *Unwellness is to be a good student.*

The generous framing of the starkly different perspectives between these students and staff could be to see them as two ships passing in the night. The staff's and students' ideas about what hurts and how to care for those hurts differ so drastically; no wonder these groups have trouble connecting. But that framing is too simple. It erases power and structure. Counseling centers are institutional creations, beholden to the larger institution. Counselors are trained in fields that are their own institutions—most often psychology and psychiatry—from which we inherit the medical model of mental health, of individual pathology to be cured. And all institutions are in the business of subject formation—of shaping us into beings that function within those institutions. Counselors and students aren't simply two equal ships unknowingly passing by each other; students are being crushed by a *Titanic* that tells them (and even thinks) it is helping them. And as they are being crushed, they are told they need to fix themselves—to learn better time management, to drink less, to procrastinate less, to tolerate distress better, to sleep more, and of course, to *go to the counseling center*—so that they can go back to being good, productive students again.[6]

"Why would you want to place yourself into the hands of an institution that seeks to resocialize you into the environment that made a mess of you in the first place?" Eliza reminds us.[7]

Unwellness

- isolation
  - ███████ structures / culture
- depression
- denial of feelings
- feeling like you have to do it alone
  → responsibility
- perfect ███████ student — "success"
  - productive   - social
  - indep.   - achievement
  - no depression — no problems

- normalized stress
  - stress as romanticized + valorized → jokes!
    ↳ glorification of busy
- devaluation of your own experiences
- hard on yourself / expectations

- pressure to be <u>positive</u>

| Unwellness cont. |

- competitiveness

- not caring for basic needs
  ↳ martyrdom

- lack of precise language for feelings / suffering

- lack of trust — in people
  in systems + structures of support

  ↳ fear of being vulnerable

  - ideas of strength + weakness
    ↳ capitalism + productivity

- power dynamics!

[2.2–2.3] Student descriptions of unwellness.

To be fair, the deans and counselors were very open to hearing from me what students have shared across my university visits. And they were open to hearing that their approaches were missing the mark. I want to be clear here that I don't think their ideas were exceptionally bad. From what I've learned from students across my visits, I would expect most university deans and counselors to answer similarly. In fact, their willingness to meet with me and have this challenging conversation demonstrates that they are ahead of other institutions, with real hope of actually engaging student needs. They actually asked what they should do differently.

So I asked them to generate a list of spaces on campus where college life happens—and asked them what it would look like to understand those spaces as also where mental health happens, and where care might happen as well. What would it look like to extend mental health care across campus, to think about building care across spaces, classrooms, units, communities—to see every person and every unit as responsible for a commitment to the well-being of all whom they encounter, to see mental health as the purview, the right, the responsibility of every person and every unit? This is the transformative work I want to see happening at every institution of higher learning, and these academic deans and counselors were willing to listen and begin the work of imagining more, real, care for their students in these ways. Who knows what has happened there in the years since my visit, but I remain hopeful—because there is no way to stop missing the mark without first doing the hard work of examining the ways you're missing it.

Harvard, on the other hand, provides us with another example of continuing to miss, for Asian American students in particular. In spring 2020, in response to rising anti-Asian racism and violence in the context of the COVID-19 pandemic, Harvard University's counseling center posted resources on its website—resources that came under scrutiny a year later in March 2021, a few days after the mass shooting in Atlanta in which eight people were murdered, six of them Asian/Asian American women. The advice, which was taken down after a Harvard student blasted it on social media, included this piece of wisdom: "When you experience racism, you can feel shame. You may wish that you weren't Asian, but remember that your ancestors likely went through similar or even worse incidents."[8] And it advised Asian Americans to find pride in their communities by seeking out positive narratives in media. Asian American students were outraged, taking offense at the normalization of internalized racism and self-hatred, the implied downplaying of their suffering by invoking supposed ancestral pain, the directive to go seek out positive media representations as a way to shore up self-worth. This psychological guidance seemed particularly absurd in the context of racist and misogynist murders in Atlanta—students were not feeling shame, did not need reminders about their supposed ancestors, did not need to watch a movie at that moment.

Two ships passing in the mass-murder-filled night?

Let us be a little bit clearer about who was steering one of those ships. erin Khuê Ninh rightly recognizes the Harvard post as an "inside job." These were the directives not of white counselors without "cultural competence" but of Asian American psychologists. "The call was coming from inside the house."[9] Asian Americans were reminding other Asian Americans how to best cope with racial violence: individualize and manage pain in order to "succeed" in the United States. This is a message every Asian American is familiar with; model minoritization has been the Asian American path to conditional belonging for centuries, if not always by that name. Immigrants—and especially their children—have been told to keep their heads down, minimize their suffering, and just muscle their way toward "functioning" as good citizens, as good students. The model minority is something you become—as Eliza shows us in her letter, and as erin shows across her work—at great cost.[10] And now here are Asian American psychologists telling students once again how to do so.

But is it really a surprise that some Asian American psychologists and psychiatrists have found a happy marriage between their own racial formation and their professional training? The medical model of individual pathology, the imperative of wellness, and the model minority all walk into a bar together. And they end up at Harvard.

erin points out what the advice does not include: educating yourself about what it means to be Asian American, about why things like this have happened, continue to happen. Joining forces with others working against injustice, finding community through shared commitments. "Process your model-minority formation," she suggests. Analyze how you've been asked over and over to be smaller, to be "good," to strive for that conditional belonging dangled in front of you that you think is yours until a gunman goes on a racist, misogynist rampage and kills people who look like you or your family, and then you remember that you don't actually belong, that you and your family are not actually safe, that Harvard will not save you. That Harvard will not save you, and instead those like you in its halls of power will actually tell you that they know what you're feeling and that you just need to watch some movies and do some deep breathing and focus on staying on track and, don't forget, *go to the counseling center.*

Students are tired of being told that they should be well, at all costs. That when they are not, when they break, it is their fault.

They want to know that we are *all* broken, together, and that the world is broken, and that there is life in that brokenness, hope not despite it but because we share it.

Does your university care about you?

The answer from students is always at first an uncomfortable chuckle. I can sense the rapid sequence of questions running through students' minds: Does it? Is it supposed to? Of course—but wait, does it? Then, ultimately, they answer: *No.* Particular people care about them—peers, some faculty, some student services folks—but the institution as a whole does not engage in this thing called "caring." At least, not in the ways the students think about it.

But universities often say they care. No university would be caught dead without a counseling center, some kind of hotline, a poster that tells you to seek help. Georgetown has caring in its mission; it bought a subscription to a deep-breathing app for all of its faculty and staff in spring 2021. I've received regular university emails about more and more resources for wellness during the pandemic.[11]

What kind of wellness is all this striving for?

And what of the ways the university itself makes us unwell?

Students at the liberal arts college in the northeast were very clear about how their university generates and feeds unwellness through a culture of hyperproductivity, overwork, and martyrdom. It bakes racialized ableism into its expectations, into normative ideas of success and failure. It creates an imperative to be the "perfect" student, and mental health structures to help students socialize into these systems, to function *well*. To pretend well.

The irony of all this university care and supposed concern for student unwellness isn't just that the university makes us all unwell. It's also that there are dire consequences in the university for failing to be well. Esmé Weijun Wang shows us how Yale "cared" for her through a mental health crisis as an undergrad, encouraging a medical leave—and then refusing to let her return afterward. The university cares until it won't. Wang had become a liability after her crisis, breaking the unspoken rule, the compulsory wellness that transmutes into student success and university success. Once broken, students must be discarded, the ones who don't "make it" clearly not meant to be there in the first place. Their failure is the sign that they actually never belonged at all. Meritocracy remains intact, upheld. After you fail so spectacularly, no amount of reperforming wellness can prove that you can be once again trusted to uphold Yale's wellness as a good student. A mental health crisis is actually perhaps the worst kind of failure: a failure not of behavior but of personhood. An endless failure, as we've learned. The permanent morphing of the Good Student into the Bad Student.[12]

But students already know all this. They know university wellness is unlivable and unsustainable. They know it is killing them. They are trying to tell us.

I always like to say that students know what the fuck is up. And while the talks have begun to blur together, a particular (prepandemic) few stand out in my memory because they were organized not by academic units but by students who already knew they needed to organize for their own lives. Students at Tufts University brought me out in fall 2017. The main organizers were student leaders of the Vietnamese Student Association (VSA) who were taking a disability studies course and reading parts of *Open in Emergency*.[13] They organized one of the larger in-person events I've done—nearly one hundred attendees, mostly students, almost entirely Asian American, on a weekday evening, for a lecture and discussion (and, of course, food). To have almost one hundred Asian American students in a room, giving them permission to talk about mental health, is something magical. Initial reticence turned into collective laughter and groans and "mmmms," shared looks of recognition, even high-fives. Individual and collective vulnerability. Mental health is something we all know and don't know at once, a taste we can't quite name but all recognize. Then suddenly it is named and we take a gasp of air together.

It was clear that students wanted and needed to talk about mental health, Asian American students especially, but there had been no spaces or mechanisms for doing this collectively. And they clearly wanted to do it collectively. They wanted to gather as a community and take that collective breath of air together.

But there were several "unicorn" aspects of this Tufts event. On college campuses, VSAs are notoriously social groups, focused on social gatherings of Vietnamese Americans and other Asian American students around things like phở and cultural fashion shows—not usually interested in advocacy, organizing, or cultural critique. (Why that is so is a topic for another essay!) I'm not sure why this VSA was different. I do know though that the two student leaders who invited me were exposed to *Open in Emergency* through a disability studies course—a course taught by an adjunct instructor who happened to be Lydia X. Z. Brown, one of the most prominent disability justice advocates in the country. Lydia themself has a short story in *Open in Emergency*, and Lydia personally has been a big influence on my own intellectual growth, especially around issues of autism, neurodivergence, and access. Lydia's approach to teaching has also been an inspiration—not simply student centered but fiercely access centered, treating students like human beings with deep needs and limits, practicing a radical pedagogy of care.

This suggests to me that disability studies and disability justice act as a catalyst for thinking about mental health. And *Open in Emergency* acts as a catalyst especially for Asian American students. Together Lydia's disability justice course and *Open in Emergency* nurtured new language and new spaces for students to name their struggles and build care for themselves. These frameworks give permission to ask questions of mental health out loud. They give permission to claim need. And they authorize students as experts of their own unwellness and agents in their own care. Students know what's up, and disability justice concepts and arts interventions like *Open in Emergency* help them take the next steps.

I'm also wondering if there was something catalytic about my own identity as a queer Vietnamese American woman scholar/writer/teacher/artist, a very different model of knowledge producer and community leader. I often describe myself as irreverent—and I'm irreverent publicly with intention: to offer a feminist and queer model of dissent and refusal and subversion; to give permission to others to find ways of moving in the world that exceed what is expected of them. I queer up spaces to try to create more breathing room for those being strangled by normative subject formation. I wonder if my two Vietnamese American women hosts saw the potentiality of that in my writing and my project. I hope so.

My visit to Tufts also reminds me that adjuncts save lives. Contingent faculty are doing the work of transformative care in the classrooms—and increasingly so, given the rapid adjunctification of academia. It is contingent rather than tenured faculty who are most often willing to explore new ways of teaching to meet students' needs. Lydia is their own unicorn, for sure; they light the way for so many of us, in everything they do, and no one can replicate what they do. But it is no coincidence that they are an adjunct, teaching a one-off course (likely for shit pay) that the university has no intention of supporting in a sustainable way, let alone growing, disconnected from any larger program or set of student resources. Lydia's course changed the lives of the students taking it, and by extension another hundred lives through the event they organized around mental health from it. These are students who now question the ableism baked into university standards and refuse to value themselves or others by those standards any longer. But that happened in spite of Tufts, not because of it. Tufts is not invested in understanding this kind of magic or supporting it. No university is.[14]

One more story. In spring 2019, Asian American student groups at the University of Chicago organized a day-and-a-half symposium on Asian American mental health called "Break the Silence" and invited me to give the keynote. This was their second time organizing this conference. That year, seventy-five students across the Chicago area from four or five different universities gathered in a lecture hall to hear me and other experts talk about Asian American mental health. I use the word *experts* here intentionally, because while organizers did program the usual "experts" of mental health—that is, psychotherapists, psychologists, and psychiatrists—they also chose unusual suspects: me, a humanities scholar and artist; local community organizers; and student peers.[15] They wanted skills, yes, but they also wanted stories, stories that would offer more than a generic list of do's and don'ts or how to "manage stress." Stories of how to understand, name, and survive the forces constraining their lives: family dynamics, toxic masculinity, stigma, domestic violence, impostor syndrome.[16] Stories to help them figure out how to live through these forces. The students recognized the need for different kinds of storytelling—and ultimately, different kinds of knowledge making and care.

For my keynote, I offered them a short talk unsettling ideas about wellness and unwellness—and then I walked them through two activities. (Workshops can work for large groups too!) First, a tarot activity in which they formed small groups and pulled cards from the Asian American Tarot to read and discuss together. Second, a discussion of understandings of success and failure—which led to a deep impromptu discussion on immigrant family dynamics and the crushing weight of their families' expectations, their filial duties, the unending and unpayable debt they feel toward their families, their desperate attempts to pay that debt while finding some measure of agency and personhood outside of that debt. In other words, their mental health as the children of immigrants. I introduce them to erin's work on what it looks and feels like to be raised as model minorities in Asian immigrant families (a process I reflect on in detail in chapter 3), and something shifts palpably across the space. Hope seeps through the cracks.

While in Chicago for "Break the Silence," I also did a workshop specifically for first-year Asian American medical students at the University of Chicago. The student who organized this had been an undergraduate at Vanderbilt in 2018 and had heard me speak there on a visit; he was also slotted as a student speaker for "Break the Silence" on their graduate student panel. He invited me to come speak with his med school peers, first years on a trajectory to become doctors, on how to think about their own mental health *and* the mental health of their future patients.[17] These medical students, often embodying the success frame, the perfect model minority lives, already knew they wanted to live better lives somehow. They wanted to know how to save their own lives while living these supposed "best lives." And they wanted to know how to be ethical in the work they were getting trained to do, realizing already the limits of their medical training and wanting to inoculate themselves against it.

Students are already looking elsewhere beyond their counseling centers, beyond those deemed the only experts. They are creating spaces that center mental health and encourage new dialogues. They are seeing the need for new resources. The students at "Break the Silence" wanted to directly interrogate the narratives around them—and were desperate for tools to make sense of the very specific pressures they experienced as racialized, model minoritized Asian Americans. It is clear to me that Asian American students want—and need—Asian American studies *as* mental health and mental health *as* Asian American studies, a synthesis that helps them move in the world in their daily lives. They wanted that at the University of Chicago. They have wanted that in every Asian American studies class I have ever taught. My sense is that this is an invisible tide across the country, a kind of student-led insurgency demanding care not only in institutional structures but also in their classrooms and curricula. They already know they deserve more; they are increasingly willing to ask for it, especially if others are willing to ask with them.

In my workshops, I invite students to directly name their unwellness, define their own sense of wellness, ask critical questions about the university's role in both of those things, and begin thinking of how to build what they need. I pose: *How might you ask the university to be accountable to the kind of mental health you want? What structures would foster this kind of mental health, and what would it take to build them?* Meaning, what would it look like to build an infrastructure for your mental health within and outside of the institution(s) you are a part of? Essentially, I ask them to deepen the work they are already conducting, performing a humanities close reading of the university, drawing upon a mental health framework grounded in disability and racial justice, and daring to unapologetically claim both unwellness and need. Students have grasped these tools tightly and turned to wield them like a torch.

Nothing (besides contingency) has helped me to see the contours of the neoliberal university more than talking with students. Their lives, and deaths, show me that wellness has become a new tool of neoliberal racial capitalism, that it works hand in hand with meritocracy, a trusty tool of neoliberal racial capitalism. Talking with Asian American students in particular reveals that the American Dream remains both horizon and chokehold for our communities, that the model minority is a death trap Asian American students continue to feel keenly—one their families desperately invest in at all costs, an investment the university and the nation happily exploit. Chapter 3 looks more closely at the immigrant family, while chapters 4 and 5 follow the logic of meritocracy through the university, across the academic profession, and in our classrooms. All three chapters continue to center students—their experiences, their expressions of need, the consequences for them in the choices universities make—because it is students who have shown me that the university is a central site of Asian American unwellness.

University ableism affects everyone in the higher ed ecosystem, but differentially; ableism's intersections with model minoritization are perhaps some of its deadliest manifestations. This is the other irony of university care and counseling centers. Counseling centers are failing our students, yes, and universities are missing the mark, yes—but on top of these failures of care is the reality that Asian American unwellness is produced most efficiently and devastatingly *in* the university. It is not simply that the university doesn't provide enough care; it is that the university is an unwellness engine for Asian Americans. An incubator.

We sort of know this, but we get there backward by way of the stats. We love to cite that Asian American students have the highest rates of suicidal ideation among college students (I did so myself earlier); the other stat often cited is that Asian American women ages eighteen to twenty-four have the second highest rates of suicidal ideation by age group, gender, and race.[18] A few more: among all Asian Americans, those ages twenty to twenty-four have the highest suicide rate. In fact, suicide is the leading cause of death for Asian Americans ages fifteen to twenty-four.[19]

We don't really ask why Asian American unwellness seems to cluster around late adolescence and young adulthood.

We simply use these stats to deny that we're the model minority.

Look, Asian Americans are suffering too! Look, we're not just success stories! Look, we need access to more mental health resources! Look, the university needs to provide more care!

Public health and psychology focus on risk factors and protective factors, when they bother to do research on Asian Americans at all. Examining mental health disparities and the social determinants of mental health begins to widen the framework ever so slightly—though it is still safely within a medical model of individual pathology. None of these approaches really ask and answer the question of what makes life feel unlivable for Asian American teens and young adults. None ask what is happening to our students. "Asian cultural values" is an Orientalist, ridiculously simplistic, woefully inadequate analytic for engaging Asian American life.[20]

But if we understand unwellness not as decontextualized individual pathology to be cured but as a direct product of structural violence—if we are all differentially unwell, in relation to the various structures of power and exploitation and degradation around us—then the question is not how to medically treat all these teens and young adults, or even how to expand access to treatment for them. The question becomes: What are the structures producing Asian American unwellness in this period of Asian American life? And how do we dismantle them?

Because I don't want students to simply "resist" suicide.[21] I want them to better understand and be able to name the systemic forces that make their lives feel unlivable. I want them to figure out how to make their lives feel more livable, together. I want them to have all those things they dream of in their definitions of mental health. I want them to figure out how to opt out of the things that stand in the way of that. What I'm seeing throughout my ongoing tour is that the university is one of the main institutions that stands in the way. (As erin teaches us, the immigrant family is the other. More on that, and how it works in lockstep with the university, in chapter 3.) Yes, racialized unwellness is produced everywhere—that is how racism works. Its violence manifests insidiously across every discursive context, every institution. But the university is an institution uniquely positioned to produce Asian American unwellness, because it is where the model minority intertwines mostly powerfully with ableist meritocracy, unwellness allowed to bloom in a discursive echo chamber under the careful "care" of capitalist education. Academia reproduces these forces in hyperfocused, largely closed-circuit form. For Asian Americans, attending college, taking classes, visiting the counseling center, and so on all constitute opting in, inescapably, to the processes of racialized subject formation.

The university produces model minorities. By way of its own meritocratic myths and culture of hyperproductivity. By way of how it bolsters racialized narratives of success and failure. By way of what it tells Asian American students they must be. And by way of how it gaslights students into thinking something is wrong with them and not the university.[22] Nowhere else in adult life (except maybe the military) will students so thoroughly be immersed in institutional messaging and control. The discursive power of the university is near absolute. Networked communication channels—recruitment and admissions, financial aid offices, orientation tours, email blasts, university websites, campus signage, registration offices, residential life, transportation and parking services, dining services, rec centers, student groups, student clubs, student services, academic departments, academic advisors, faculty, teaching assistants, syllabi, course pages and student portals, libraries and librarians, research portals, career advising, work study—are all telling students, *We are getting the best education in the world! We are on our way to bright, successful futures! The university is the mechanism by which we achieve more wellness! Work hard, in the ways that the university tells you, and you will succeed. You will be worth something. Trust in the university; it will save you, and your family, and deliver everything you think you owe to the world.* This messaging comes precisely at the developmental moment students are pulling away from parents and family environments, becoming adults, and being vested legally and socially with decision-making powers.

The university makes us unwell while telling us that it cares. It tells us that we're not actually unwell, that everything is fine—that everything is more than fine. This gaslighting is particularly devastating for Asian American students and BIPOC students more generally. BIPOC students struggle in predominantly white institutions not just because of racial biases, differential treatment, lack of community, and institutional neglect. They struggle also because the university tells them that their experiences of harm are not real and that they don't actually deserve care. Meritocracy meets neoliberalism meets ableist myth of independence meets racialized pressure to prove you belong. Embody these myths, and don't you dare fall apart, don't you dare fail. The stakes are higher, the abandonment more stark. Asian American students have to work harder than white students for this conditional belonging, but they also think they deserve care less. College is both the training ground and the final test for model minorities. This is for all the marbles. Succeed and become what you're supposed to be, or fail and—no, there is no room for failure.

One more irony: the university is also where students most likely will encounter Asian American studies—and critical race more broadly, and gender and feminist studies, and LGBT and queer studies, and disability studies—for the first time, maybe the only time, and that's if their university even offers these classes and if students manage to find their way over from their majors on the other side of campus. When done well, these are the classes that work to undo that gaslighting, that begin pointing to the structural conditions of students' lives. When done *as* mental health, they can save students' lives. But universities are continually dismantling these very programs, cutting funding, cutting faculty, restructuring. Critical race and gender and disability studies face their own precarity and unwellness within the university—another irony. Actually it's not very ironic; it makes perfect sense. The very tools that would help students save their own lives by dismantling the institutional ideologies and structures that are harming them are of course what threaten the institution the most. This tension is at the heart of these fields and of students' experiences in the early twenty-first-century university.

If you're doing mental health, you have to be looking at the university. You have to be willing to ask how the university contributes to unwellness, both within its boundaries and beyond in the kinds of subject formation it enacts. The model minority leaves Harvard—what happens from there?

The flip side: if you are examining the university, you have to be looking at Asian American mental health. The Asian American mental health epidemic is a central by-product of university functioning. I talk about students being the canaries in the coal mine, and Asian American students are perhaps the best at this (ha, we can be exceptional even in the ways we are unwell!). Want to understand the workings of this institutional machinery? Follow the Asian American student's unwellness; it'll take you to where the sausage is really made.

Somewhere along this journey of discovering the death grip the university has on Asian American students, I've also learned the terrible truth that faculty and staff are the university's magistrates.[23] We execute university policy and culture, we are the upholders of meritocracy, the adjudicators of wellness and therefore belonging and worth. We give assignments, set deadlines, assign grades, create rules, enforce consequences. We normalize the ableist structures of the university, and unfortunately, we align ourselves with those structures. Often we even innovate them, evolving their brutal efficacies. Students do not trust us to see their complex personhood—nor should they. We fail students spectacularly, every day.[24]

We fail ourselves, too.

When *Open in Emergency* sold out its initial print run by late 2017, less than a year after initial publication, Lawrence and I began planning a reprint and knew from the start that *OiE* 2.0 needed to have a Student card in the tarot deck. Designing tarot cards has actually been an assignment professors have used in *Open in Emergency*'s teaching program, to get students to catalog their affective lives and think about the structural conditions of those lives. But to create an official Student card for the expanded tarot deck, we knew we had to develop a new process—it couldn't be us, it couldn't even be a student single-authoring it. We would need to crowdsource this card, to channel the cacophony of voices I've listened to for the last decade-plus of my teaching and the last six years of my mental health speaking tour. Community curation in yet another form: we developed prompts for students to submit ideas, experiences, fragments on several of my 2019 visits (most notably Harvard and the Chicago area), and assembled a student editorial team to brainstorm, synthesize, and write.[25] Lawrence and I oversaw this process and finalized the card, trying to ensure it covered everything students have taught us about their lives. Our hope with this card was that every student who read it would be able to see themselves in it, that it would do some justice to the unbearability of their lives and to their dreaming work toward a different futurity.

The Student: Art by Matt Huynh, Text by Students Everywhere

See plates 3 and 4 for full card

The Student is the twenty-ninth card in the major arcana, sometimes known as the lost card. The Student cried the day of graduation. They play one role for the Mother, another for schools, another as the Daughter, another for workforces, another as the Model Minority, another for the state, always in the pull of the annihilating void. The Student is, at essence, a note-taker: be grateful / always be ok / chase the promise of / this, for hours / never complain never be sick keep going / nothing is ever enough the work goes impossibly on / is college life normal stress? / ~~what would it mean to leave~~ / we are finishing our parents' immigration stories / leaving behind the fact of living / we are not grades / a condition of what can't / ~~don't feel guilty~~. Drawing the Student card in a reading reminds you that Student debt extends forward and backward across our collective lifetimes. But ask yourself, what is it you actually owe? Your entire personhood, and then more. *We gave you your past, now give us your future.* The Student urges us to refuse. If schools are a feeder system for churning out good citizens, embrace being a bad citizen. Embrace being a bad subject, a bad student, a bad child, a bad person: a revolutionary. Remember that the Asian American Movement was birthed in the fires of student protest.
✱ *students everywhere*

We finalized the card in late 2019, and I began sharing it on the road. I'm not sure I've seen a tarot card so powerfully wreck its readers. There is something about the fragments in the middle of the card, set off with slashes, that leave people breathless; audiences hold their breaths as I, or a few of them, read that section of the card out loud. Those fragments are direct quotes, pulled from the writing of various students. The strikethroughs are the most, well, striking. How to read out loud what has been stricken? How to voice what is not allowed to be said, or even thought? Our eyes linger on those redactions, those "errors" of writing, of feeling, of thought. We wonder when and how to move on.

I've watched students weep upon reading this card. I want to weep every time I read it.

What are we doing to our students? How have we let student life be . . . this?

The last lines of the card are hopeful. They give direction. All the tarot cards end with reminders and imperatives, what the card means for you when you draw it in a reading, but to echo the students I've listened to, I especially wanted The Student to end with a sense of agency. I wanted to help students, on a larger scale, do that work of looking around and realizing they are not alone—and not hopeless. But the imperative to be a bad student, to embrace "failure," to reject normative subjectivity, to defy structures of power that have told them who they have to be their whole lives—this is absolutely terrifying. The card suggests that freedom and social death are intertwined. Students know the cost of noncompliance perhaps more keenly than the rest of us—I hope this card also reminds them of the possibility in it as well.

Academic life took a wild left turn in early 2020 when the pandemic hit. I stopped touring; all my in-person gigs were canceled. At this point, I was starting at Georgetown in a visiting position, teaching and mentoring students in the Disability Studies Program. I wasn't meeting students all over the country anymore, but I had my own students to care for as Georgetown shut down abruptly in the middle of its spring break, telling students to fly "home" and lock down, telling faculty to immediately switch to remote teaching. In a later chapter, I reflect on what teaching has looked like, has had to look like, in pandemic times. Here, I will just mention that I introduced The Student card to my own students that spring and fall (and the following spring while teaching at University of California, Santa Barbara) during remote learning. And though the card was not written with the pandemic as context at all, students still found it deeply resonant—the work went impossibly on *even during a fucking pandemic*. In fact, getting off the merry-go-round seemed to be even harder, as we all tried to continue our working lives in quarantine, on Zoom, with no child care, with more familial obligations, with fewer jobs, sometimes stuck in toxic living situations, all of us surrounded by seemingly uncontrollable death.

In early 2021, as we closed out the first year of the pandemic and moved into the second, I began touring on the road again—but virtually. By this point, we had all settled into our new Zoom lives and a near-constant stream of virtual events. I received speaking invitations almost every week in those first months, the need for mental health resources more universally recognized than perhaps ever before.

Picking public speaking back up in 2021 required several shifts. Speaking into a screen of black boxes posed new challenges, while using the chat function and breakout rooms helped to create new kinds of engagement. Creating spaces of intentional vulnerability and care was harder to do across virtual space, requiring more energy, less silence. I had to be "on" more, projecting my presence into the ether, often with little of the visual and auditory feedback—nods, laughter, mm-hmms—that I've relied on for energy and connection.

But community and care are possible, even within these constraints. All you have to do is keep asking what hurts.

It became very clear that we all needed space to share/process/just let ourselves feel the deep suffering of the pandemic. Asking what unwellness looked like in that moment became an urgent necessity. By early 2021, unwellness for students looked like even more exhaustion, even more terror: family members dying, anti-Asian violence, saying goodbye on iPads in hospitals. Toilet paper shortages. Getting COVID. Fear of getting your family sick. No hugs. Having to return to live with toxic families of origin. Or having no place to live at all. Doing classes on Zoom in the bathroom. Hiding with the laptop away from your parents so they don't overhear the "controversial" content of your classes. Taking care of younger siblings now out of school too. Losing jobs. Getting new "essential" jobs. Wearing masks. Not wearing the right masks. Seeing others not wear masks. Seeing loved ones through glass or across a yard. Your universities and professors saying they care, but everyone trying to continue business as usual anyway. "Instructional continuity" feeling like a cruel fucking joke.

Everything failing you, but you feel like the failure.

The ableism of the WHO definition of mental health has become even more clear now to students. Productivity feels both more pressurized and more ridiculous. It's a merry-go-round—no wait, it's a train, already fallen off the track, veering wildly to god knows where, but we are all still riding it, still can't get off. They want to get off.

People who attended my many virtual events in the first half of 2021 wanted and needed to catalog these losses almost more than anything else. This tells me that ableism left us no space to mourn 2020. It gave us no language and no structures to grieve—and connect—in all the ways we needed. So we were trying to do it over Zoom, staring more often than not at little boxes on a screen while sitting alone in our rooms.

But connection is possible, even through our screens. I have seen it, over and over in the last year and a half. I have created spaces of vulnerability even through the awkward mechanism of a Zoom webinar, by asking the right kinds of questions, by cultivating the Zoom chat as a space of sharing, by being vulnerable myself. The care work that I usually do during in-person visits—body language, eye contact, handshakes, after-talk one-on-ones, dinners, coffees, walks, and don't forget crying, people always stay after my talks and cry—this care work has had to find translation in the Zoom world.

Part of that translation has been to nurture virtual spaces not simply of vulnerability but also of collective creation. We have needed spaces to mourn in ways that resist the ephemeral nature of events, especially virtual ones that can feel disembodied—our bodies don't even get to have the memory of going somewhere, of being in a different space, of being with other bodies. And so I started dreaming up ways to make *stuff*. I like to say I make cool shit. Well, let's make cool shit together on Zoom.

I introduced The Student in a public collective tarot reading at a virtual event hosted by the University of Connecticut in fall 2020, discussing its meanings and resonances with several student panelists, using it as a foundation for opening a critical conversation on what makes the student experience feel unlivable. Students used the card to give themselves new language—and permission—to make sense of their own lives. This is what the tarot cards were meant to do. Watching The Student card take on this life as tool, as impetus, as lexicon, in action was an incredible and meaningful moment for me. But what if we could continue to let students into the creation process as well? What if The Student card could "do" even more in these public spaces? How might we transform The Student card into an iterating process, a foundation for collective creation? I gotta give full credit to Lawrence for this one. When I began planning a collective tarot reading for the Disability Studies Program at Georgetown as one of my in-residence events in early 2021, Lawrence suggested: How about taking the Mad Libs form we used to create tarot cards and using it as a structure to ask the Georgetown students about their experiences? And then compare their answers with *OiE*'s official Student card to see what is revealed.

So I made a Student Mad Libs for that event.

The Student is the twenty-ninth card in the major arcana.

The Student feels _____.

The Student dreams of _____.

To the Student, failure is _____.

The Student's experience of _____ tells us that _____.

Drawing this card means _____.

Remember that _____.

Over a hundred students joined that Zoom, writing their answers to each Mad Libs phrase in the chat. The answers poured in faster than I could read out loud. There were only these six lines but students answered endlessly, filling in the blanks over and over for forty-five minutes. The Mad Libs form not only gives permission for vulnerability—it demands it. It asks directly what you feel, what you fear, what you dream of. Starting these sentences for students gives them permission to finish them, compels them to finish them. The blanks call to be filled, like a test where every answer is the right one. Students know tests. They know fill-in-the-blanks. They don't know the safety of answering every single one right no matter how you answer.

When Jim Lee texts you, "Hey I'm applying for a grant to do some mental health stuff at my university, do you want to be part of it?"—you say yes. Even if it's the beginning of a pandemic. And thus the "Open in Emergency Series" at University of California, Irvine, was born, with me at its curatorial helm. A series of virtual events exploring critical arts as care spanning the 2020–21 academic year, it represented an opportunity for me to do sustained mental health work. Working within a supportive institutional structure (in Jim), I could build care over time instead of just dropping in for a one-off event. I could bring *OiE* to life in new ways, and push myself to rethink community making and care in this pandemic and this new Zoom world. The series was also a chance to bring in co-conspirators! I learned through creating the special issue that editorial and curatorial work are acts of faith and trust. And now programming could be as well.

I opened the series in the fall with my "What Is Mental Health?" workshop, laying the foundation by cataloging that moment's unwellness, and beginning to unsettle our frameworks around mental health, detaching our ideas from (racialized) productivity and compulsory wellness. Next, I invited Simi Kang to facilitate a discussion of "emergency" and finding agency during crisis. In the winter quarter, Yanyi and Shana Haydock joined the series, crafting workshops inviting explorations of intergenerational trauma and "healthy" interpersonal relationships respectively. Across these events, facilitators and participants worked together to create archives of feeling and new languages for feeling. Yanyi even took the language offered by the participants to craft collective poems live—which gave me the idea for the culminating event of the series in the spring of 2021. We would collectively create a new tarot card, The Pandemic, via a process similar to what I had done at Georgetown but more elaborate and fine-tuned, with live writing and editing to pull together a draft. And a live illustrator to start rendering the image!

I brought back Simi, Yanyi, and Shana to facilitate the breakout groups that would generate language for the card, and invited artist Nguyên Khôi Nguyễn to join as the illustrator. Nguyên and I would move around the Zoom rooms to listen to the discussions. Additionally, I would watch each group's Google doc as it populated with ideas, language, and imagery. And to help guide the discussions and generate all the elements of my version of a tarot card, I created another Mad Libs.

The Pandemic

The Pandemic is the thirtieth card in the major arcana.

The Pandemic has been a year of _____.

I miss _____.

I don't remember _____.

I'm scared of _____.

Now, when I hear/see _____, I think of _____.

When will I _____ again?

I wonder _____.

In the center of the image is a _____.

The image is full of _____.

When you pull The Pandemic card, it means _____.

The Pandemic teaches you _____.

The Pandemic is to The Emergency as _____ is to _____.

Ask yourself _____.

Remember that _____.

Know that _____.

Tell yourself _____.

The audience was relatively small, a mixed group of about twenty students, faculty, artists, and community members. The breakout rooms became spaces of deep vulnerability, each facilitator using their own methods of creating safety and care. It was mesmerizing to watch, and listen, like witnessing that collective first breath. Again, mental health, this thing we all know the flavor of but don't quite know how to name, and then we are collectively given permission to name it, to luxuriate in it, to explore what it looks and feels like.

Then the Google docs started populating. Three of them, quickly, with depth and candor and gut-wrenching pain. I started panicking, because I had never had to edit/curate/write in such a drastic time crunch before. So I yelled out to Lawrence, who was at the time downstairs feeding our daughter dinner: Anh!! Come help!! The two of us hunkered down with two laptops and four Google docs—the three from the breakout rooms and the one we created to pull the draft together—speed editing like never before. We read across the docs, pulling lines from each, and dropping them into our shared doc. Lawrence began "Frankensteining" them together. I oversaw the process, continually pulling lines as new ones appeared, while discussing out loud with Lawrence how to stitch them together. We argued over which lines to choose and how to revise them. Whether to keep the "I" or change to "we." Which lines to be combined, paraphrased, massaged. Which to keep verbatim. Whether to keep jokes. How the card should end, what the imperatives would be. Part of me wishes the participants could have seen this part of how the sausage gets made. The rest of me relishes the intimacy of this work that my partner and I share, that we do only with each other, like a bridge we've built across our minds and hearts, or, better, a muscle or limb we've somehow grown and learned to use together. Our magic.

Here's what we came up with.

The Pandemic: Art by Nguyên Khôi Nguyễn, Text Generated Collectively, Edited by Mimi Khúc and Lawrence-Minh Bùi Davis

See plates 5 and 6 for full card

The Pandemic is the thirtieth card in the major arcana. It has been a long year like a long decade, one of atrophying time. We miss the way it feels to walk in a city, in the current of everyone going somewhere. We don't remember why certain things felt important in the beforetimes, do remember seeing a classmate in a casket on YouTube livestream. The Pandemic unmasks the lie of the word essential: who provides care, who deserves care, death visited disproportionately on the poor, the black and brown, the lower caste. Returning to normal is an impossibility brimming with longing and terror. In the center of the card is a discarded mask, an iPad by a hospital bed: say our goodbyes however we can. Toilet paper has become a totem of survival, sweatpants an emblem of refusal, sourdough a gift of renewal. All things will pass, like a kidney stone. When will we hold our brother's hand again? Will our kids remember this as the worst time of their lives or as something strange and tender? Will our dogs forgive us when we return to work? Drawing The Pandemic card in a reading means a portal is opening. Where it leads is unclear, but remember people have always slept in doorways, huddled under them during bombings. Who knows if The Pandemic will ever end. ✳ a collective card

When I began touring in late 2016, I brought with me a few ideas from *OiE*, some questions and approaches to mental health, and some critical arts practices — but I was also just meeting and listening and learning from students. I facilitated conversations that expanded my own language around what hurts for students. The Student card is the culmination, the product, of several years of touring, an attempt to synthesize and create something from what I witnessed, something to capture student experience but also to help students continue this work of developing language, of figuring out what hurts and why, and how to care for themselves and each other. I watch The Student card's life in the world now as it helps create spaces of conversation, vulnerability, grieving, care. I love the card itself, but I love even more what the process of reading and writing a card opens up for students. Agency, voice, a chance to generate language and frameworks for themselves. Community. The Pandemic card was born from the latter part of this tour, a collective creation made by reaching across the expanse of pandemic isolation, of virtual space, of unspeakable loss—and connecting not despite it all but through it. If you let them, students will go to the edge of the abyss and speak into it.[26] erin was the first person I've read who asked directly in her scholarly writing, "What hurts?" I've taken that question into the center of my own work, animating everything that I do. I want to know what hurts, and I want to give people permission to say what hurts, together. I've seen firsthand the effects of asking students what hurts. And helping them connect those things to structures, not just individual pathology. Giving them space to think about their pain, to name it, to connect with others. To figure out what they need. To create.

The lesson is simple: listen to students. They are dreaming of more than what universities are giving them. They are trying to claw their way out from the harm institutions are doing to them. From the harm their families are doing to them. Teaching and touring taught me about students' needs, the ways universities do and do not meet those needs, the ways so many of us are failing to meet those needs—and how students are trying to save their own lives.

What can student unwellness and desire for new language for their pain and new structures for their care teach us? What can we learn about mental health, the neoliberal university, our own unwellness, our own complicity? How might we begin asking—and answering—along with students, *how do we live?*

How might we who are not students stay beside them at the edge of the abyss, recognize it as ours too, and speak into it, together?

interlude 2
the suicide tarot

[Inter2.1] Suicide: art by Matt Huynh, text by Terisa Siagatonu.
See plates 7 and 8 for full card.

How do we usually talk about suicide? We think of it as tragic. But often also as selfish and shameful. Common social scripts tell us the person was weak, that they couldn't "handle it," that they "gave up." We accuse people who try to kill themselves of burdening their families, abandoning their responsibilities, seeking attention, being ungrateful. We say something is wrong with them. Sure, we might say they need help. Psychology and psychiatry, the fields chiefly entrusted with understanding and addressing suicide, often frame it as an isolated, discrete illness unto itself, as if the only response to suicidal ideation is to stop the suicide from happening: suicide prevention, they call it. Stop someone's ability to harm themselves. To me, that always seemed so ass-backward: it's taking away someone's way of addressing a problem without any understanding of the problem. People want to die because their lives feel unlivable. Suicide is not an "insane" response to a "sane" world; it's a desperate response to an unbearable existence.

I have wanted to die many times in my life, sometimes more intensely than others. I tell you this because I want you to know that wanting to die is a normal response to pain. I want you to know that your pain matters. You are allowed to want it to stop.

But I want you to live, and I know the only way that happens is if we figure out how to make life feel more livable.

I don't know too many others who approach suicide this way. Eliza's approach was the first I encountered that told me wanting to die is not only normal under unlivable conditions but that it might actually be a form of resistance to those unlivable conditions. Eliza's letter locates suicide at the forefront of what it means to make Asian American art and do Asian American studies—Eliza taught me that my pain, our pain as Asian Americans, matters, and that I'm allowed, we are allowed, to say, *No more*. But I have not encountered many like Eliza since my first reading of "A Letter to My Sister."

Which is why I did not curate a Suicide card in the first edition of *Open in Emergency*'s Asian American Tarot. I did not trust others to write about suicide without falling into the pitfalls of compulsory gratitude or inspirational narratives of "the will to live." I did not trust others to not apologize for wanting to die, to not recuperate their own journeys into the abyss through narratives of "overcoming" and triumph and healing. Until I heard a poem by Terisa Siagatonu, a queer Samoan woman poet based in the Bay Area, including the line: "Wanting to die is only frightening to those who have never been exhausted by the audacity of their own survival."[1] Terisa opens her tarot card for the Asian American Tarot with that same line:

Wanting to die is only frightening to those who have never been exhausted by the audacity of their own survival. Killing yourself is only terrifying to those who have always put their faith in a light ahead of them—rather than bearing the ancestral duty to be the light itself. Suicide is the twenty-eighth card in the major arcana. It speaks not simply to suffering, but to the life that holds the suffering as long as it can. You, who must endure being your ancestors' wildest dreams amidst the colonial terror that killed them, and left you with . . . what? Intergenerational trauma? Your war-torn homeland, bloodied by the genocide of your people? No wonder you chose this card at this moment. Or rather: this card chose you. Its image of a tired hand reaching to extinguish the flame of a candle symbolizes that yes, the light goes out, but like all candles: it can be lit again. What often goes unnoticed in the image on this card is what the rest of the body is doing that we cannot see. When chosen, Suicide is not a destiny. You are never to blame for what colonization has made you believe is your fault. This card chose you as a sign to pause and feel everything, rather than end. You're left to interpret what the rest of the body is doing while you're still here. Alive. ✳ Terisa Siagatonu

Folks are sometimes frightened when they pull the Suicide card in a reading. Is this card foretelling their death by their own hand? Of course not. What it does is give us all permission to admit that sometimes things hurt so much we don't want to live anymore. I have come to know that needing this permission is a critical dimension of Asian American life. But it also stretches across communities differentially, and here in this card a queer Pacific Islander poet draws on her communities' experiences to guide us in our own dwellings in unwellness. To think about what it means to try to live under unlivable conditions. To recognize that life is a struggle to stay alive. To reflect on what it is we need in order to stay alive.

I am pulling this card for you and me right now. What makes life feel unlivable for you? What do you need in order to stay alive? Whatever it is, you deserve it, unequivocally. How can we get you what you need, together? What do we need to build, and from what unbearable worlds do we need an exit strategy?

3 how to save your asian american life in an hour

I wouldn't be here if it wasn't for this class.
This was the most important course I've ever taken.
Your class saved my life.
—*excerpts from student evals*

Dear second-gen Asian Americans,

I started teaching many of you in Asian American studies classes in 2009 for that Program-That-Must-Not-Be-Named at the University of Maryland, all the way up through 2017, then more of you for a short stint in American studies at UMBC in 2018, then a few of you here and there in disability studies classes at Georgetown since 2020, plus a full class of you remotely during the pandemic in Asian American studies at UCSB in 2021.[1] I also unofficially taught many of you at public talks and workshops at universities all over the country in the years after the publication of *Open in Emergency*.

I've lost count of how many Asian American students I've taught, and I've lost count of how many of you told me I saved your life: too many to count. But I know precisely how many times I've taught the one-hour unit that saves lives. At the time of this writing in early 2022: twelve times in courses across UMD, UMBC, and UCSB, and nine times in stand-alone workshops for students at UMD, University of Pennsylvania, Tufts, Ohio State University, Princeton, Vanderbilt, Williams, and Georgetown.

Twenty-one times. I don't know how many students' lives I've saved, but I know definitively, without a doubt, that I've done lifesaving work twenty-one times over the last dozen years.

In chapter 2, I located student unwellness in university ableism and the medical model of mental health—and for Asian American students in particular, as intersecting with processes of model minoritization. Universities tell you that you must be well and must do well, at all costs. They tether your hopes for your future to unreachable visions of wellness. But Asian American students, you come to my classrooms *already* unwell. Asian American unwellness blooms around the college years, but it begins much earlier. Remember: suicide is the leading cause of death for Asian Americans ages fifteen to nineteen.[2]

This is why I start my classes with Eliza's letter. "The Asian 'model minority' is *not* doing well," she writes. Students need to hear this up front. They need to have it said out loud because it is not said out loud anywhere else. They need to know that we see their unwellness, that their pain *matters*, that we will make sense of it together. Eliza puts mental health at the center of understanding Asian American life by claiming unwellness and locating that unwellness not in individual medical pathology but in complex relationship with model minoritization. And the immigrant family. She writes to her dead sister to make visible her sister's pain—and also the conditions surrounding that pain. "I must bear witness to the crimes committed against you (and against us) that led to your suicide," she writes. Over the years I have returned to this letter over and over in my teaching, in my writing, in my creating, because it so resolutely pulls back the veil that covers over our unwellness. We are not supposed to look directly at what hurts; we are supposed to find ways to move on, forget, erase. Eliza does not let us forget. She will not let us pretend. I quote her here at length because these passages are so searingly important to outlining the scope of the problem:

> The first time was different in many ways. First of all, no professional psychologists or mental health experts knew about it. Everyone in our family kept your suicide attempt secret and normalized it as if it had never happened. Secondly, I know you did not want to die, but to get our attention. I remember coming home and discovering you in bed with your wrists bandaged and the bathtub full of blood and water. You thrust your limp arms into the air and cried, pleading for my help. I was devastated, broken-hearted, sickened, and bizarrely nervous all the while about what our parents would do if they had to be interrupted at work! I looked to our brothers for direction, but they

acted as if there was no big emergency. I convinced myself that you were not dying, that your slashed wrists were not much worse than a cut finger. When our parents finally discovered you, they became hysterical and burst into wails of anguish—I was so taken aback by their rare show of sympathy that I began crying myself, throwing my body onto yours, because only then did I feel safe enough to reach out to you. Once our mother wondered aloud why I had not told them right away about your suicide attempt. I did not explain myself to her, but it was because all the violence in our lives, both physical and emotional, made your suicide attempt seem normal, everyday. It was not that I was unaware of what a crisis looked like, but that I was used to having to assimilate them into quotidian experience. I was more worried about controlling the "disruption" than about what was actually happening to you...I knew there was an emergency, I was ready to do something! But then I felt I was supposed to walk away, like all the other times when one of us was in distress. Silence was disciplined into us.

And:

The Asian "model minority" is *not* doing well. Do you see what a lie it is and how it is used to reinforce the American Dream and punish those of us who don't "succeed," or who succeed "too much"? It is making me mad knowing the truth of this culture, which is so obvious and yet so strategically dissimulated in the everyday that it becomes invisible, and nothing is left but the violence that results from its disappearance. How do you point out the horror of something that is so fundamentally banal and routine that it ceases to appear traumatic?

Our inclusion into the American process turned out to be our worst form of oppression.

Isn't our madness often the only evidence we have at all to show for this civilizing terror?[3]

Eliza reminds us that there is something invisible and horrific about Asian American life, and that that something has taught us to swallow the traumas of our lives to the point where they cease being recognizable as traumas, and we are left choking on a pain we can't name or even see.[4] Sometimes, we even say it's good for us.

If you want to embark upon a journey to save your Asian American life, Eliza's work is an essential place to start.

erin's is the other.

To save their lives, I teach students ingratitude.

I met erin Khuê Ninh in her first years as faculty in Asian American studies at UCSB while I was a PhD student in religious studies and feminist studies there. I read her dissertation, before, in 2011, it became the book *Ingratitude: The Debt-Bound Daughter in Asian American Literature*, at the urging of Jim Lee, my then-professor in an Asian American studies grad seminar. It's 2022 now, and the three of us somehow find ourselves in an almost-daily group text through which we repeatedly save each other's lives.

To save my students' lives, I give them what I gleaned from reading erin's dissertation all those formative years ago. Lawrence jokes that I'm erin's PR department. erin and I recently discovered the hilarious fact that I have now given more talks about her book than she has. What I want to make sense of here is the life the book and its central ideas, and maybe its unspoken hopes, have taken on in the frictional space of my classrooms and workshops over the years, and the interpretive ownership students have taken of *Ingratitude*, the small salvations they've kindled from it.

Asian American reader, indulge me this activity on *Ingratitude*. I know I could describe it to you relatively quickly, but I think it's better if I just show you. Don't worry, this won't take the full hour here.

Do you feel like you owe your parents for their sacrifices?

You should be nodding right now. When I ask my students, "Who here feels they owe their parents for their sacrifices?," almost every single Asian American hand raises. This happens every time, every course, every university at which I've taught.

Next question:

What is it that you owe? In other words, how do you repay this debt?

Let's actually take a few moments to answer these questions. Write down five things that you feel you have to do in order to repay this debt.

1 _____

2 _____

3 _____

4 _____

5 _____

Now take a few moments to expand on each a bit in more detail. Surely there are more specifics. What does each thing you have to do actually entail? What are the options, or nonoptions, within each? Build out each one some more.

1 _____

2 _____

3 _____

4 _____

5 _____

I've done this activity with hundreds of students, and the answers are always almost exactly the same. Let's see if yours are too.

- Take care of my parents in their old age
- Financial stability
- Success

Did your list start in these same places?

But what does "success" actually mean? Students explain: *The right kind of job—high-paying, high-status, acceptable to their parents' social circles, something "braggable" to their aunties. A better job than their cousins'.*

What is the right kind of job? *Doctor, engineer, lawyer. Something STEM. Maybe finance/economics/business. Not art.*

This obviously requires the right kind of major in college as well. *Pre-med, engineering, computer science. Not English.*

Did you list marriage? My past students always get there eventually. To have a successful life also means to get married, have children, have a house. But wait! Not just any kind of married. It has to be to the "right" kind of person, one who is of the right race and/or ethnicity and/or religion, from a "good family," whatever that means, and with a "good career," likely from that same approved list above. Don't forget, a spouse must be the right gender too.[5]

Marriage also has to come at the right time, in the right ways. Some students have said they have to magically get married without having dated first. No dating in high school, maybe even in college. No sex before marriage, obviously. Then after this miraculous marriage, there must be children, to give their parents grandchildren. And all this must happen at the right time—not too early, not too late—*and* in the right order: marriage *then* children, not the other way around!

The house and suburban, upwardly mobile, middle-class life naturally come with this picture. Sometimes there's even a pool! Maybe the parents will live in this large suburban house with them too. *No nursing homes!*, my students have exclaimed with laughter.

Anything else? Have we left anything out? Is that everything you owe? Is there anything left *to* owe?

Because once the list feels exhaustive, once it covers the entire whiteboard, a student will inevitably raise their hand and say in quiet horror, "That's my whole life."

Look at your list. That's your whole life.

This is the first moment of horror in the process of saving your own life.

The debt is "selfhood," erin writes. Because what is owed is not simply thank-yous but *to be the right kind of person*. And rightness of personhood is something we must express over and over, in every act, every choice. The time of personhood is endless, all-consuming, both in rightness and failure.

Why do we owe our very selves to our parents? My students have always wanted to know this, the why and how of it all. Where does this sense of filial debt come from?

To begin answering that question, we first must throw out—and I mean into the garbage—the idea of "Asian Cultural Values." It does not exist. There is no such thing as a monolithic "Asian culture" that we all share. This enduring myth stems from Orientalism, a colonialist construction of "The East" that imagines it as the opposite of something called "The West," flattening all difference across geography, ethnicity, culture, and history (which is particularly galling for those of us colonized by others of us!). This racial construction benefits many, and endures because of continuing desire for it—including ours and our parents'. It is an easy story to tell. It is an easy story to deploy.[6]

The myth also stems from an attachment to Confucianism as a way of explaining immigrant family values, another easy story to tell. Part of what is considered "traditional" about Asian immigrant parents is their supposed Confucianism, a worldview and cultural system developed from the teachings of the fifth-century BCE Chinese philosopher Confucius. "Confucian values" has become shorthand for a sense of family duty and rigid familial hierarchy. "Respecting your elders" has become its paraphrase. But not all of us actually come from cultures that have been touched by Confucianism and Chinese colonization. While Confucian values may play a role for some immigrant families from various countries in East Asia and Vietnam, it clearly does not for those from South Asia, Central Asia, and other Southeast Asian countries. At best, Confucian values may be one layer upon which intergenerational conflict shapes itself (and explains itself), and at worst, it may be another Orientalist construction that reflects more our desires and anxieties, or those imposed upon us, than what is actually happening in Asian American families.

Another version of Asian Cultural Values is cultural psychology's framework of "collectivist" and "individualist" cultures. My students will sometimes come into my classroom armed with this framework that they've learned in their other (non–Asian American studies or very bad Asian American studies!) classes. Their attachment to it makes sense: it explains the very real distance between their sense of themselves and their parents' demands, and it puts "American culture" and their families' cultures of origin into neat categories that make sense of students' complex lives in simple and desirable ways. But the binary is suspect from the start, a construction grounded in an Orientalist assumption that "Eastern" cultures are more collectivist and "Western" ones are more individualist. Why are cultures measured along this spectrum in the first place? How do we actually measure the strength of social ties? By some studies and measurements, American culture demonstrates a very strong orientation to community (and here, one has to wonder who counts as representing "American culture," and then remember this question applies equally well to many radically diverse Asian countries, too). Even beyond interrogating these processes of measurement and operationalization, I would press that any analysis of social ties must take into account the historical and structural forces that shape sociality. Cultures are not monolithic and unchanging; the depths and meaning of social ties have to change over time as well. The overarching label of collectivism is just not nuanced enough to capture these dynamics.

I also question the very concepts of individualism and collectivism as opposites—as if wanting agency for yourself and being committed to community are mutually exclusive. I would hope that we do not have to choose one over the other; we should be able to be part of a community on terms that we have a say in. And we should be able to ask for care from our community—this is not selfish. We deserve for our communities to care for us. We deserve for our communities to care about our personhoods. Choosing agency is not inherently a betrayal of community, no matter how much some might want us to believe that.

I care deeply about how to be in ethical community and feel great responsibility for the well-being of those I am in community with—and these feelings are not a result of either my "Confucian" or my "collectivist" Vietnamese background. They stem from an ethics I have cultivated from Asian American studies, women of color feminisms, queer of color critique, and disability justice—all things I've encountered in a US context. Indeed, it does not get more collectivist than the crip value of interdependence! But I care just as deeply about my and others' rights to personhood on our own terms. And it does not get more agentive than demanding the recognition of each person's full humanity within a community.[7]

So I'm sorry/not sorry to say that intergenerational conflict in Asian immigrant families does not come simply out of a cultural clash between traditional or Confucian or collectivist parents and their Americanized or individualistic children, no matter how seductive this narrative might be. And it is seductive to our community for many reasons. It allows parents to frame themselves as bastions of authenticity and tradition and as absolute cultural authorities, while their children are shameful assimilationists giving in to the depravity of their American environment. This allows parents to be critical of parts of American life, an outlet for frustration and grief and anger at the broken promise of the American Dream. For the children of immigrant parents, this narrative allows them to dismiss their parents as "backward," "old-school," and see themselves as progressive, modern, democratic—and thus more "American" in an America that does not ever truly allow them to be fully American, but more American than their parents. For the United States, this narrative is critical for bolstering its sacred myths of American meritocracy and exceptionalism and the Orientalism that undergirds them.

But the narrative doesn't actually hold up upon scrutiny. There is no monolithic Asianness to draw from, across time and space. There is no static culture that immigrants maintain. Culture is adaptive and selective—no one brings their culture wholesale, unchanging, when they immigrate. Immigrants have always had to figure out how to survive in new environments, strategically reshaping their practices, even beliefs. Immigrants draw selectively from traditions of their upbringing as they negotiate experiences of immigration and living in a new country (alongside many other immigrant groups, with their own adaptations). In other words, assimilation isn't the only kind of change possible. Immigrants (and their children) are not simply keeping old ways or shedding them, not simply resisting or acquiescing to assimilation. Change is always happening, and not simply along a binary.

Look closely and you'll find that immigrants invoke their cultures of origin much more discursively than in actual practice—we say we're maintaining traditions much more than we actually are able to exactly replicate them. We say we're maintaining them because that positions us as cultural and moral authorities—as representatives of our immigrant communities, as "good" community members, and, especially for erin's work, as parents to unruly children. But parenting is not a tradition handed down and brought over unadulterated and outside of history either. For immigrants to the United States, it is shaped, driven, by "the demands of surviving in capitalist America."[8]

And the environment in which Asian immigrants have found themselves in the United States has been historically harsh. This context is crucially important. As erin explains, struggling families see themselves, and reorganize themselves, as economic units. Everyone in the family must contribute to its survival. Precarity redefines family relations so that the child becomes the debtor and the parent the creditor. Parental care transmutes to sacrifice; children's survival becomes debt. Hence debt is less a cultural value brought over from Asian countries of origin and more a product, a constituent element, of immigrant struggle in capitalist America.

The ways that debt plays out bolsters this argument. Children accrue debt for their very lives. They owe their continued existence to their parents' labors. Parental sacrifice takes on new meaning in a new land, the stakes unbearably high, the sense of economic danger and imminent class failure unbearably urgent. Of course parents must sacrifice in this context, and of course their children's survival is not a given.

If your survival—your entire existence—is something directly owed to your parents' work and sacrifice, then of course your existence, your selfhood, is how the debt must be paid. Because you would literally be nothing without your parents. Or so they say.

One pays this debt of selfhood by being a good child, the right kind of person, at all times. If one fails—and you will fail, at some point, perhaps often, because you are set up to fail, because perfection is a horizon meant to keep you obedient, not to actually be reached—then one is the bad child, the ungrateful child, a waste of all the sacrifices that have been made on your behalf. An investment with negative returns. A failure of the worst kind: a failure of personhood that reverberates outward to hurt everyone who loves you.

Children of immigrants and refugees, this is why being "ungrateful" is one of our greatest fears.

What non-Asian Americans often don't understand about second-generation Asian American mental health is how high the stakes are for failure, and what it feels like to live in perpetual near-failure. I've called this the slow death of not being enough—because in this system you are always not enough. erin calls it "designated failure," a technology of power that creates compliance through failure. Model minority-ness and "good child"-ness are all aspirational—horizons to desperately perform toward and maybe embody for brief moments but never permanently hold, because "rightness" has to be constantly performed. Rightness can't be achieved and then sustained on its own; there are always more choices to make, more right behaviors to enact, with failure dogging every step. You are set up to fail, you see. So that you can be continually redisciplined into correct being, shown once again what you are supposed to be.

This plays out differently across various pan- and ethnic-specific Asian American communities. For viet refugees, I know intimately, failure means our torturous escape from Vietnam, our abandonment of everything we had, the separation of family members, *the loss of a country, all the people who died at sea*—all are rendered meaningless. Children of refugees are forced to perform rightness within this narrative, carrying the burden of making meaning out of the worst kinds of death and destruction. For other communities, with their own, distinct migration histories, sacrifice takes entirely different shapes and names: perhaps downward mobility for South Asian doctors, for example, or the work of small businesses like liquor stores, dry cleaners, and restaurants—wherever geopolitics and immigration circuits and economic forces and geographical particularities intersect. There is no singular Asianness to point to, but America makes a Model Minority™ of us all.

Some failures are worse than others. The worst earn disownment. Fuck up badly enough and your family will throw you away. Achieve failed personhood so thoroughly and there is no redemption possible. You are ungrateful beyond repair. You are a disgrace, and you have to be ejected from the community. The investment tanks; the family needs to cut its losses.

The threat of disownment is always there, part of the aforementioned technology of power, part of the logic of indebted selfhood. It has to be there, or else the demands on selfhood have no teeth. We have to believe that our parents might throw us away if we fail—otherwise we wouldn't try so hard not to.

We have to believe that we deserve being thrown away—otherwise we would never fear it.

We have to believe that feeling like we are always failing, that we deserve to be thrown away, don't deserve unconditional love, don't deserve safety in our relationships, bring nothing but pain and shame to those we love, is normal. Otherwise, we would never accept it.

Let's say we do everything right. We don't fail, or we fail only in minor ways and manage to get back on track. We become a paragon of success, the pride of our family and our community and even the nation. Is it done? Has the debt been paid?

Remember, we listed out our entire lives. Because it doesn't actually end. This is a debt, erin teaches us, that cannot actually be paid off.

You see, the more you succeed, the more you actually owe.

Let me explain: if immigrant parental sacrifice is meant for the second generation to have more, precarity is supposed to work itself out of existence—right? That's the story. Parents sacrifice so that the kids can have better lives. And once things are more secure, that sacrifice doesn't have to happen anymore. Stability should mean a different set of familial relations. Then why doesn't the language of debt and obligation actually decrease? The child's success "simply demonstrates the immeasurable value of her debt to [her parents]. . . . If her success she owes to her parents, then paradoxically whatever she makes or achieves *compounds* her debt—adding interest onto interest, rather than paying against the principal."[9] This means that success *retroactively increases* the debt. The more successful you are, the more valuable what your parents did to get you there, and the more you owe.

You can never pay off this debt. It only grows.

This is the second moment of horror.

———

Wait. But this is love, right? This is how our parents show us they love us. Not with "I love you" or "I'm proud of you" but with sacrifice and high expectations. Our parents work their asses off so that we can have better lives. And they cut us fruit! "Are you hungry? Here's some food" is the Asian American "I love you," we say. Food is missing from the wildly popular (very white) system of "love languages" developed by Gary Chapman in the 1990s, but even adding food to the typology fails to explain what is happening in Asian American families.[10]

My students often insist their parents love them, that their parents enact this system of debt out of love. As if love and abuse are mutually exclusive.

In the end, the fact of parental love does not obviate the need for us to examine and understand the nature of its power, its logic and technologies. It is valid and necessary to discover the particular forms and meanings of anything we call love—how it is interpolated by power, or power interpolated by it, as neither power nor love makes the other less true.[11]

Here I quote erin's dissertation, because this beautiful paragraph didn't make the cut for the final book! But I found it so transformative—and so have my students. erin gives us permission to question the things we call love. Students have needed this permission because the cloak of love has made their pain illegible even to themselves. I actually agree with them when they insist their parents are acting out of love. "Love" just isn't the rejoinder they think it is. Indeed, it leads us to a new set of questions: What does love look and feel like in Asian American families? And is this the kind of love we want?

Turns out Asian American love isn't expressed by words or touch or acts of service, but through a system of parenting and a lifetime of subject formation. Crafted at the intersection of immigration and racialization, the Asian American love language is a mixture of sacrifice and debt, guilt and shame. Our love language is buying into the ideology of the American Dream, working ourselves to death, and asking our children to work themselves to death to achieve ideal personhood in that ideology. Our love language is model minoritization.

I'm reminded of what Ta-Nehisi Coates writes about Black parental love, not because it is analogous to Asian American parental love, but because it operates within the same ecosystem of racism. Coates describes parental love under the weight of knowing the extreme vulnerability of the Black body and knowing you cannot protect your children from the ones who can and will harm their bodies:

> Black people love their children with a kind of obsession. You are all we have, and you come to us endangered. I think we would like to kill you ourselves before seeing you killed by the streets that America made. That is a philosophy of the disembodied. Of a people who control nothing, who can protect nothing, who are made to fear not just the criminals among them but the police who lord over them with all the moral authority of a protection racket.[12]

Look at what racism does to love. How it shapes love, distorts it into forms that kill us. I think of other Black writers trying to trace the contours of what racism limits their love to and then trying to love, and write, their way out of those impoverished shapes. Coates writes to his Black son, Imani Perry to her two Black sons, Camille T. Dungy to her Black daughter.[13] This book is an Asian American letter to my Asian American daughter, to a generation of Asian American children, to explain our inheritances of pain. I join that chorus, that lament and prophetic call. I am asking us to look directly at the version of love we have been forced to contort ourselves to express, to accept, to die for. Asian American parental love—love that tells its children they have to be particular kinds of perfection in order to deserve it, because that is what it takes to survive here in this land and to give the ugliness of that survival meaning—is killing us. And I for one don't want it anymore.

"However compromised, your suicide was also a form of resistance, a refusal to carry on under such brutal conditions."[14]

How do we get out of this? My heart both breaks and fills with hope when a student asks this question, voicing the collective desperation, and sometimes anger, that wells up in the room. Eyes turn to me, stricken.

I don't have an easy answer.

In my classes and workshops, we first talk about negotiations. There are different pressure points in different families; most of us negotiate by compliance in some areas to alleviate pressure in other areas. There are different ways we must be good children, and each family, each community, has its own flavor of the Good Child. Most of us learn what are deal breakers in our families and what might not be. For instance, doing computer science might be an acceptable alternative to med school. Getting straight As might mean that parents look the other way in terms of your social activities. Not dating in high school might mean that getting that B is okay. Going to church every weekend and performing dutifully in front of the larger community might give enough cover so small discretions go unpunished. Historically, being queer has usually been a big deal breaker, so when suspected, performing straightness can earn a get-out-of-jail-free card, continually renewable. We figure out how much of ourselves we can devote to this project of self-as-payment. We calculate how much self can be given up, how much we might get to keep. We tell ourselves this is love; this is good for us; this is necessary. We find pockets, moments, of agency. Sometimes, in these negotiations, we find a livable balance. Sometimes we don't.

But even when we find something possibly livable, that is not the same thing as "getting out." When students ask about getting out, they are asking not about a difference in degree but a difference in kind, not about being less indebted but being actually debt free.

So I tell them what I learned when I read erin's dissertation all those years ago. I learned that we need to cultivate what she calls "a sustained commitment to injury." We need to be okay with hurting our parents. Because, remember, they will claim injury—we are hurting them with our willful, ungrateful choices. We are "doing this" to them. They are not lying when they say it hurts. So we have to be okay with them hurting.

We have to do this over and over and over again. Defiance requires perseverance. The opposite of obedience, it functions similarly—it is something you do over and over again to be the person you want to be and not the person asked of you. Because if you only defy once or twice and then capitulate, you are simply a bad child in need of censure—you have not actually gotten out.

Ironically like obedience, defiance is an exercise never done and over, but performed and renewed each day. It is not once but everyday that one is a writer instead of a lawyer, a runaway or drop-out instead of a valedictorian, a single mother instead of a culturally sanctioned wife.... Defiance is a choice constantly being re-made, because it requires that the subject consciously know that what she does inflicts pain, and actively reassert her desire to do it nonetheless (or all the more): it takes a sustained commitment to injury.[15]

This is the third moment of horror. Some of my students visibly recoil at this prospect. Some exult.

I always share my own experience of coming out as queer in my midtwenties, to help them see what the process might look and feel like. Queerness has often been a deal breaker in many of our families. But as I came into my own queer identity, I realized that queerness was a deal breaker for *me*. I cannot *not* be queer. And I won't be not-queer for someone else's sake—that idea seemed patently ridiculous. And I am not "doing" anything to my parents by being queer. They may claim injury (and may really feel it!), but I am not doing the injuring simply by being queer. The shame was theirs, not mine.

How incredibly freeing this was for me, to realize that I had my own deal breaker. And then—what if other aspects of my life are deal breakers for me as well? What if all the choices of self my parents had claimed for themselves didn't actually belong to them? What if these other realms of self belonged to me, just as clearly as queerness did? What if being a self that I want to be has nothing to do with being ungrateful or not loving my parents or not appreciating their sacrifices or being a bad child?

A startling discovery: erin's advice to defy, to nurture a commitment to injury, does not exist in the final book form of *Ingratitude*. This was something I discovered only as I was writing this chapter, searching in the book for the updated version of the dissertation quote that I had long treasured and taught. Somewhere between the dissertation and the book, erin stopped giving this directive directly, and when I asked her about it, she reported not remembering why. I will hazard a guess: an academic book cannot provide advice or guidance or solution in such a way without particular kinds of research and "rigor" and qualifications. We in the humanities are not medical doctors, nor are we therapists, authorized to prescribe "treatment" directly. But erin had imagined a way out for herself, which she included in the coda of her dissertation—she dared to imagine what none of the texts she studied could, what even her published book could not include. In that daring, she saved my life and has saved countless others, this daring living on in all the writing and teaching—and living—I've done over the last decade and a half of my career.

It could not exist in her scholarly book. But it exists at the meeting place of the scholarly, the literary imagination, the personal, the pedagogical. Because she needed it. Because I needed it. Because students have needed it and continue to need it. I write it here, this book a moment in that meeting place, because you need it.

What are *your* deal breakers? Who are you outside of your family's expectations? Who are you outside of your compulsory gratitude? What parts of you will you insist on keeping, will you refuse to excise?

What does life look like outside of debt?

A few years ago Jim shared with me a writing assignment he developed that I've since adapted and used in every Asian American studies class I teach:

Write a letter to your parents. What is the letter you wish you could write? What are things you haven't said but wish you could? What would you say if you didn't have to worry about being "grateful"? What would you ask for? What do you need? This letter is not meant to be sent unless you want to send it; only I will be reading it.

Let's actually take some time to do this. Take a few minutes, an hour, a day. Write your letter. It doesn't have to be perfect. No one else will read it. The letter is to them but it's for you.

But if you want, feel free to send it to me. I'd be honored to read it.

Dear _____ ,

_____

_____

_____

_____

_____

_____

_____

Back to "this is love." Yes, this is love. But can we imagine a love without debt? A love without the erasure of one's personhood. What might love on different terms look and feel like? When I pose this question, my students usually stare at me, bewildered, like I have asked them to imagine life without air—or essentially a world without parents. How impoverished is our language around love, even with the advent of Chapman's supposedly universal love languages, that my students have no language for love outside of this sacrifice/debt/shame system. So I supply some suggestions: reciprocity, mutual respect, mutual accountability, mutual commitment to each other's well-being. Mutual recognition of each other's suffering. The second generation is constantly asked to recognize the first generation's suffering—this suffering is *deployed* in Asian American immigrant parenting as parental strategy, the backbone of subject formation. It forms the basis for much of the second generation's compulsory gratitude. How would it change the parent-child relationship to have the second generation's own suffering acknowledged—and not put on a scale opposite "ancestral pain"?

No amount of sacrifice should earn ownership over someone else's personhood. No amount of suffering gives permission to ignore the suffering of others—especially suffering one is inflicting.

No amount of love justifies abuse.

We can all learn to love differently.

In one of my workshops at Georgetown, my students wanted to know how they might talk to their parents about this system of filial debt, because they wanted to reject the system but not their actual parents. They wanted to salvage something in those relationships. The work, it seems, is not simply rejection but rebuilding too—rebuilding themselves, their ideas about love and family, and their actual relationships with their families.

I didn't have an answer for them. I had so much trouble imagining this conversation. In all honesty, I haven't been able to have this conversation with my own parents. Or more accurately, the version of the conversation I've had with my parents is probably not the version my students are looking for—a hard setting of boundaries, over and over again, distancing myself, not allowing them input into my personhood, focusing almost entirely on access to their grandchild. Basically, I stopped allowing them to parent me. They can give some forms of limited care, they can access and give love to their grandchild, but they cannot parent me in any sense of the word that they had known before. I became parentless, or maybe I became my own parent? I know reparenting yourself is a thing lots of folks on healing journeys talk about these days. Giving yourself the unconditional love and care that you didn't get as a child. Perhaps that's a name for what I've done. I'm also okay with just being an adult without parents. Perhaps I'm too okay with this, and that is why I can't advise my students on how to keep theirs while also keeping their own lives. I don't know how to do that. I don't know if that is even possible. Perhaps you, reader, will figure out another way.

It would need to begin with asking exactly what it is we hope our parents understand. That this system of debt is a function of structural forces? That it harms us? That the stakes are life and death? That we are not actually failures? That they have taken something precious from us, and we want it back? That we want their love to transform into something that does not exact such cost. That we want to love them without giving up ourselves. That we want them to love us without hurting us.

What would it take for parents to be willing to listen to this?

Sometimes it takes a suicide attempt. That is the "wake-up call" some of my students have described to me. That when their parents finally noticed them at the edge of the abyss, halfway falling in, their parents pulled them back and relearned how to love them in the ways they needed. Is this an Asian American happy ending? Because it is simultaneously beautiful and awful. No one should have to live on the edge of the abyss for most of their lives. No one should need to fall in before anyone notices.

But sometimes there is no wake-up call. Sometimes our parents don't pull us back; sometimes they actively turn away as we fall in, washing their hands of the bad investment causing them so much injury. These parents could not divest from the Good Child and what that means for them. They could not stray from the pathways of model minoritization offered to them, thrust upon them. Even when it meant losing a child. Such is the power of conditional belonging in the United States.

Ultimately, what is needed is divesting from model minoritization as survival. And creating some healthier boundaries.

My relationship with my father is a good example. Early on, he thought providing me financial support meant he could have a say in my life—and I had to make it clear that I would not take his money if it came with any strings. His financial support must be unconditional, not debt peonage. I did not need it, I did not need him. I set a hard boundary/ultimatum: if you want to be in my life, it will be on my terms. So he changed. He stopped asking for anything in return, stopped trying to mold my personhood. Occasionally, a conflict would arise, and I would have to remind him by resetting the boundary. He backed off. Now, over two decades into this process, there are no strings attached, ever. My gratitude is not in personhood but in care—time, kindness, curated access to my life, access to his grandchild, as much as I am able to safely provide.

He also had to let go of some of his ideas of "success" for me. Not a medical doctor, but yes a PhD. No steady professorial job, but yes some prestigious gigs. No steady income, but yes marriage and a child and a house. A divorce, but who doesn't get divorced these days?—and then a remarriage that looks respectable enough from a distance. My dad brags about certain aspects of my life to his friends but also has managed to let go of much of his anxiety about what my life says about *him*. The joke in my extended family is that no one can tell Mimi shit—and my dad has made his peace with that somehow. He has his own life, his own successes and failures, and he surely has not divested from model minoritization for himself, but he somehow has accepted the boundaries that I've set, finding meaning and joy in them and not despite them, and somewhere along the way, without ever really talking openly about filial debt, he and I found balance and peace. During the pandemic we started a lovely practice of monthly trades: he brings me viet food he buys at the markets near him (he lives in a viet enclave), and I bake a variety of goodies for him and my stepmom to try. He stops by at the beginning of the month, says a quick hello, hands over the chả lụa and khô bò and bánh cuốn, receives the milk bread or coconut bao or mochi muffins, and then is off to the next thing on his social calendar. We trade food and joy, but not many words. This is also love, and I would take it over that other form of love every day of the week and twice on Sundays.

But this peaceable arrangement isn't always possible. A different kind of example: I keep a kind of distance from my mom, too, with hard boundaries that often give her very little access to my life. The intermittent access I do grant is so my daughter can know her grandmother and her grandmother can know her. That is one joy I can give my mom, albeit constrainedly. My mom makes different demands on my personhood than the usual model minority ones, but boundary setting is still necessary. I find it much harder than with my dad; it pains her. She accepts the boundaries I set begrudgingly and inconsistently. It's a dance we do, never in perfect synchronicity but always in tandem. Always in pain. Because she wants more, because she used to have so much more. There is a deep loss I have to keep maintaining, even nurturing, and that is devastating work. A commitment to injury is hard to sustain precisely because it is painful for everyone. But this pain is better than the other kind of pain—of strangled personhood and failed daughterhood—and I'll take this pain every day of the week and twice on Sundays, too.

I credit both my parents for the work they do. It takes a special person to be a parent to me. I do the hard work of setting tough boundaries, and my parents, to the degrees they are able, do the hard work of respecting those boundaries. Perhaps it all comes down to that. Because no amount of explaining will work if we can't set boundaries and if our parents aren't willing to respect them. Which leads to an interesting question of whether the familial dynamics erin outlines might be a form of enmeshment: a lack of healthy boundaries between parent and child, in which personhoods overlap, children are made to be responsible for their parents' feelings/well-being/suffering, and parents feel their own sense of success and failure through their children. A group of Asian American therapists asked me this in a workshop, and it blew my mind. A racialized form of enmeshment, operating at a larger, cultural, structural level?! While I am deeply uncomfortable with medicalized language in mental health—and the ease with which psychology might pathologize Asian immigrants and their families as a whole—there is something profound about framing immigrant parent-child relationships as a lack of boundaries nurtured, made necessary even, by historical forces. Avoid white prescriptions of familial "health" and racist vilification of nonnormative family structures we must; but we also must face head-on the reality that immigrant family dynamics are a love that kills.

I do not know what is possible with your parents, or with my students' parents, or with immigrant parents more broadly. I do know that the work begins with understanding the constraints on possibility: the shape of what we are currently trying to survive, the entry points, the possible exits.

I asked my students at UCSB in spring 2021, after an hour-long discussion on filial debt, to reflect on their takeaways in a collective document, and I share them here, with permission, because they give me hope, and I want them to give you hope too. I want you to know you are not alone.

- Today's discussion really made me think back to all those times growing up where I in fact felt I had to navigate and "negotiate" with my parents over seemingly benign things because I was afraid of their reactions and their opinions of me. That tiptoeing around my parents of all people really is not conducive to any sort of open relationship/

communication. Sounds easy to write, but harder to actually realize and process in all of its depths.

- How do we break the cycle of the relationship between parent and child that shouldn't be transactional?
- I am my own person and I deserve respect as much as my parents deserve respect. However, voicing my concerns and boundaries in the face of being hated, shunned, etc. is scary. Parents and children should be able to communicate with love and respect.
- How can I grow as a person if I need permission to do everything based on the desires of my parents?
- People are valuable from the moment they are born, not because of any tangible accomplishments.
- Mutual respect/love/expectations with parents, but not owing your entire selfhood to them.
- I am capable of deciding what boundaries can exist between parent and child. Also that many of these expectations are universal. It's not just me that feels stuck.
- Being critical of my parents (even in my head) is not necessarily indicative of ungratefulness. I should live for myself and not them or their image.
- I might have to create boundaries with my parents for my own sake . . .
- Setting boundaries is not a form of punishment against my parents.
- I can look toward friendships to understand what healthy boundaries are as well as what it means to love someone without the need for payback.
- It's okay to put your wants and needs before your parents' expectations of you and not feel guilty about it!!!
- Being defiant does not mean I do not love my parents. It means I am learning to show up for myself.
- Defiance is a form of self love!!!!!!
- Needing to break out of the system of debt or we continue guilt/ struggle—but how do we be defiant for the rest of our lives?
- "You have to be okay with hurting your parents." These words are reframing how I am thinking about boundaries. One of the hardest parts of setting boundaries for me is constantly feeling guilty that I am being ungrateful or hurting my parents for being critical of something they do or trying to draw a line. A lot of the time my mom will "claim injury" which makes it hard to set that boundary but this

line and our conversation in class is helping me realize that it's not done to hurt our parents. Trying to set boundaries is not something to be ashamed of because boundaries are healthy for us.

- How do we get our parents to understand this?
- The big question for me is how can we open and make transparent conversations for filial debt so future generations of Asian Americans don't need to go through this?

At a UCSB event I did the following year, a participant offered this reflection that I see as a powerful model, one that had me weeping at my own event:

- Hurting my parents feels like a heavy burden that I cannot carry a lot of the time so I am trying to reframe it as they are grieving who they thought I was and I am grieving the parents that I wish I had (mostly about being queer and trans).

Do any of the above resonate for you? Let's reflect on your takeaways from this discussion on filial debt. What are you feeling? What questions are you left with? What do you hope for, and what are you afraid of?

Thank you for coming with me on this journey. The rest of your Asian American life begins here.

Dear reader,

Indulge me in a closing reflection on the why of this work. In this chapter, I've walked through what I've done to save Asian American lives in my classrooms and workshops, and I write it all down in the hopes it will save your life here. Because I don't know where else Asian Americans can turn when desperately trying to stay alive. I've watched schools, counseling centers, and the mental health industry fail us over and over.

Of course they fail. They are predicated on ableist ideas about wellness and productivity and achievement that ensure they fail all students, as we discussed in chapter 2. They fail Asian Americans in very specific ways because they don't understand the conditions of Asian American suffering. They don't understand the interweaving of model minoritization and immigrant family dynamics to create a high-stakes, pressurized form of living or, really, dying. They don't understand how the slow death of not being enough can speed up quite a bit in the ableist environment of college. The university makes this worse, not better.[16]

I am not making a call for more "cultural competence" in the field of mental health. I do not want more diversity training or an Asian American psychology class that ends up essentializing these family dynamics once again into something called Asian Cultural Values. Cultural competence cannot simply be additive. What Asian American mental health—Asian American suicide—teaches us is that we must stop decontextualizing mental health from race and institutionalized ableism. Asian American mental health cannot be done without Asian American studies. And Asian American studies cannot be done without Asian American mental health, because it is only this form of Asian American studies—one that sees the stakes, understands these deathly dynamics, attempts to intervene in them, rejects ableism and model minoritization—that is an ethical project accountable to Asian American life and Asian American death. As my friend and colleague Linda Luu writes, "There are many ways to teach an Intro to Asian American Studies course, and I do not want all of them."[17] There are many ways to do Asian American studies and many ways to do Asian American mental health, and I do not want all of them. (Indeed, there are many ways to study Asian Americans and many ways to provide services to Asian Americans, and I definitely do not want most of them.)

The fact that in the years since I began preaching the gospel of *Ingratitude* I've given more talks about erin's work than she has tells me that universities don't know where to look or what questions to ask when thinking about mental health. Neither does the field of Asian American studies, or Asian American students themselves. Counseling centers don't know the term *filial debt*. Mental health professionals rarely ever encounter erin's work. When students across the country approach me to come speak at their campuses, they don't ask me to do a workshop specifically on filial debt; they just want something "on mental health." I suggest a discussion on filial debt as one possibility out of several, and as I briefly describe the workshop, it is like I've yanked opened a door they didn't know even existed, and now all they want is to keep it open.

Faculty don't know where to look and what questions to ask either. To invite erin to come share her work with students requires that colleagues themselves understand her work, see its value, and frame it in a way to draw students. It requires that they have some understanding of what students need in the first place. While some faculty attune themselves to student needs, the majority do not. In fact, they are structurally encouraged not to. More on this in the next two chapters.

Asian American students are dying because no one knows how to give them what they need. The university doesn't know—but it also doesn't want to, because model minority success dovetails so nicely with university baselines of meritocratic ableism and hyperproductivity. The university benefits from the drives that are killing its students. Hence the university is invested in seeing (and promoting) Asian American distress as individual pathology to be managed, many singular problems to be treated singularly, individual Asian American students stitched back up to go back to business as usual, being good students.[18]

It both is ironic and makes complete sense that university spaces are where so many Asian Americans are holding conversations on mental health. The years in college are perhaps the first time many students experience a kind of independence from their immigrant families of origin. The university offers the opportunity to shape personhood outside of family expectations, even as it simultaneously doubles down on racialized ableist meritocracy. The university's increasing commitment to "wellness," especially in the past decade, and even more so during the pandemic, is another painful contradiction for students: the kind of wellness the university commits itself to is tied inextricably to productivity. Asian American students feel these contradictions perhaps most keenly, and it is in these contradictions—a university that both opens and forecloses possibility, a university wellness that speeds up their racialized premature dying—that they desperately seek alternate, underground ways of engaging mental health. I've seen this striving throughout my tour across the country; I see it in my students at the universities at which I currently teach. The pandemic has made both the contradictions and strivings clearer.

What *Ingratitude* offers, in erin's ideas and in the life of those ideas I've nurtured in my classrooms, is not simply something to help Asian Americans with their mental health. It is teaching a generation of Asian Americans—and there are always new waves of first-generation Asian immigrant parents and second-generation Asian American children—to divest from their parents' dreams for them, from the university's imperatives, from the model minority. I have taught thousands of students to identify the forces in their lives that have made their lives feel unlivable, and I have offered them tools to name and interrogate and disrupt these forces. I have told them that their lives and their pain matter. But even more than all that, I have been asking them to reject the pathway to belonging the United States offers them *by way of their parents.* Universities peddle seductive narratives of "success" and achieving the American Dream to students, yes, but there is nothing more insidious than recruiting *parents* in the project of racial subject formation and *calling it love.* And there is possibly nothing more difficult than rejecting that love.

I've been offering Asian American students something other than "cultural competence." In speaking the language of their feelings and naming the pressures they face, I have been giving them permission to opt out of the racialized system that is killing them, helping them see their family lives as part of this system, and then giving them permission to *reject their family lives.* In rejecting these systems of love, they might begin to dream new ways of creating relationships and new vocabularies of love—and ultimately, new forms of personhood outside of model minoritization.

What I'm offering you, and asking of you, is not simply to save your own Asian American life, but to save all of us, together. How might we dream a different Asian America into being, a different America into being, by rejecting the narrowed futures forced upon us? How might we, in expanding our agency and hope and love, expand agency and hope and love for others?

I am raising one of these future Asian Americans. I have not completely figured out how to transform my relationships with my own parents, but I have worked to cultivate my relationship with my daughter in transformative ways. On top of not replicating the parenting I received is the hard, steady labor of creating something new. In the work of parenting, I've had to create a different set of relational rules and a different love language.

I imagine a relationship for the two of us based on mutual commitment and reciprocity and care for each other's needs, with healthy boundaries, no one's needs subsumed by another's, no one's self sacrificed for another. I imagine never asking her to be smaller. I imagine creating space for her to be unwell, for us to be unwell together. I imagine nurturing vulnerability and continually earning each other's trust. I imagine learning together how to navigate all the institutions that fail us. I imagine holding each other accountable, and helping each other hold others accountable. I imagine letting her decide when to toe the line and when to burn shit down, when to choose safety and when to choose risk. I imagine being there to catch her when she chooses risk. I imagine pushing each other toward greatest courage and inspiration. I imagine staying with each other at the edge of the abyss, always.

I feel hopeful about this. Trying to shift our parents to this kind of system may be impossible, but perhaps it is not our job to change our parents so much as it is to make the conditions of our lives and the next generation's lives livable, at which point we can ask our parents to join us on the other side, when they are ready, when, or if, they can.

[PLATES 1 & 2]
The Hangman: art by Camille Chew, text by James Kyung-Jin Lee.

The Hangman is the twenty-first card in the major arcana. The Hangman is the body rent asunder by the violence of empire, racism, patriarchy, and ableism. As people pass him hanging there, they thank God that they are not him, until they are. Then, they begin to think differently about this hanged body, because theirs is being hoisted and harnessed to their own suffering borne of empire, racism, patriarchy, age, everyday violence, bodily failure. Then they realize that she who seemed so alone as she hangs there was in fact not so, but instead hung there as witness to the violence but not fully consumed by it. Because even here, in the cataclysm of her hanging, another witnesses her in her suffering and thus liberates her suffering for an altogether different—dare we say—utopian impulse. And so now, they, who are also being hanged, can join in a community of sufferers, a brotherhood and sisterhood who bear the marks of pain, and invite others into such solidarity, so that when they, when we, meet our ends, we will know that we are surely not alone. Receiving this card may feel like the worst fate imaginable, but take heart! The very cosmos weeps with you. ✳ James Kyung-jin Lee

THE STUDENT

[PLATES 3 & 4]
The Student: art by Matt Huynh, text by students everywhere.

The Student is the twenty-ninth card in the major arcana, sometimes known as the lost card. The Student cried the day of graduation. They play one role for the Mother, another for schools, another as the Daughter, another for workforces, another as the Model Minority, another for the state, always in the pull of the annihilating void. The Student is, at essence, a note-taker: be grateful / always be ok / chase the promise of / this, for hours / never complain never be sick keep going / nothing is ever enough the work goes impossibly on / is college life normal stress? / ~~what would it mean to leave~~ / we are finishing our parents' immigration stories / leaving behind the fact of living / we are not grades / a condition of what can't / ~~don't feel guilty~~. Drawing the Student card in a reading reminds you that Student debt extends forward and backward across our collective lifetimes. But ask yourself, what is it you actually owe? Your entire personhood, and then more. *We gave you your past, now give us your future.* The Student urges us to refuse. If schools are a feeder system for churning out good citizens, embrace being a bad citizen. Embrace being a bad subject, a bad student, a bad child, a bad person: a revolutionary. Remember that the Asian American Movement was birthed in the fires of student protest. ✳ *students everywhere*

THE PANDEMIC

[PLATES 5 & 6]
The Pandemic: art by Nguyên Khôi Nguyễn, text generated collectively,
edited by Mimi Khúc and Lawrence-Minh Bùi Davis. This tarot card was
collectively created in the culminating event of the UCI Center for Medical
Humanities' 2020–21 Open in Emergency Series curated by Mimi Khúc. (*continues*)

The Pandemic is the thirtieth card in the major arcana. It has been a long year like a long decade, one of atrophying time. We miss the way it feels to walk in a city, in the current of everyone going somewhere. We don't remember why certain things felt important in the beforetimes, do remember seeing a classmate in a casket on YouTube livestream. The Pandemic unmasks the lie of the word essential: who provides care, who deserves care, death visited disproportionately on the poor, the black and brown, the lower caste. Returning to normal is an impossibility brimming with longing and terror. In the center of the card is a discarded mask, an iPad by a hospital bed: say our goodbyes however we can. Toilet paper has become a totem of survival, sweatpants an emblem of refusal, sourdough a gift of renewal. All things will pass, like a kidney stone. When will we hold our brother's hand again? Will our kids remember this as the worst time of their lives or as something strange and tender? Will our dogs forgive us when we return to work? Drawing The Pandemic card in a reading means a portal is opening. Where it leads is unclear, but remember people have always slept in doorways, huddled under them during bombings. Who knows if The Pandemic will ever end. ✳ a collective card

CREATED WITH THE SUPPORT OF THE UCI CENTER FOR MEDICAL HUMANITIES

(Plates 5 & 6, *cont'd*)
Series facilitators Simi Kang, Yanyi, and Shana Bulhan Haydock returned to lead breakout groups to generate language for this card, while Nguyên Khôi Nguyễn joined to live illustrate. Mimi Khúc and Lawrence-Minh Bùi Davis drew upon the breakout groups' discussions to coedit this card for the Asian American Tarot project, documenting our collective unwellness during the COVID-19 pandemic.

[PLATES 7 & 8]
Suicide: art by Matt Huynh, text by Terisa Siagatonu.

Wanting to die is only frightening to those who have never been exhausted by the audacity of their own survival. Killing yourself is only terrifying to those who have always put their faith in a light ahead of them—rather than bearing the ancestral duty to be the light itself. Suicide is the twenty-eighth card in the major arcana. It speaks not simply to suffering, but to the life that holds the suffering as long as it can. You, who must endure being your ancestors' wildest dreams amidst the colonial terror that killed them, and left you with... what? Intergenerational trauma? Your war-torn homeland, bloodied by the genocide of your people? No wonder you chose this card at this moment. Or rather: this card chose you. Its image of a tired hand reaching to extinguish the flame of a candle symbolizes that yes, the light goes out, but like all candles: it can be lit again. What often goes unnoticed in the image on this card is what the rest of the body is doing that we cannot see. When chosen, Suicide is not a destiny. You are never to blame for what colonization has made you believe is your fault. This card chose you as a sign to pause and feel everything, rather than end. You're left to interpret what the rest of the body is doing while you're still here. Alive. ✳ Terisa Siagatonu

interlude 3
the professor is _____

Let's play a game. You know Mad Libs? The fill-in-the-blank game many of us loved as kids in the 1980s and '90s. I've mentioned it a few times in previous chapters. We're going to fill in the blanks below to reflect on what it means to be a Professor. Maybe afterward, we could even turn this into a new Asian American Tarot card!

The Professor

The Professor is not well.

The Professor pretends they are well because _____
_____.

The Professor desires _____
_____.

The Professor fears _____
_____.

The Professor works hard because _____
_____.

The Professor is grateful for _____
_____.

The Professor is to tenure as _____ is to
_____ .

The Professor will _____
after tenure.

A Good Professor always _____
_____ .

The Professor imagines a future in which _____
_____ .

In a reading, drawing The Professor is a reminder that _____
_____ .

To succeed in the academy, you must _____
_____ .

To survive the academy, you must _____
_____ .

————

Was this hard to do? How did it feel to complete these sentences? Did your
own answers surprise you? Do you think your answers have changed over
time? Which lines were more difficult to complete, and why? Which ones
felt scary? Which ones felt meaningful?

My Mad Libs tarot activities are meant to capture feelings and experiences—but also the structural aspects of both of those. What do our feelings
tell us about the underlying forces that shape Professorhood and ultimately
our mental health in the academy?

————

Now ask a friend to do this activity, and compare your answers. What do the
similarities and differences reveal?

4 the professor is ill

Dear colleagues,

We seem to think we can take our CVs with us to our graves. Like our students, we are unwell, though most of us won't admit it. We are afraid to be unwell, afraid of not being enough, afraid of not only failing in the academy but revealing the "truth" that we never succeeded into belonging in the first place. I teach my students to interrogate "success" and "failure" in their lives, and they throw themselves into this hard, transformative work. My colleagues, though: you refuse with a vehemence that is both laughable and bewildering. You need to know that the only way to survive the academy, to figure out how to make the conditions of your life livable, is to begin with the recognition that you are unwell. That notions of academic success and failure, especially for faculty of color, especially for Asian Americans, constitute a high-stakes gambit that makes us sick. We are dying excruciating, premature deaths, like our students. And even more so than our students, our dying might be accompanied by applause: we'll be lauded for our achievements all the way to the grave.

I am unwell. In previous chapters, I wrote about dwelling in that unwellness in *Open in Emergency*, and in my teaching and speaking since. Let us now dwell in the unwellness engine that is the academy. Let us look at our unwellness as scholars and teachers, together.[1]

We already know the university is not kind to those of us who are sick.[2] We also already know the university is not kind to those of us from vulnerable communities.[3] Some of us know that the university is not kind to an underclass of workers it has created: adjuncts.[4] What most of us don't want to admit aloud is that the university is ableist and racist in more insidious ways than just those. The university is killing us not simply by preying on our vulnerabilities. It is killing us not only by denying access and policing bodies, but also via what it asks us to aspire toward. The university is killing us through wellness.

Let me back up for a moment. In the academy, we as scholars are producers, of knowledge, of teaching, of publications, of institutional service. We are weighed and measured at all times for our quantified "contribution." Academia is a frenzy of quantifiable production, documented in number of publications, number of citations, number of grants, number of invitations, number of committees. Our CVs read as absurdly long, desperate lists that we hope present the totality of our achievements and convince others (and ourselves) of our worth.

Academic hyperproductivity across university strata is a kind of unrelenting dehumanization that relies on the conflation of that productivity with wellness. But for scholars, wellness is woven together with meritocracy in particularly lethal ways. Wellness is not just productivity but achievement. Wellness for us is the ability to achieve, accomplish, at the highest levels of intellectual inquiry and institutional positionality. Wellness becomes conflated with success, structures of access and inaccess conflated with individual merit.

We live and work in a machine that makes us unwell while not allowing us to be unwell and punishes us for being unwell and asks us to punish others for being unwell *so that we can prove we are well.*

Let's do a self-care activity that I assign my students. List five things that you appreciate about yourself—that are *not* related to productivity or achievement.

1 _____

2 _____

3 _____

4 _____

5 _____

Was that difficult? My students have always found the directive to avoid productivity challenging. They don't know how to value much else about themselves, especially in the context of school.

Now for comparison: List five things you appreciate about a loved one in your life.

1 _____

2 _____

3 _____

4 _____

5 _____

Now share this list with that person! And then ask them to share five things they appreciate about you in return.

How many of the things that you listed for your loved one were related to productivity or achievement? How many of the things they listed for you were? I'm going to guess very few. My students report that their loved ones' lists look very different from the one they write for themselves, and this is startling to them. Their loved ones (at least some of them) often value them very differently from how they value themselves. And they value their loved ones very differently from how they value themselves.

How do you value yourself? How do you value yourself *as a scholar, an academic, a professor?*

Another activity I do with my students: I ask them, "What is a good student?" Let me ask you now: What is a good professor?

I'll be a bit more precise: What does your field, your institution, your department think is a good professor? What do you have to do and be in order to be a good professor, to your colleagues, your university, and academia broadly?

Let's actually make a list. I'm serious. Write it down.

_____

_____

_____

_____

_____

_____

_____

Now looking at this list, answer me a final question: *Can you be sick and be a good professor?* In other words, can you be disabled, chronically ill, neurodivergent, traumatized, exhausted, grieving, depressed, anxious, and/or overwhelmed and still do all those things you're supposed to do to be a good professor?

If the answer is no, maybe it's time to consider being a bad professor.

Those of us in the academy, especially those in the increasingly tiny tenure stream, are the ones who made it. We are the smartest, the most productive, the most accomplished, the successful ones. We worked hard to be here. We earned our place.

These aren't exactly lies. But they aren't exactly truths either.

Ethnic studies critique has always revealed the lie that is American meritocracy. The United States is not structured for success by merit or will or hard work. Meritocracy is a sacred myth, a story we tell ourselves in order to make invisible our social stratifications and the violences directed at the most vulnerable for the benefit of the least vulnerable. Our inculcation into meritocracy happens everywhere, but perhaps nowhere more deeply than in our educational systems.

For those of us who have "made it" through the educational systems, especially against the odds, it is hard to remember that merit does not structure achievement. It is true that we worked hard, maybe twice as hard. It is true that we deserve to be here. It is *not* true that we simply merited our way to success. We all know of brilliant scholars of color, women scholars, queer scholars, disabled scholars whose hard work hasn't been enough to make them successful in the academy. (We all also know plenty of mediocre how-are-they-even-here?! scholars.) We watch our fellow colleagues "fail"—not finishing their PhDs, not getting jobs, being stuck in the adjunct underclass, not getting promotions or tenure—and we distance ourselves from them. We got our PhD, our job, our tenure, our promotion because we worked hard, we earned it, we deserve it. The corollary we conveniently forget: we imply that our failing colleagues didn't work hard, didn't earn things, possibly deserve what's happening to them. They weren't cut out for academia, we think mostly to ourselves but sometimes out loud to each other too.

While I was finishing my PhD, I read Karen Kelsky's blog on The Professor Is In religiously for its advice on how to write a cover letter, how to write a teaching statement, how to write a research statement, how to interview for jobs, how to apply for postdocs and fellowships. In the years following, her blog turned into an academic coaching business, then into a book, now into a podcast and an expanded array of webinars, courses, and individual coaching services, under the organizing umbrella of The Professor Is In: Guidance for All Things PhD: Grad School, Job Market, Careers in the Academy and Out. I think every single one of my academic contemporaries in the last decade knows of The Professor Is In. Most have read at least an article or two of her advice, many relying heavily on that advice during their years on the market. Her advice has been particularly helpful for those of us unfamiliar with the academy and its many unwritten, unspoken rules. She told us what the rules were.

Full disclosure: I anonymously guest posted for her once in 2012 on mental health and the academy during my postpartum depression recovery process. It was the beginning of my own writing journey and the beginning of my work identifying structures of unwellness.

Looking back now, I cringe at all the advice on her blog that blurs the line between strategic essentialism and internalized racialized ableism. Advice on how to navigate the terrible process of going on the market can quickly turn into reification of that process and its implicit and not-so-implicit values. It can also quickly turn into a meritocratic success formula: do these things, and do them right, and you will get that job! Kelsky doesn't explicitly promise the job, but she's running a business, and what is it that people are buying if not a path to academic success? The testimonials make this particularly clear: a client who, after five years on the market and 325 applications, finally landed their dream tenure-track job in their dream city; another who learned to "respect [themself] enough on the market to get what [they] want"; another who became confident enough to "take the reins and drive the offer negotiation process."[5] The messaging here: Kelsky offers the skills one needs for academic success, and if you don't learn them, you will fail. Implicit is the corollary: if you are failing, it's because you're not "respecting yourself" enough or "taking the reins" enough or doing enough of any of the myriad pieces of advice new PhDs get.

What is that advice? Most pieces are well intentioned, seemingly helpful, or even crucially necessary. But beneath each is the subtext that there are right ways and wrong ways to be an academic, and that all those things are within your control. Let's look at some of the advice I've heard over the years:

What we say:

And what it means:

1 Before you go on the market, publish at least one article, the more the better, in peer-reviewed journals. Don't waste publications in anthologies.[6] Don't do projects that aren't legible for tenure.

Publishing is the most important thing to show that you are tenurable and have value to the university. Your value is in your publishing. Your value is tied to the prestige of the publication. If you work on things that aren't legible to the academy, you are wasting time and energy—and it is your own fault then if you don't get that job or promotion.

2 Apply widely, market yourself widely.

Apply to dozens of jobs, all over the country. Apply for jobs for which you barely fit the description. Apply for jobs at small schools in the middle of nowhere, far from any family or friends or support networks. Apply for departments and universities that are predominantly white, even historically hostile to people of color. Be willing to be the only Asian American/Black/Latinx/ SWANA/Indigenous person in that department (or university!). Don't set any boundaries for yourself or prioritize your needs over getting a job, any job. Don't complain if you have to move. Be grateful you have a job.

3 Say yes to everything in interviews.

Pretend you can do everything. Because you don't have value unless you can do everything. Don't complain when they actually make you do everything. Be grateful you have a job.

4 Keep trying! You can do this!

If you just keep trying, you'll get that job! This is a meritocracy—try harder, try longer, and eventually it'll work out! You deserve a job, so you will get one! Those who can't get jobs don't deserve them.

5 Don't tell them you're pregnant or plan to get pregnant. Don't tell them you have children.

> *Getting pregnant or having children makes you a liability to the university—you'll have to take time off, you won't be as productive, you won't be as tenurable. Having children makes you less valuable as a worker. Your academic work is more important than your family life; you are your work, not a whole person with identities and responsibilities outside of work.*

> I've heard this advice from colleagues of all genders and all ranks. This is about as basic as it gets in terms of sexism and the motherhood penalty.

6 Wait until after tenure to have kids.

> *Tenure is the most important thing, and having children at the wrong time is potentially destructive to your career. Focus on your work, your publications, in these pretenure years. You have to structure your family life around the academic calendar and career trajectory. If you don't, it's your own fault if you fail.*

7 Don't tell them you're sick or need accommodations.

> *Being sick or needing accommodations is a weakness. It demonstrates that you are a burden to the university and your colleagues. You need "special" exceptions that are "unfair." You should need nothing beyond what is offered, what is "universal." You should be well, at all times. Being unwell is unprofessional. Being unwell is a failure.*

8 You have to really want it.

> The fuck? I'm not even going to dignify this one with a close read.

9 Teach a little to get experience. But not too much, lest they think you're just an adjunct.

Don't be "just an adjunct." Work hard to stay out of that underclass. You don't belong there. Unless you fail, and then maybe you do belong there.

10 Be tenurable.

Show that you can produce scholarship, at the correct rigor, amounts, and frequency. Show that you will be able to do this no matter what, and that other obligations will not get in the way. Show the department, college, university that their investment in you is worth it.

11 Be professional! In clothing, in speech, in emailing, in social etiquette.

Be middle class, white, straight, able bodied, neurotypical. Preferably cis male. Learn to perform these things at all times so you can prove you belong. Failing to perform any of these means you are choosing unprofessionalism and therefore don't belong.

12 You'll be fine!

As advice given to a new PhD, this *might* be the most innocuous of them all. But what it means:

Smarts are what it takes to get a job, and you are smart enough, don't worry. You deserve to get a job and tenure, so you will. Those who don't get jobs just weren't smart enough. When you don't get a job, maybe they were wrong and you just weren't smart enough too.

What is intended as reassurance places both achievement and failure at the individual's feet. It neatly erases all the barriers, uneven junctures of access, and forms of suffering in the job process, gaslighting us into believing those things don't exist, didn't happen, only happen to others.

As new PhDs languish on the market over several years, especially if they are adjuncts, the advice gets more aggressive and more anti-adjunct:

13 Just keep trying! Don't give up!

> What does "giving up" mean here?

> *If you give up, you must not have really wanted it. Or you just weren't good enough.*

14 Don't adjunct for a department you want to get hired in as tenure track. It will permanently track you as an adjunct.

> *We recognize adjuncts form a second-class tier, but one we think we can meritocratically stay out of. It is natural(izing): those who are there, after a certain amount of time, must belong there. If you don't belong there, make sure to do everything you can to not get mistaken for one of the people who do. Teaching is second-class work; do not get labeled as "just" a teacher.*

15 As you adjunct, make sure you continue being interesting and tenurable. Keep publishing to show you're not just an adjunct.

> *Keep writing and publishing even while applying to dozens of jobs and spending three or four months of the year being on the market, while also teaching two to six classes a semester, sometimes at several different universities. If you don't keep up your publishing, you're not proving your tenurability. You'll become stale, and then you won't deserve that job anymore anyway.*

Graduate students and junior faculty need to learn these fundamental rules of higher education, don't they? They need to know how the academy operates so they can successfully navigate it. They need to professionalize. Knowing the above, doing the above, gives them the best chance possible not to wash out of academia. This is mentoring. Right?

What was so alluring to me about The Professor Is In and other forms of professorial career advice was that they gave me a window into a world I had not had access to before and had never learned the rules of, as a child of Vietnamese refugees and immigrants, not the first in my family to go to college but definitely the first to pursue academia. Academia (and its particular forms of whiteness) was a foreign language I had to quickly, frantically learn during my years in graduate school. These professionalizing resources made that language accessible.

I cannot deny that these resources can be lifelines, especially for students of color. Especially for those facing a paucity of mentoring. But the well-meaning advice of "here's how things work" and "what you should do" turns into "what you must do" turns into "what you're not doing and that's why you're failing." It's a slippery slope—one that graduate students and new PhDs and even junior faculty, in their desperate attempts to sustain a foothold in academia, consistently descend.

The advice on writing and promotion demonstrates this descent even more starkly. The Professor Is In offers a writing webinar called "Unstuck: The Art of Productivity," a "self-directed course devoted to changing your writing habits and getting your work from stalled to submitted." The focus of the month-long course is identifying your "negative habits" and then creating new, better ones. It "challenges you to examine your writing process, identify your mental roadblocks, apply those insights to creating a new skill set, and finally practice those skills in a way that overwrites your old patterns." The main obstacle to your productivity, this course argues, is your own mentality: your own lack of desire, bad habits, and bad brain wiring. All you need to do to become extremely productive is "rewire your brain," "break through being stalled and get to submitted." Individual problem, straightforward individual solution. Implied: since the solution is so clear, if you don't do this, well, it's your own fault if you're not writing. I won't deny that there are many feelings and narratives surrounding writing, and that processing what writing means to us is an important thing to do—this chapter actually is trying to do just that. I won't deny that reorienting our relationships to our work would contribute greatly to our mental health—this chapter is trying to do that as well. But I am wary of a model that individualizes both problem and solution, and holds up hyperproductivity as a given ideal. (A testimonial claims that in the eight months after taking this webinar, the scholar was able to easily complete three articles and one book chapter!)[7]

A source for writing support that many faculty of color have turned to in the last few years is the National Center for Faculty Diversity and Development. Brainchild of founder Kerry Ann Rockquemore, NCFDD is an independent professional development business offering workshops, coaching, and mentoring for faculty of color, designed to help us achieve our highest potential as academics. Its mission is to teach faculty of color "how to thrive in academia" and help us "achieve extraordinary writing and research productivity while maintaining a full and healthy life off campus." This is especially important for junior faculty of color; NCFDD fills the gap in mentoring they often face.

A lot of people love NCFDD. So brace yourself for this next part.

The National Center for Faculty Diversity and Development operates on a subscription/membership model, meaning individuals and institutions can pay annual fees to have access to its resources. Let me repeat: *individuals* and *institutions* can pay annual fees. Individuals and institutions are very different animals. As an adjunct, I recognize this difference most sorely, because I as an individual am never securely attached to an institution and the resources to which affiliation might give access. Every university is different in terms of what resources it allows adjuncts to access (and access easily). As contract-based teachers, we have access only for the duration of our contracts. There is no guarantee beyond the term of a contract, and even if you know they'll offer you more classes, semesterly contracts create gaps in institutional affiliation even when consecutive, and these gaps have consequences in terms of access (to libraries, professional resources, course pages, even buildings and email accounts). Full-time faculty can make use of their institutional membership in NCFDD easily; contingent faculty cannot. Individually an adjunct would have to pay hundreds of dollars to access annual resources, thousands of dollars for the specialty professionalizing program. For some of us, that is equivalent to an entire semester's income. Full-time faculty not only have more, steady income to pay these fees, NCFDD offers a *discount* for institutional members. Plus full-time faculty often have institutional funding to cover professional development anyway. The difference in structural access and privilege is mind-boggling. But wait, it gets worse: the specialty program NCFDD offers is actually only for tenure-track and tenured faculty— contingent faculty can't access it even if we have the money.

Let's look at what NCFDD actually offers. An annual membership gets you access to webinars, multiweek courses, online discussion groups, weekly motivator emails, and its Core Curriculum. Its signature twelve-week intensive Faculty Success Program, for tenure-track and tenured faculty only and available for an additional fee, aims to help you "improve research productivity through intense accountability, coaching, and peer support." All of the offerings are grounded in NCFDD's focus on four key areas:

1 Strategic Planning
2 Explosive Productivity
3 Work-Life Balance
4 Healthy Relationships

Its Core Curriculum further breaks down these four key areas into ten key skills that revolve around time management, making plans, reprioritization, setting boundaries with colleagues, and building a professional network of mentors. These skills seem particularly helpful for becoming more intentional about managing our time, taking more control over the things that demand our time, and souping up our overall executive function skills.[8]

I have to admit that I would benefit from more planning, better time management, more organization, better boundaries. Perhaps it would help me feel more in control of my life, less overwhelmed. Here is that slippery slope again: the skills I need to better navigate the academy easily become reification of the academy's systems, its structures, its values. This is a model of hyperproductivity and meritocracy: learn how to work better, more efficiently, so you can produce more. Find resources so you can succeed—without questioning what we mean by success (defined by the institution) and what that kind of institutional success extracts from us and others in the ecosystem (tenured versus adjunct). Follow these guidelines for "explosive productivity"—that phrase alone should make your skin crawl—without regard to differential capacities and limits. Learn these skills and you can produce in the right ways, amounts, and frequencies. The fourteen-day writing challenge in NCFDD's program, for which you commit to writing every day and engage "accountability" by checking in with your small groups on your progress, assumes a universal able-bodied, normative-minded, neurotypical scholar-worker whose only obstacle to becoming more productive is motivation and the lack of a writing habit. In this model, there is no room for unwellness, disability, and neurodivergence. There is no room for doing work in different ways, with different goals and different priorities that don't align with the institution's. There is no understanding of the varied and fluctuating demands you might face, say, if you are a parent or caregiver. This model seems to make room for some needs in its desire to support "healthy work-life balance"—but I am just as skeptical about this nebulous idea as I am about productivity-defined success. What counts as "work" and what counts as "life" and what relationship is allowed between those arenas? What is "balance" and who gets to say it's been achieved? What is a "healthy work-life balance" when you are unwell? In other words, can you be sick, disabled, traumatized, depressed, neurodivergent, and follow this structure and find "balance" in academia? Does this model account for unwellness that is not temporary, curable, aberration? Does it acknowledge the ways the institution's demands actually harm us? It clearly doesn't recognize that we should never see "explosive productivity" as an ideal. It clearly doesn't recognize that telling someone they should "write every day" is ableist bullshit.

Repeat after me: the advice to "write every day" is ableist bullshit.

It is ableist because it presumes not only that everyone has the ability to do this but that everyone has the structures in place to enable this kind of writing. In fact it makes invisible the structures that are necessary to enable writing, such as financial stability, resources for research, emotional support, tech support, professional validation, child care, time, spoons, therapy, a cat, not a pandemic, someone to cook and clean and do the fucking laundry— implying that writing is simply an individual act of will and habit. It makes you individually responsible for your lack of productivity. It makes you feel like a failure when you can't manage to write every day. It makes every day guilt and failure laden. It makes you unwell and tells you it's your fault.[9]

I'm also concerned that The Professor Is In and NCFDD, in addition to being unintentionally ableist, run the risk of being unintentionally exploitative in a specifically racialized capitalist sense. They are creating markets for their services by naming and codifying "failure" and "success" in ways that amplify anxiety built into the myth of meritocracy, then charging those who most need help but can least afford it, most often those QTBIPOC outsiders without other access to these unspoken rules. Yes, The Professor Is In and NCFDD are providing services to fill a need for those disadvantaged in the academic system, but anyone doing this must continually ask the hard question of whether inclusion by way of teaching the vulnerable how to navigate a deeply flawed system is for the sake of the vulnerable, the system, or the teachers. They run the risk of creating *more* of that need, growing a market for their business—because let's be real, these are businesses—and pushing all of us to meet ideals that they unquestioningly uphold and reify and press upon the most vulnerable. And it is the most vulnerable who will feel they need these services the most, paying disproportionate amounts of money to access what they've been told they so direly need, compounding greater anxiety with greater financial precarity.

Let's say it all works. You followed all the job market advice and landed that dream tenure-track job, and now you're working your ass off being "explosively productive" and taking names on the way to tenure. Or maybe you already have tenure, and you're rising in the institutional ranks at your university. You're a success, and that means something important to you. Perhaps success means that you're a good person, that you're worthy, that you belong. Perhaps it means you *got out*. Perhaps it means you're different, special, better than those who haven't succeeded. Perhaps it means you're safe.

But the time of personhood is endless, we already know. Just as the Good Child requires continual performance, so does the Good Professor.[10] You have to keep proving you belong. You have to keep proving that you have earned everything you have achieved, that the merit continues to be yours. If it was hard work that got you there, hard work must be what will keep you there.

Remember that there are never-ending ways to fail. Even when you meet the benchmarks of success, maybe you didn't do it fast enough or easily enough or often enough or rigorously enough—there are always others who seem to be succeeding at all this *better*. You have to continuously keep failure at bay because failure at any moment would mean you never belonged in the first place. Failure would mean you'd be discovered for the fraud you are. Those of us already in the margins of the academy whose belonging is always under question, we feel this terror most keenly. We have to believe the story of meritocracy for ourselves because deep down we are terrified that we don't actually deserve to be here. We are terrified that we will be discovered as impostors and then everything can be taken away from us. We live in perpetual precarity, even at the highest levels. Because deep down, we know the institution does not want us.

For Asian Americans, believing in meritocracy and following a narrowly delineated path to success is old hat. The model minority formation dogs our every racialized step in the United States, and it is no surprise to discover academia has its particular version.[11] It is no surprise it is hard for us to disinvest in this version of our story; the stakes have always felt so high, the rewards so valuable.

It is also no surprise that in our investment we visit meritocracy's violence upon those around us and those under us.

Faculty, especially tenure stream, are tasked with the administering of academia: teaching and evaluating students, evaluating each other, hiring and firing. For faculty, it is easy to think that our job is to weigh and measure students and colleagues for their individual achievements, to evaluate their merits. It is easy, even satisfying, to demand from those under us the kind of dehumanization we ourselves have endured: we went through this; this is what it takes to make it in academia. In fact, demanding this helps to prove our own worth. We were able to survive, even advance, under these conditions— this proves we belong. This kind of suffering is given meaning through the narrative of meritocracy and neoliberal achievement. Violence as rigor, wellness as success, unwellness as failure.

Meritocracy is a whip across our collective, intergenerational psyche. We forget that our students, our colleagues—we—are human. We forget that they and we are whole people, and that whole people are broken. A pedagogy of unwellness acknowledges that we are all differentially unwell—breaking in different ways at different moments in our lives, with different and shifting relations to structures of unwellness. Do we as scholars know this about ourselves? Do we know all the ways in which we are broken by the structures in which we live?

Let me ask this another way: What would it take for you to stop pretending that you always have your shit together?

Here are all the ways in which I'm a bad professor/scholar/academic, for your reading pleasure:

I don't read much.

I write sporadically, sometimes go full years without writing.

I always turn essays/articles/chapters in late.

I don't apply for grants or fellowships.

I don't answer emails quickly, or sometimes at all.

I lose track of emails, forgetting which ones I need to respond to and by when.

I don't prep for teaching. I don't do my own readings.

I miss deadlines. I forget to register for things, forget to renew memberships, forget to apply to things.

I don't publish regularly. I've published one peer-reviewed journal article, ever.

I don't cite well, or enough. I also never remember or follow citation style guides.

I don't attend department or university events. I rarely go to colleagues' talks. I register for things and then don't show up.

I forget to respond to my students' emails, sometimes timely ones related to class assignments.

I cancel class, several times a semester.

I turn grades in late.

I let my students call me by my first name, let them turn things in late, sometimes not at all.

I don't read my colleagues' books. I don't keep up with the latest books in my fields.

I write my conference papers the week of, sometimes the day of, and lately I just recycle something I wrote before.

Actually, I don't even really present research at conferences anymore. I barely even attend any conferences. When I do, I don't go to any panels.

During the pandemic, I have been even worse about all of these things. I didn't do any reading, writing, speaking, or administrative emailing for most of 2020. In the summer of 2020, I didn't work academically *at all*.

(Consider this your academic Rorschach: Which of the above made you squirm the most?)

But I don't (usually) feel like a failure. Or a bad scholar. Or a bad teacher. Or a bad person. In fact, I often feel like a success: a good scholar, an amazing teacher, a pretty darn good human. I am thoughtful and caring, ethical and discerning. I take care of myself, my colleagues, my friends, my students, my children, as much as I can. I am generous, and feelingful, and expressively joyful. I am fucking hilarious. I think hard and feel hard. I create, when I can and when I want, how I can and how I want. I cultivate joy, with great intention, for myself and others. I rest. A lot. I laze about as much as possible, and that perhaps is one of my greatest successes. I am lazy as fuck, and I luxuriate in it.

I call this Sloth Professoring.

———

I forgot one item on my "bad professor" list above, maybe the most important one: I'm an adjunct.

As we already know, being an adjunct by definition means I have already failed, permanently exiled myself into the academic underclass of underachievers, of instructors not researchers, teachers not thinkers, lecturers not decision makers. I often teach intro classes that senior scholars don't want to teach; I cover classes when tenure-track faculty get grants for course releases or go on sabbatical; I fill in gaps in the curriculum that the full-time faculty can't cover. I get paid a fraction of what my tenured colleagues are paid. And I'm supposed to be everlastingly grateful for it.

A primer on the academic system of tenure for those who don't know: a limited number of faculty are hired into tenure-track lines, meaning full-time employment positions that begin with a multiyear probationary period in which new professors work to prove they deserve to be granted permanent employment, usually through meeting threshold amounts of published scholarship. Once they earn tenure, faculty are essentially unfireable. The majority of university courses today, however, are taught not by tenured faculty but by adjuncts—faculty hired on contingent semesterly or annual contracts, often hired and fired at will by tenured faculty who are in charge of running departments. Adjuncts teach the classes and often support the students; tenured faculty teach but also do their own research and administer their departments and the wider university—and get paid up to fifty times more than their adjunct counterparts. Adjuncts form an underclass labor force whose exploitation tenured faculty depend upon for their own job security. There is no university as it exists right now without adjuncts. Most academics know this. What they often won't admit is that there is no tenured class as it exists right now without adjuncts. All that precious research and writing and publishing that makes tenure and promotion—their very careers—possible? All that happens on the backs of adjuncts.

Let me finally tell you that story I've been promising.[12]

It is a difficult story to tell. Lawrence and I have talked a lot over the years about when we would give this accounting, and where and how. Especially the how, because stories like these break the social rules of institutions. We the aggrieved are not supposed to name what happens to us—that is unseemly. It is petty and self-indulgent. But whose rules are these, and whom do they protect? Institutions insulate themselves and their middle managers by labeling complaints "uncivil" and not worthy of retelling or scholarly attention.[13] As Lawrence has written elsewhere, shame is among institutions' chief affective weaponry, their means of naturalizing certain modes of discourse and silencing dissent.[14] Naming names these days gets placed under the broad reactionary label of cancel culture. I want to resist this norming of discourse and affect, even as, especially as, it makes me and you uncomfortable. This is what it means to ask myself *what hurts?* and then actually listen, and share.

I am breaking the rules of respectable academic behavior, and many will not like it. Many have not liked it over the years. I have been dismissed as bitter and petty and inappropriate, "holding a grudge," "unable to let things go," unwilling to handle what happened in the "right" ways. I am guessing this sounds familiar to some readers—many of us, especially women of color and queer of color scholars, are regularly dismissed in these ways.[15] This is all gaslighting. This is how institutional power maintains itself. If we turn critical university studies and disability studies approaches onto adjunctification, we must examine the processes by which adjuncts are exploited and discarded and give the fullest accounting possible of this aspect of university unwellness. A full accounting includes the ugly, the unseemly, the affective, the excessive. The structures of feeling here matter.

I have learned slowly over the years to embrace these derisions and let go of the fear upon which their power relies. I *am* that bitter, petty bitch who holds grudges and holds people and institutions accountable (cue hair fan). I have no interest in the unwellness and violence that is respectability. I like to think that many of us are ready to be done with it.

A friend reminded me as I was writing this chapter that I have actually already told this story, verbally, many times over the years, in different ways to different audiences for different purposes, usually in the context of a larger institutional critique and advocacy for contingent faculty.[16] Legibility has forced me to streamline the story, smooth its edges, flatten its complexity, because otherwise how will the people hearing it actually understand—and care? But now I am writing the story, in a space that is fully my own, and while legibility is always a factor because you, reader, bring your own sets of understandings, here I might be able to more effectively create for you an epistemic shift. Here, I can lay the groundwork for over a hundred pages leading up to this story so hopefully you more readily meet me. And here, this story can shape the understanding of unwellness we are working on together.

I began teaching in the Asian American Studies Program (AAST) at the University of Maryland in 2009.

I was pushed out in 2017, partly via this email:

From: <NewDirectorAAST@umd.edu>
To: <Contingent1AAST@umd.edu>, <Contingent2AAST@umd.edu>, <Contingent3AAST@umd.edu> . . .

Dear all,

I hope your semester is going well. I am writing to confirm that according to your current appointment agreements, your Fall semester part-time employment will end on January 7, 2018 and that your contracts will not be renewed for the Spring semester. As mentioned when the contract was offered, updated university policy requires that I notify you of this. For reference, please refer to paragraph three of your signed appointment agreement that states *"This appointment creates no right, preference, entitlement or expectancy on behalf of the Appointee to be employed by the University for any other term or purpose."*

If you have any questions, please feel free to contact me.

Many thanks for teaching and I wish you a continued successful Fall semester.

Best,

The New Director

This is how all of the adjuncts in AAST were notified by the New Director in fall 2017 that we were fired. We as adjuncts had no right to assume any further employment, any further inclusion in the program, any treatment as community members and stakeholders and collaborators—we were just contract-based employees who deserved only basic notification of policies. The New Director, despite being a relative stranger to the unit over the prior nine years, with minimal to no involvement in its program building, curriculum development, mentoring, work with student groups, community engagement, public programs, or fundraising, had, as tenured faculty and now the newly appointed director of the program, the right to do whatever the fuck she wanted. No moral authority; absolute institutional authority.

Here's the backstory to the email. The spring before, the Former Director converted my ad-hoc lecturer position into a full-time non-tenure-track line because the university would not give her another tenure line and because the "new" position would give me more security, approved for three-year contracts instead of just semesterly or annual. This triggered the formal process of a national search. The Former Director, thinking it would be a cursory process, relinquished stewardship and handed the search over to three tenured faculty, one of whom was jointly appointed to AAST for the previous eight years but spent most of her time in her tenure home, and the other two affiliates who rarely engaged the program at all. That was where things went horribly wrong. That jointly appointed faculty member was the aforementioned soon-to-become New Director. And at the end of the search that spring, that soon-to-be New Director decided not to rehire me into the "new" position but to hire someone new in my place. My Former Director was horrified, admitting to me (and Lawrence) that she had royally fucked up, that losing me would be a "devastating loss to the program" given all I had done to help build it and how much I meant to the students—and that she would do everything in her power to try to fix this and get me retained. When she came back a week later with "it's really tough, I don't think there's anything I can do," I asked her to really fight for me, to press both the New Director and the Dean to find a way to retain me, to directly tell the New Director and the Dean that cutting me out of the program was unconscionable, given my value to the program, given my history with it, and given the Former Director's soft promise to retain me. The Former Director responded, aghast, "I have to work with her!"—meaning the New Director. The Former Director didn't *have to* work with me. The New Director didn't have to work with me either and could *choose* not to work with me. Here were two tenured Asian Americanists, naturalizing both their institutional power and the institutional disposability of adjuncts. The only relationships worth preserving are the ones structurally enabled. The Former Director is a tenured full professor. The New Director is a tenured associate professor and now also the incoming director. Lawrence and I, we were just adjuncts. We were already gone. We were gone before this even happened. We were never there at all.

Lawrence and I had been with AAST for eleven and five-plus years respectively, teaching and program building for it. Lawrence had taught more classes for the program than anyone in its history, through five different directors. But no one ever "has to" work with us.

Let me go back even further. In 2008, I moved from California back to Maryland to be near family, planning to finish my dissertation from my hometown. I lived right next to the University of Maryland, where I did my undergrad; its Asian American studies certificate program during my college years had grown into a fledgling Asian American studies minor program with two (jointly appointed) tenure lines, a slew of graduate student instructors and researchers, and a handful of adjuncts, supported in large part by a recently won federal grant. I introduced myself to the then-director, the Former Former Director, a different (also tenured) Asian Americanist scholar, who offered me a part-time teaching position to fill out his curriculum but also to draw me under his wing, as he did with many young, female, Asian and Asian American graduate students during his tenure. (He offered to become my mentor, dangling the prospect of future postdocs and tenure-track positions that he could somehow line up. Before you worry: I got away unscathed. Many others didn't, but that is another story.) I taught one semester and then decided to distance myself—better to focus on finishing the dissertation and not get involved in what was clearly a sketchy situation. The many UMD graduate students mired in that situation whom I befriended (including Lawrence) regularly reported to me the shady-ass shit that was happening. This director would eventually lose tenure and be fired from UMD, thanks to brave students and staff who spoke up. But by then AAST had run out of that federal funding and, with no director, was on the brink of collapse. A new director was hired in 2012 to rebuild the program. This director, the Former Director, an acquaintance with whom I shared mutual friends and colleagues, offered me, one of the only floating PhDs in Asian American studies in the DC area, some teaching to fill out her curriculum, and, likely, to throw me a bone. One course, one semester. I said sure; I had just finished the PhD, was jobless, and could use the additional experience. I also wanted to develop a new course on some things I'd been thinking about (ahem: Asian American mental health). The Former Director gave me free rein over the course topic and syllabus and pedagogy, and this felt so full of possibility. This was the beginning of what would become a deep personal and professional relationship. I did not think the market or tenure would serve me—but I still thought an Asian American studies program and Asian American studies colleagues would. By 2016, I would be teaching a full-time lecturer's load, advising many of the minors, running an internship and fellows leadership training I developed, serving on the program's advisory committee, chairing the program's financial aid committee, helping with curriculum development, helping with grant writing, applying for necessary "Gen Ed" designations for our courses, collaborating with student services on programming, and hosting phở parties with Lawrence for the program. The Former Director would officiate my and Lawrence's wedding. All of our children played together. The three of us felt like a dream team. Sure, Lawrence and I were severely underpaid—our combined salaries were less than half of the director's, and in previous years had been less than a third—but that was just the nature of things, and we were loved and appreciated and given the ability to grow the program according to our vision. We were "geniuses," she raved. By this point, Lawrence and I were teaching a large portion of the courses the program offered, interacting with most of the minors, supporting almost every aspect of the program's workings. Students flocked to our classes and to the minor program. In addition to our teaching and program building, we also grew our own intellectual work, dreaming into being a critical arts project—*Open in Emergency*—that would change the face of Asian American mental health. We had built a home, and we were making magic from it.

A search-gone-wrong later in 2017, that home would die, and I would find myself, and Lawrence, no longer welcome in the program we had helped build. The geniuses were no longer geniuses. In fact, to our friend now rotating off the directorship, the Former Director, and to the tenured prof preparing to rotate on, the New Director, Lawrence and I were now a problem, a disruption to the "actual" functioning of the program. Somehow we found ourselves very neatly removed from the center of the program and placed not simply at its margins but beyond its borders. The Former Director publicly called me a liar. The New Director cleaned out my cubicle and threw away all my things, including a Polaroid of my daughter at an AAST student event, my daughter who had grown up in this program, running up and down its halls, attending its events, meeting its students, playing with its grown-ups and their children. My then-six-year-old was fair game for excision too.

That year, the tenured faculty, staff, and administrators closed ranks on us, as we and students organized to ask for accountability, transparency, and community governance.[17] The questions we asked: Why was it that three tenured faculty from other departments—and here I include the jointly appointed incoming director who had been relatively absent from AAST while she focused on getting tenure in her other department—were in charge of hiring for a program that was fought for and founded by students and adjuncts? Why were there no real stakeholders on the search committee, especially students? What was the vision for the program moving forward if they were cutting out the two instructors (because Lawrence, who had been on semesterly contracts, would just quietly never be offered a course again) who taught its humanities, literature, critical arts, Vietnamese American studies, mixed race studies, film studies, women and gender feminist studies, and mental health coursework? Why were they pushing out the two instructors who had most actively mentored students for the last five to eleven years? Students wanted answers, but mostly they just wanted to keep their beloved teachers. They were fighting for me. I will never forget that. In response, admin—the Dean, the New Director, and even the Former Director—mostly playing good cop, made sympathetic noises and did mollifying hand-waving from a distance while maintaining their stonewalling. And they deployed the perhaps most effective institutional strategy of all: they just waited us out.

This was a lesson in the inherent violence of institutions and those empowered within them, no matter how "good" those people are. It was a lesson that contingency is both structural and personal. That structural violence has a vast affective life, that our affective lives and intimate relationships are shaped insidiously by structure. That structure necessarily dehumanizes to enable otherwise good people to enact exploitation. That good people can do bad things; that they can start and stop being good at will. That institutions do not care, and even caring people learn to not care, because caring puts them in danger. That my friendship with the Former Director could not bear the weight of academic structural violence, of the siren calls of power and privilege and respectability. That it makes perfect sense I would lose my job and one of my closest friends, who was also my boss, at the same time. That Asian American studies is and is not a home.[18]

"I have to work with her!" my Former Director and former friend had said. This was in a meeting soon after she privately admitted she had fucked up the search and Lawrence and I publicly shared on social media about our devastation that I was not getting rehired. She lamented how this situation was so hard for her, how she had to work with the New Director and the Dean, how she was mad at Lawrence for being angry and yelling at her, how she still had feeling in her heart for me because I hadn't yelled at her, how this situation was just so tough, so tough, for her. She confessed how upset she was that we'd complained publicly, even as we never mentioned her name or her role in this debacle. She still felt attacked, and hurt, and publicly embarrassed. I listened to the absurd indulgence of all her feelings, in shocked silence, my face forming a mask of polite sympathy as I suddenly realized I needed to be careful here. Proceed with caution, like one does with white people up in their feelings. Handle with care, do not provoke their fragility and defensiveness, allow them to see themselves as allies, appeal to their desire to be a "good guy," stroke their ego, make them feel safe, ask nicely, smile, *so that they won't harm you*. There is nothing more dangerous than a white woman who feels under attack—but in that moment I began to understand that tenured faculty, even when Asian American, occupy a strangely analogous structural position. In a university, there is nothing more dangerous to folks at the bottom of the academic hierarchy—adjuncts and students—than tenured faculty who feel attacked. Tenured privilege is a helluva drug. Tenured fragility will be the death of us all.

I'm including here Lawrence's and my social media posts from that time. I want to be as transparent as possible, because I will surely be dinged for supposed elisions and inaccuracies and misrepresentations. I have been dinged for those throughout the process. That is another key institutional strategy—to gaslight by way of poking holes in a victim's narrative, undermining their credibility as victim and thus their ability to narrate a story at all. One detail "wrong," one "omission," and the whole thing must be a lie. Those in power, arbiters of truth. In a post-#MeToo world, this should be all too familiar.

My post:

Mimi Khúc updated her status
April 4, 2017

No good deed goes unpunished.

It's official today, so I can finally announce it here: I will not be rehired as the full-time lecturer for Asian American Studies at UMD. They—the incoming director and the hiring committee of outside faculty—have hired someone new.

Some background: This program was founded by student protest and is sustained by community buy-in. The dedication (and free labor) of contingent faculty and staff is the lifeblood of the program. And that dedication is first and foremost to the students, and then to each other. Some more background: When I came to this program 5 years ago, it was a heap of ashes, burnt bridges and burnt souls, just beginning its climb out of the wreckage that many in the field have since heard about. Over the last 5 years, I, along with other committed faculty and staff, led by the current director, rebuilt the program, repairing immeasurable damage and breathing new life into it. We saved it. And grew it into something amazing.

Apparently, none of that matters. The principles and spirit and history of the program mean nothing. My years of devotion to this program, teaching hundreds of students, closely mentoring dozens, creating new courses, developing innovative curriculum, creating unique leadership opportunities for students, fostering student-driven programming, rebuilding trust with other units on campus, cultivating relationships with student groups, representing the program to other units and to the field nationally, and SAVING LIVES—most of which was volunteer and unpaid—mean nothing. The fact that I've just published a project that is some of the most exciting work that's ever come out of the program means nothing. The vision and needs and voices of the stakeholders of the program—the current director, contingent faculty, staff, and, most importantly, current and past students—mean nothing.

I feel like my home is being taken from me. Our home. Lawrence has an even longer history here, 11 years of service, teaching more classes and students than any other faculty since the program's inception. The loss—for us, for the program—is staggering.

I'm guessing this is what a tenure denial feels like. Perhaps this is what tenure-denial looks like at the contingent level.

I will miss the students so fucking much.

To the person hired in my place: Welcome to the house I built. I have no ill will towards you; I wish you the best. Please serve the students well. Please take care of the program—and don't forget that I helped build it. Also: know you have big fucking shoes to fill.

To my colleagues across all of Asian American studies: please join me in condemnation of what's happened at UMD and support me as I close the door to

this chapter of my professional life and embark on the next, terrifyingly financially unstable and heartbroken.

[EDIT to clarify: there was an open search, which is why this is "fair."]

And Lawrence's post:

Lawrence-Minh Bùi Davis updated his status
April 4, 2017

Today we learned my wife will not be hired as a full-time lecturer with the University of Maryland's Asian American Studies Program.

A little over 20 years ago, as a high school student, I worked a summer job
with a young UMD undergrad. He told me that he + some other students were
fighting to get Asian American studies classes offered regularly at UMD. Then
he had to explain to me what Asian American studies classes were. His name
was Linh-Thong Nguyen. He was my friend.

Fast-forward 10 years, and I found myself at the very Asian American Studies Program that Thong had helped to found. I was a new grad student and
teacher, teaching Asian American literature. I wanted to reconnect with Thong,
but to my horror I learned he'd been killed by a drunk driver. He barely got to
see the home he built. I have taught in this home for the last 11 years, in large
part to honor Thong's memory and thank him for being my first Asian American studies teacher, by being that teacher for others. His program is mine, his
vision for a program mine: a program always just coming into being, something to fight for, something to wish for.

I love this program.

Mimi and I were thinking about it, and 11 years of 2–4 classes a year probably means I've taught more classes for the program than anyone in its history.
That doesn't make me its best teacher, or its most devoted. The legendary
Franklin Odo has taught here. And Deepa Iyer. I count myself lucky to have
worked alongside them, and alongside the people who make up the program's beating heart: Gem P Daus, who also just celebrated a 10-year teaching anniversary with AAST, and Phil Tajitsu Nash, who's been with the program
since before it was a program, who taught and counseled Thong and the
other student founders in the 90s.

Then there's my wife. Rather than list out her CV or all the intangible work she's done to program-build over the last 5+ years, I'll just point to the UMD students already mobilizing, in groups, individually, as student orgs, separately and together, to protest the decision and voice their support for her and testify as to how she's changed their lives. That's the truest index of her importance to the program, esp one birthed in protest.

Let me say it plain: the decision not to hire her is a sacrilege to this program's history and spirit.

There is a lineage here, a thick genealogy of struggle and caring, and it fucking matters.

Not recognizing what Mimi has done, what she does, what she can do for this program is an abject failure to be accountable to its guiding ethos and the communities it was founded to serve.

How did this decision happen? By way of a committee of 3 strangers to the program. 2 of whom have zero stake in it, not even a fleeting moment of participation, and who will go merrily back on their ways oblivious to its striving and stumbling and the damage their decision wreaks. Meanwhile no adjunct faculty who teach the majority of the classes, no staff, no allied student services, no alumni, no current students, no minors or fellows or student org leaders, were involved. Were informed of anything. Zero transparency. All major stakeholders in the program, all the people with the most to lose and gain, were cut out. This is an unacceptable, abysmal failure of leadership and conscience.

I know the person who has been hired. I've worked with him, and I like and respect him — many of you know him, and some of you whose opinions I value speak very highly of him. I think he will help the program, and I will work with him and support him because none of this is his fault, and because I love the program. But he's not the best candidate for the job, and the decision and process that got him here are unconscionable.

I don't know what's next. I don't know whether we will be welcome in this program that's been our home for so long. Esp after taking public stances, and after the student protests to come. I do not want to leave. Well, I do want to leave, I feel heartbroken and betrayed, but leaving is not what's best for the program. I want to stay. And I think I've earned, I think Mimi and I have earned, in our 16+ years of combined service, the countless unpaid hours of mentoring students, working with them in winters and summers, writing and getting grants for the program, developing curricula, creating public programs, and on and on—we have earned a motherfucking say in the futures of the program.

Born by fire, live by fire. The student protests are coming. I'm going to go hug my wife now, and we'll figure this shit out. Thank you for your support and standing with us as we demand some accountability and demand that the people making decisions about this program care about it as much as its stakeholders, or at least get the fuck out of the way.

I reread these posts now with such heartache for Mimi and Lawrence of 2017—what happened to us was awful, and it hurt so goddamn much. We felt the betrayal and loss so deeply. Something precious had been ripped away from us, so casually by those so assured of their right to do so. That assuredness still astounds me. My and Lawrence's work and our claims to the program were so easily erased by that assuredness. I reread the posts now with the distance of five years and much reflection and healing, and I'm happy and relieved to say it doesn't hurt anywhere near as much anymore. But I can also say unequivocally that I stand by every fucking word of those posts. Lawrence and I have always stood by everything we write and say. That is our ethos, our ethic, our commitment to looking back at power and looking toward what hurts. You may not agree with our choices, and I can admit that there were things I could have done differently in the aftermath, but you have to acknowledge that Lawrence and I always act from a place of integrity. You can call us many things, but unethical cannot be one of them.

I stand by these words still, even Lawrence's "strangers to the program," the phrase for which I would ultimately be punished.

I met with the Dean of my college that summer, after student organizing and a national petition made little traction, and tried to make a case for why I should be rehired, why I was an important part of the program, my own sense of ownership and belonging in this program that I had helped to build for the past five years. I cringe now at my own naivete: that I thought I could convince a dean of my worth, that I thought this was even the point of the meeting. He listened with polite interest, nodding, "taking notes"—again, cringe-worthy naivete that I believed taking notes showed goodwill—and let me talk for over an hour. His response to all the work I had done? "Well, you actually shouldn't have done all of that. It wasn't in your contract. You really should've stayed within your contract. In the future please stay within your contract." Not only was my work dismissed, but now it was being reframed as transgression. I actually did something wrong by putting in that extra, free labor that the program—and all the tenured faculty—benefited from. An adjunct must not be allowed to feel entitled to anything beyond the terms of their contract. That was my real transgression, you see: daring to lay claim to more than what they had doled out to me. When I asked about the possibility of a targeted hire, he actually laughed at me; the idea was preposterous. What didn't need to be said: targeted hires are to recruit superstars with dazzling research, not to retain mere adjuncts good at teaching and program building. When I finally asked him directly whether he would agree to retain me as a lecturer, he responded, "There's no programmatic need for you anymore." With the polite firmness and self-assuredness only mediocre white men in positions of power can express. He said it, so it must be so. He, a white man who was new to the deanship and barely knew anything about this ethnic studies program that students had fought for, that had blossomed despite terrible mismanagement over the years, that adjuncts had worked so damn hard for. I then asked him if I would be fairly considered for a different, administrative position now available in the program. His answer: well, he and the Former Director and the New Director all felt attacked. By the student organizing. By letters of support for me. By calls for transparency. He quoted Lawrence's Facebook post as evidence of the obvious harm we had done to the New Director: "You called her a stranger to the program! She's one of its tenured faculty!" As if institutionally conferred tenure were the surest claim to belonging, more important than time, labor, commitments, relationships. Tenured entitlement, tenured fragility, so dangerous. Then he told me that if I wanted to be considered for the administrative position, I needed to go meet with the New Director to apologize and make her feel better, since she would be doing the hiring and anyone who got that position would be working directly with her. I should go apologize to the colleague who essentially just fired me. In the hopes it would allow me fair consideration for a job working directly under her. Tenured privilege, a grotesquerie.

I did end up meeting with her that summer, right after her appointment as the New Director became official. She had actually refused to meet with anyone prior to that, avoiding all student requests to discuss the decision not to hire me. She refused to answer emails and canceled all her office hours. She even canceled the community welcome the Former Director had organized to introduce her to students as the incoming director. She essentially hid from students. Until she had the power of the directorship. I went into this meeting with teeth gritted and ego in check; I had no intention of apologizing for anything—I hadn't done anything to her!—but I was willing to try to smooth things over for the sake of moving forward and for the sake of the program. (I still thought of AAST as mine, still thought its welfare, and the welfare of its students, was my responsibility—again, how naive.) I sat through an hour of her crying, actual tears in her eyes, about how hard these last months had been for her, the hardest time she had ever experienced at UMD, even harder than the years under mismanagement by the sexual harasser. ("You remember that, Mimi." As if I and an entire cadre of graduate students hadn't been even more vulnerable than her under his unchecked power. And as if students asking to meet to talk about my retention is somehow comparable to sexual harassment. Tenured victimhood, so absurd.) A White Woman Deanlet was present, tasked to observe and "mediate"—cover the university's ass—and she listened and murmured empathetic noises, validating how hard it had been *for the New Director*. My mask slid into place faster and more firmly than it had with the Former Director—there was no semblance of goodwill or friendship here, only a set of fragile administrators totally unwilling to critically examine their power, looking at me as the entitled, troublemaking adjunct. Ungratefulness, an adjunct's greatest sin. Like white tears, tenured tears filled the room, ate the air, left no space for anything that might be called justice or collaboration or restoration or even just plain old communication. So I swallowed my pride again. I told the New Director I recognized it'd been hard for her, I would like to move past this, would like to remain part of the program, would work with her in good faith for the benefit of the program. I let her cry some more.

Two months later she sent that email to all the adjuncts. Three months after that, right as my final contract ended, she cleaned out my cubicle and threw out all my things.

I guess I didn't let her cry enough.

As for the Former Director, she would eventually withdraw from me and take the administrative party line. She met with students and told them that she understood their pain but there was nothing to be done; they should stop protesting. She didn't answer my desperate emails wondering why my final contract was suddenly truncated, later telling me she took so long to answer because she had been too busy finishing her second book—a detail I think is important to include and set alongside the fact that the Former Director largely excused the New Director from service to the program throughout the latter's tenure process. Research time and career trajectories of tenure-track faculty must be protected at all costs; they are what really matter. After the New Director's email in the fall of 2017 informing all adjuncts that they were entitled to no future employment, I knew my time at UMD had come to its quiet end (because the easiest—and very legal—way to get rid of an adjunct is to simply not renew their contract). So I wrote a final mass email to stakeholders laying out concerns and asking for transparency from leadership, a last attempt to hold the program accountable to those it was supposed to be accountable to, knowing full well that if I hadn't already been permanently blacklisted from the program by then, I would after this email. I would not go as quietly as they hoped. Upon receiving this email, the Former Director privately forwarded it to some of my mentors outside of UMD, senior scholars in our field, to show them how I was behaving badly. She also responded to that email, reply all, that she could attest "as the former director" that I was providing misinformation, though also "as the former director" she could not actually share any details on what I was lying about because of "personnel" issues. No receipts needed. A former director is perfectly authorized to publicly call a soon-to-be-jobless adjunct a liar to every stakeholder in the program.

What I have been outlining here is not simply the particular harms inflicted upon me by these particular people but an invisible culture of academia we all operate in: the hierarchies that we naturalize, the mythologies we rely upon, the things we internalize that enable and sanction institutional violence, the feelings we are allowed and not allowed to feel, the things we are allowed and not allowed to say. The consequences for those who disrupt its mechanics.

For ethnic studies programs, this culture also includes slippage between two forms of academic governance: community governance and top-down institutional governance. Ethnic studies programs such as AAST form and grow because of student demand, and function, at least early on, through a kind of community governance, a coalition of student organizers, allied staff and faculty, invested community members, alums, and donors. Ethnic studies programs have stakeholders in ways that traditional departments do not. And ethnic studies programs rely on community relationships in ways that traditional departments do not. Asian American studies programs draw upon local Asian American community for research, student mentorship, student internship/service opportunities, public programs, and fundraising. These programs require reciprocity, and various parties can reasonably ask: What is my money supporting? What is my time and energy helping to grow? What are the directions of this program and why? In community governance of a burgeoning, barely-off-the-ground unit, participation from many is necessary and valued. Everyone has to pitch in; sweat equity is a thing. Participation makes you an inherent stakeholder. You are invested in the unit; the unit invests in you back. You are accountable to each other.

What is a stakeholder in a top-down institutional governance model? To whom is the unit—and its leadership—accountable?

At UMD, the Dean, the Former Director, and the New Director engaged in something we might call *strategic slippage* between those two models of governance. They allowed the lines to blur, or intentionally blurred the lines, when it benefited them, strategically allowing slippage when they wanted and needed community buy-in, when they wanted to extract resources from the community for the benefit of the institution or their individual careers, when they wanted to maintain a public image, and simply when they got program building and relationship building for free. Without cataloging exhaustively, I'm thinking not only of my and Lawrence's labor but of that of countless other adjuncts, alums, community partners, and student organizers. I'm thinking of research initiatives and fundraisers in local DC-area Asian American communities, all built on webs of relationships, trust, and cultivated goodwill.

The lines between the two models of governance became crystal clear, though, when the Dean, the Former Director, and the New Director needed to maintain power and avoid accountability, and when major decisions, like hiring, were being made—because they don't *actually* want to allow anyone other than tenure-track faculty and administrators into decision making. Academic divine right, bestowed upon deans, directors, and tenured professors, crystalizing the academic hierarchy. They were happy to take advantage of what community governance had built but not willing to relinquish any power to that community or be accountable to that community. They refused to respond to requests for budget transparency, for the program's strategic plan and why that plan was best for the program and the populations it served. Accountability lay elsewhere: with the institution, with the culture of meritocracy, with tenured privilege, with tenured careers.

Ethnic studies programs are happy to let students advocate for jobs—NONE of us in ethnic studies fields would have jobs if it wasn't for students demanding them—and of course happy to have students boost course enrollments to justify those jobs, but few of us are willing to allow students into institutional governance. Few of us comfortably align ourselves with our students. This is actually part and parcel of the culture of academia: the university renders students and faculty differentially unwell but effectively silos them from each other, leaving both ignorant of the other's unwellness. Students at UMD understood nothing about adjunctification and the hierarchies of power in their beloved program, until that program fell apart. Students everywhere are kept totally in the dark about the institutional workings and labor issues of their universities. Meanwhile faculty are not encouraged to see how the university is making students sick, and instead are tasked with being the institutional magistrates executing the very policies and culture that make students sick. In fact the university pits students and faculty against each other, defining success for each in ways that not only alienate one from the other but frame the other as obstacle.[19] Accountability to the institution (and to meritocracy) requires us to refuse accountability to each other.

This is our unwellness in the academy.

Unwellness is institutional violence against you made invisible, and you are gaslighted into believing it never happened, it never mattered, but if it did, well, you must've deserved it anyway because this is the natural order of things, and those in positions of structural authority get to tell the story, not you, and the story they tell from the cushy chairs of their offices is the "actual" truth, because they and we all believe in their benevolent leadership, a leadership grounded in an academic version of divine right bestowed through tenure and "fair" hiring processes and meritocracy. I'm telling this story because I need to.

Unwellness is also turning away and pretending you don't see this happening all around you, under you. Unwellness is believing that doing everything right will protect you, has protected you, and that those set below you belong there, having not "merited" their way up as you did. Unwellness is a complicity that affords you some structural advantage and security while demanding parts of your humanity in the process. I'm telling this story because you need to hear it too.

We have trouble seeing our students' full humanity and our contingent colleagues' full humanity — indeed, we are invested in that not-seeing — because to face them would mean to face the ugly truth that the Good Professor is a lovely, destructive myth.

———

Soon after I was pushed out of UMD, a friend posted on social media the desire to form a group to cultivate "academic accountability." This sounded exciting to me, given the clear lack of structural and interpersonal accountability I had experienced. Then I realized all this person meant was that they wanted a writing group to help them meet their writing goals. Apparently *academic accountability* means something very different to me than it does to a lot of other people. The NCFDD includes something called "Accountability

Calls" to help you meet your writing goals, and touts that its Faculty Success Program will increase your productivity through "intense accountability."

What people mean when using the term *accountability* this way is that they want to meet their writing deadlines and complete the (arbitrary) amount of work they are "supposed" to do. When we ask each other to form groups to "hold ourselves accountable" in our writing, what we really mean is that we'd like a structure of support to enable us to write, to make meeting deadlines more possible, to care for us. But instead we use language that implies we are betraying something when we don't write. Who or what are we being accountable to here? Are we failing to be accountable to ourselves and our careers? To the academic writing gods? To the institution? That last is the saddest form, I think, an example of what Mimi Thi Nguyen, Other Mimi, names "scenes of misplaced faith" or Lauren Berlant's "cruel optimism."[20] We believe in the institution. We believe it believes in us. If we work hard enough, it will love us back.

Adjuncts know most intimately how the institution does not love. Adjuncts also know most intimately the harm caused by those Academic True Believers through their misplaced faith, their cruel optimism. The cruelty extends well beyond the self.

To me, academic accountability means holding ourselves in ethical relation to those around us in the academy—our colleagues, both tenured and contingent; our fellow university laborers, from maintenance to staff to upper admin; our students. The land, unquestionably stolen, and its original Indigenous peoples. The local community in which our university resides. Ourselves. Disability justice has taught me that to do so requires a commitment to seeing and meeting our needs and others' needs as much as possible. Mental health has taught me that it also requires allowing ourselves to acknowledge all the ways in which we hurt, are unwell, are trying to make sense of pain—and to do so together, because care can only happen collectively. Accountability is access and care.

Ethical relationship also requires an understanding of power differentials. For whom do we enable access; for whom do we allot care—and who gets to make these decisions? This is how community organizers usually use the term *accountability*: to discuss responsibility and acts of harm. We want to hold perpetrators of interpersonal violence accountable to those they've hurt. We want to hold institutions accountable for the kinds of environments they cultivate that cause harm. We want to hold leadership accountable to those they are supposed to represent, govern, and care for. Accountability is responsibility.

For whom do we feel responsible? To what do we feel responsible? Transformative justice has taught me that accountability requires a holistic understanding of relationships, contexts, and structures. Responsibility exists in a complex web. Responsibility is collective, but also differential.[21]

I have tried to figure out with contingent and/or disabled colleagues and students how to hold Asian American studies accountable. I may not believe in the university, but I still believe in our field. I believe our courses save lives by giving students the tools they need to understand the systems and structures and histories they find themselves (dying) in. Our courses are often the first time Asian American students see themselves in their education and learn that their experiences matter and are worth studying. At our best, we create knowledge that helps our students, and each other, survive. I believe Asian American studies can be this best version of itself by drawing on its historical commitment to justice, its origins in Third World Liberation Front coalitional politics, and deepening those commitments through what disability justice, mental health, and transformative justice teach us in terms of interdependence and community care. But to do so we will have to reckon with our institutional place in universities and the structures our professionalization and growth have relied upon. Our departments used to be programs which used to be a few regularly offered classes which used to be a random smattering of classes offered inconsistently and begrudgingly across several departments. At every stage, the majority of classes have often been taught by adjuncts. (Case in point: AAST at UMD has only ever had two tenure lines in its twenty-five-plus-year history—both of which have course releases from the program—and so during any given semester, there are anywhere from four to six adjuncts teaching most of the classes.)[22] The crisis of contingency in Asian American studies is not just that so many of us can't find tenure-track jobs and are stuck in low-paying, insecure, second-class contingent positions. It's also that our very programs have been built and sustained by those low-paying, insecure, second-class contingent positions. It's that the tenured are the ones creating those nontenured positions and managing them—often with that benevolent, self-assured, institutionally backed, meritocratically earned, academic-divine-right leadership. It's that tenure-track faculty are able to build their careers—by having full salaries and benefits, lower course loads, fewer students, sabbaticals, time and resources for research, access to fellowships and awards and professional development and mentoring—through their contingent colleagues' low-wage labor and disposability. Add to that the psychic privilege of never having to worry whether they will have a contract next term or whether their employment paperwork will go through in time or whether their paychecks will get mailed to the right place. And that psychic privilege of academic divine right.

Adjuncts, even in Asian American studies, have to do their academic or creative work unpaid, possibly on top of a full load of adjunct teaching across several institutions. Adjuncts, even in Asian American studies, have to watch colleagues get paid to *not teach* while adjuncts teach their classes for them, for less money.[23] Adjuncts, even in Asian American studies, have to watch colleagues get institutional rewards they won't ever have access to while their lack of opportunity is normalized. Adjuncts, even in Asian American studies, have to watch their colleagues' research and writing be valued exponentially over their own. Adjuncts, even in Asian American studies, have to support their colleagues' tenure and advancement through their own exploited labor and disposability. Adjuncts, even in Asian American studies, have to languish— professionally, emotionally, physically—so that others can thrive. Asian American studies as a professional academic field, both institutionally and individually, has been built upon the backs—and deaths—of adjuncts.

These dynamics I name are structural dynamics endemic to the university in the twenty-first century as it becomes increasingly "adjunctified," not just in Asian American studies. But for Asian American studies, and the other small, insurgent fields that have had to fight for a place in the university over the past five decades, our institutional purchase has relied—and still relies— disproportionately on adjuncts.[24] Our programs face that institutional bind: the university will not grant us more tenure lines—in fact it is always threatening to slash us altogether—unless we can demonstrate need by putting more butts in seats, but we can't get more butts in seats if we don't offer more classes, and we can't offer more classes if we don't hire adjuncts, as cheaply as possible, to teach them. We have holes in our curriculum because we don't have enough tenure-track faculty, so we plug those holes by hiring adjuncts. And we tell ourselves this is the right thing to do because (1) we are growing (and sometimes simply fighting to sustain) our programs; (2) we serve students, and students need these classes; and (3) we are giving opportunities to new PhDs and those who haven't (yet) secured a tenure-track position.

The last is the one I need us to look at more closely, because it is the most supposedly benevolent rationale and often cited as the *only* thing tenured folks can do to help new PhDs. We think we are giving people opportunities: teaching experience, some institutional affiliation, definitely some much-needed income, even mentoring. The Former Director was throwing me a bone. (She even offered to ameliorate the situation in 2017 by hiring me as her research assistant so she could provide me some income from her research budget—this is not unmeaningful personally [albeit a bit insulting], but structurally it is an absurd, unsustainable, unreproducible solution.) But as Other Mimi teaches us, with gifts of rescue comes the imposition of debt.[25] Adjuncts are supposed to be grateful for anything they are given, a compulsory gratitude that when not performed breaks academic social rules and hierarchies—and hurts tenured feelings. The tenured owe the nontenured nothing but a thank-you (if even that). The nontenured owe the tenured affective labor—and adjuncts' ability to keep their jobs depends heavily on it. Be nice, be grateful, never complain about labor conditions, never expect more than what you're given—or else you may not get renewed next term. Even if you are nice, ask nicely, take care of their feelings, let them cry, you might not get renewed anyway.

In the last two decades, we as a field have been taking stock of the project of Asian American studies, evaluating the representational politics and justice commitments of our field, the problems of representation that arise from institutionalization, our place in the "diversity management" of the neoliberal university, how we might work against the "planned obsolescence" of our programs, how we find stable "homes" in our institutions, the political utility of an identity-based framework for our field, and how we make our work matter outside of the ivory tower to a broader public.[26] But we have yet to evaluate Asian American studies through the lens of adjunctification. Or from the other direction: to do Asian American mental health, we must look at the university as a central site, and while the Asian American mental health epidemic is most clearly illustrated by students, it is also devastatingly manifest in the university's adjuncts. We have to ask what Asian American studies' relationship is to the university's project of producing unwellness. Where does our field fit into *that* project?

Asian American studies as institutionalized academic field creates a class of Asian American academics located within the university—and tied inextricably, if unwittingly, to its projects. We invest in the university because that is where our jobs are, where we might find institutional support for the liberatory work we want to do, where our research and teaching might matter. We want recognition as a "real" field, a legitimate mode of intellectual and political inquiry. We place our faith in the university to give us all these things, even as it makes us unwell and then *trains us to make others unwell*. We have worried as a field about Asian American studies being co-opted by the university—our overprofessionalization, the siloing of knowledge, the disconnect from community, our model minoritization as diversity poster child—but we have yet to realize that we as a field are also being co-opted into the university's project of unwellness. When we reproduce meritocracy and hyper-productivity, which I've argued in earlier chapters is particularly insidious for Asian Americans because of model minoritization, we produce unwellness. I am worried that a central part of what it means to be a "successful" Asian Americanist scholar is to be unwell and produce unwellness in succeeding waves of new scholars and students. I am arguing that the university is an epicenter of Asian American unwellness, unwellness that the field of Asian American studies is beginning to recognize—but the field isn't asking what higher education's role, let alone what its own role, is in that unwellness.

These deep contradictions call us all to account.

I am the wrong kind of doctor to my viet family but perhaps I am the right kind of doctor for this. I will hazard an Rx, humanities style, for how we might start being accountable for the unwellness we imbibe and reproduce in the university. Here are its beginnings.

Witness and Dwell

I was elected to the board of directors of the Association for Asian American Studies (AAAS) as its inaugural contingent faculty representative in 2018, immediately after I was pushed out at UMD. It felt like vindication and agency: look, an institutional body sees my value and wants me, and now I can actually do something about the plight of adjuncts instead of just helplessly absorbing institutional violence. Also, look, my home field, for the first time, sees contingent representation as important and contingent struggles as worthy of some attention; the moral compass missing at UMD might be put in place on the national level. As the first person to hold this position, I got to make it up as I went along, with the support of other contingent organizers in the field.[27] In my first year, I had one goal: bring the plight of adjuncts to the forefront of the association and make tenured faculty see their complicity in adjunct exploitation. It was important, though, to take care not to seem like I was simply airing personal grievances. I did not want to run the risk of the advocacy work being dismissed as individual vendetta, as opposed to demands for broad-scale justice.[28] So instead of calling out the particular people who had harmed me (and they were not at all interested in being called in!), I could point to the structural conditions of our work in the academy, the lines of power and privilege striating our community, and I could make everyone *care*. My students cared for me during the drawn-out fallout at UMD, and individual colleagues all across the country cared for me. Now I would ask the entire field of Asian American studies to care, for me and for those structurally positioned like me—because wounds deserve tending, especially when they are collective and especially when our own are inflicting them.

I asked for one of the high-profile presidential plenary sessions for AAAS's 2019 conference, and then-AAAS-president Theodore Gonzalves agreed. I organized it in collaboration with fellow contingent prof Laura Sachiko Fugikawa, and we devoted the session entirely to adjunct testimonies, the first of its kind in AAAS history. *You all will hear us*, I thought, *and you cannot turn away.* Because what I found most unbearable at that time was the pretense that all this institutional and interpersonal violence along academic hierarchies wasn't happening in our Asian American studies community. The ease with which so many of my tenured colleagues could look away. We could not let them look away anymore.

I titled it "Our Institutions Don't Care about Us, but Maybe AAAS Can" because I saw this as an affective intervention. The year prior, I had organized a AAAS conference session on contingency with several fellow adjuncts and one tenured ally, beginning to explore the exploitation in our field as things were unraveling at UMD. In that 2018 session, my friend and colleague Jennifer Hayashida talked about wanting tenured colleagues to understand "what it feels like to work alongside people who don't care if you live or die." She talked about being pushed out of her program at Hunter (she was the director for seven years, and had just gotten a $1.2 million grant!) and shared about the shame she felt continuing on campus during her "dead year"—and her continued feelings of shame and alienation at AAAS itself, her home association and field and supposed community. The 2019 plenary was born out of this critique of AAAS and a hope that remained; Jen had lost faith in institutions but still had faith in AAAS to do better by its contingent members. Maybe AAAS could change. Maybe AAAS could care.

The structure of the session was inspired by a student listening session organized at Clark University by my friend and colleague Betsy Huang, then serving as Clark's chief diversity officer (and the tenured ally on that 2018 panel). In response to protests by students of color about racism at Clark, linked with the national racial uprisings around the police shooting of Michael Brown in Ferguson, Missouri, in 2014, Betsy advised the president of Clark to hold a listening session to hear out student concerns and grievances. What is especially remarkable about this session, as Betsy has described it to me, was that all faculty and upper admin were required to come—*and were not allowed to speak.* Students would be the only ones speaking, with no defensive responses allowed from faculty and admin. Betsy described the event as incredibly powerful, with student pain and testimonies of injury made visible in incontrovertible ways. It's hard to gaslight when you're not allowed to respond.[29]

I found this structure incredibly appealing. Listening is what I wanted. Witness, and then dwell in what you've seen and heard. We cannot look away. I started collecting testimonies. I put out a call on social media, and adjuncts across the field answered. Not many—some were worried about blowback, some uncomfortable being publicly vulnerable, some just too tired and too busy trying to survive—but enough, most in excruciating, gut-wrenching detail. Irony of ironies, almost all of the adjuncts who submitted testimonies would not be attending the AAAS conference that year because they had no institutional support for it and couldn't afford to pay out of pocket. So I decided to print out their testimonies and have audience members read them out loud. Theo introduced the session; about seventy-five conference attendees joined, ranging from students to the tenured to senior scholars and AAAS leadership. Volunteers read the testimonies out loud, one after another, for almost an hour. We all did the work of listening. Some of us wept.

Here is the prompt I presented to contingent contributors:

What does it feel like to die, differentially, in the academy's halls? What does it feel like to be treated like a second-class citizen, to slowly have one's spirit crushed, to have one's career slip away? What does it feel like to "follow the rules" of academia, to do everything right—and yet still "fail"?

What follows are excerpts of the responses I received, portions of what we read aloud at the session. I include long excerpts of many of the testimonies here because I want you to dwell, like the attendees of the session, in the collective grief and pain of that moment.[30]

ANONYMOUS: Reading this question makes me cry. You've really hit it on the nose. It feels like shit. I feel invisible sometimes, even though I publish, teach, and attend conferences. I feel embarrassed that I couldn't get a tenure-track job, even if I've had other accomplishments in my career. I never know how other academics will treat me. I'm pleasantly surprised and encouraged when tenure-track and tenured colleagues actually treat me like a colleague (rereading this last sentence makes me sad).

Today I attended an event for graduating seniors on campus. There were the typical uplifting "you can do anything you want" and "don't let anything stop you from reaching your dreams" type of encouraging statements. As someone who once dreamed of having a tenure-track job and has given that up, I now find these kinds of statements sad. Just when I'm becoming okay with my situation and not wanting a tenure-track job anymore, I hear something like this and it makes me wonder if I've given up too soon, and just didn't try hard enough. It makes me feel like a failure for giving up, rather than proud of myself for moving on with my life. I think for the rest of my life I will always wonder "what if." I can rationalize that it's a structural problem of too many PhDs in a bad economy, etc., etc., but part of me will always feel like I just wasn't good enough.

ANH THANG DAO-SHAH: I was teaching up to 5 classes at 3 schools per semester.

I did not make enough to support myself. I was lucky to have a spouse who had a full-time job who supported our family and provided insurance. In addition to teaching I had side jobs which I did in the evening and on weekends. I also taught over the summer in a different city and would stay at a relative's house for 8 weeks at a time.

I think we need to stop accepting adjuncting as the norm. Once I got out of adjuncting I realized how abusive that life was, how it was structured to make me feel like a failure constantly. It took me 3 years to rebuild my professional self esteem, with a lot of support from mentors and friends inside and outside of academia.

ANONYMOUS: Most tenured or TT faculty treated me like I was invisible (at best) or like I had a communicable disease, was a worthless doormat, or a threat (at worst).

Our labor enabled them to write their books, publish, go on leave, do self-care, keep an extra chunk of their research funds, avoid teaching Gen Ed courses.... They got to where they are because they got lucky and/or had privileges that enabled them to succeed. In another set of circumstances, they could have been us.

ANONYMOUS: I felt like a second-class citizen. Anthro provided an office space for me to use and I noticed the furniture kept changing from new desks to older used desks. One time during my office hours, a staff member came into the office with a newly hired tenure-track faculty member to shop for a new desk of her choice—including examining the one I was sitting at. The staff at least sort of apologized while walking into the office but said nothing upon leaving. The faculty member ignored me altogether and treated me like I wasn't there.

I am tired of tenured faculty who, despite having good intentions, keep telling me to *just* hang in there and *just* publish a bit more and a job will happen.

I am astounded when I hear that some tenured faculty are against having some form of job security or entitlement for adjuncts after a certain amount of teaching because they feel like it is a "back door" to get hired when they had to go through a full job search—never mind the fact that we have to reapply for positions every year and departments make the decision to keep hiring.

ANONYMOUS: I've wasted so much of the last handful of years of my life applying to jobs for which I didn't even make the short list.

I think it's important that we acknowledge that we are fed a bunch of lies: "If you do x, y, z, something will click eventually, you just have to be patient." When I think of the sacrifices my partner and I would have made if I had gotten some of the contingent work I applied to—like a 3 year VAP gig in Indiana—I am grateful that I got rejected. Because you can get these jobs (that you don't actually want) hoping they will lead you to jobs you do want, you can keep moving from state to state, you can be separated from your partner or make your partner uproot their life too, and do everything right, jump through all the hoops, and end up with nothing.

We deserve to have good lives, to be in control of where we live, to not be exploited, to be seen and valued. We shouldn't have to throw years of our lives away doing jobs that overwork us, underpay us, just to MAYBE have a shot of something good later.

ANONYMOUS: I feel like I am drowning, and there is no end in sight. I feel my chest tightening and shortness of breath when I stop and think about how much longer this will last. I am only in my first year as an adjunct so my experience is limited but even a year of demanding work hours alongside uncertainty and limited resources has been challenging. If I'm not preparing lessons, I am grading, advising, mentoring, or trying to work on a publication. I've been disconnected from friends and family to get the work done. As an adjunct taking on new classes, developing new syllabi, I feel great anxiety before every class thinking "do I know enough to teach this class?" Of course I am fully qualified to teach these courses but I am always in a state of feeling like an impostor as a woman of color lecturer.

Being that I have yet to be offered a more secure position, I already know another year of this is coming, which is difficult to process.

LINTA VARGHESE: For years I experienced cognitive dissonance in AAAS and other academic spaces when people spoke of "contingency and the neoliberal university" but mainly in abstract terms or as hard numbers, not as the reality of the majority of people they worked with. Where people talked about the future of the field without consideration to the outsized role that labor conditions play in intellectual production.

I quickly came to realize how non-contingency and the research, writing, publishing that result from that are the basis of many networks and collaborations. Thus setting mirroring systems in which people with resources keep getting more resources.

I have come to dislike the d-word—deserve—that often accompanies landing an academic position. This is not to say that I don't feel moved and seen when folks have said this to me. I do. But the word now signals in some sense our enduring belief in merit.

ROSIE KAR: I live in near poverty. I teach 5 different classes a semester, for a total of 10 per year, and have no teaching assistants. That means 5 different preps. Every year, I am told to teach/create a new course. I make 75% less money than my white tenure-track counterparts and teach twice as many courses. My husband and I have the good fortune of living with my mom and dad, so as to save on the expense of rent or a house payment. We have delayed having children because we cannot afford it.

My department is run by tenured faculty who routinely teach classes online, go on sabbatical, and get course releases. Adjuncts bear the brunt of all the work.

I am tired. We have been sold a lie. We are doing your work and not being paid for it.

GENEVIEVE ERIN O'BRIEN: Most days I have to triple check what day it is to ensure I head to the right campus. On average, I make $500/week per class, and I spend anywhere from $100–175 per week on gas, parking, and a dog walker. As a part-time worker I am not eligible for benefits. I have no job security and work contract to contract, quarter to quarter or semester to semester. I have been asked to teach a class with as little as three weeks notice. More often than not, I am offered classes for the following quarter/semester in the current quarter/semester. This means, in October I might find out if I have a job in January. My classes, although under contract, are not guaranteed. They can be canceled at any time.

I get paid once a month. As a temporary contract worker, every quarter or semester I am also a new hire, so my first paycheck often gets lost or mailed instead of direct deposited. I have often had to call HR to hunt down my paycheck. Once, I worked for six weeks before my first paycheck was even processed.

During the winter and summer months, I am on unemployment and work other jobs where possible. My career as an artist does not generate much income. To supplement, I babysit the children and/or walk the dog of a few tenured faculty families. I am also a private chef for a family of two tenured professors. I spend my only day off cooking their meals for the week and delivering them so that these professors have more time to write and do their research. While I love these families, I have to acknowledge the irony of this situation.

The cost for me to attend one conference can be anywhere from $800–$1500. I remember one year for AAAS all of my colleagues were attending from Thursday through Sunday in San Francisco. I teach Thursdays and Fridays so I had to fly up Saturday morning and go straight to my panel for my presentation. My panel chair and the chair for another panel decided to combine the two panels since they were similar in topic. With twice as many panelists my time got shrunken by 10 minutes. As academics do, everyone went over their time ever so slightly. The moderator leaned over to me and whispered apologetically, "We might not have time for your talk." I fought back tears thinking of how much it cost me to get there that morning. Once, I found a letter on the copy machine at one of the campuses I teach at. The letter was for one of the tenured faculty, detailing a travel funds grant in the amount of $1700 to attend the same conference I had paid out of pocket to attend.[31]

JENNIFER HAYASHIDA: The facts never helped me, but for those of you who don't know, I was hired as an adjunct in the Asian American Studies Program at Hunter College and eventually came to be Director of that program. My glorified contingent title was Distinguished Lecturer.

Even the act of admitting that I was hired into a contingent position brings with it a sense of shame. I willingly entered into a position of institutional precarity where I had all of the responsibilities of the tenure track, with none of the rights.

At that point, I still trusted the institution. There is a photograph of our college President holding my first-born child, whom I brought with me the day I went to sign my contract.

Other facts include that I spun straw into gold and grew that program, put it back on the map in New York City, and ultimately obtained nearly two million dollars in grants and gifts. I also had two children, completed my first poetry collection, and developed vertigo and insomnia.

Being a contingent faculty member meant that I was simultaneously in the wrong place at the wrong time, and in the right place at the right time. I cherished a job where I was erased, exploited, and beloved all at once.

The Provost notified me of my non-reappointment two days after our program was awarded a 1.7 million-dollar AANAPISI grant, and two days after students took their long-standing campaign for the Asian American Studies Program to the floor of our faculty senate.

The Provost had no tissues in his office, so fetched me his hankie, which I should have burned.

People look at you differently when they find out that you are not at the institution on the same terms as they are. Some look at you with sympathy or dismay. Others look at you with indignant rage. I was often met with shock, since everyone knew that I ran an academic program and, in many cases, did more institutional labor than tenure-track and tenured faculty.

"I get it: it's rough to adjunct, but what about my workload?" some said, as if it's a zero-sum game. Please don't say that.

How do adjunct faculty look at tenure-track and tenured faculty, and how do you meet their gaze? Looking away is not an option.

I hired friends and acquaintances, established artists and graduate students. I was the gateway to chronic exploitation. I adopted the ability to look at new hires with chagrin when that program grew because people would work for nothing.

To call adjunct positions "part-time positions" is an offensive misnomer, since no adjunct I ever hired had a part-time investment in their position, the students, or the institution. Please refuse to use that term.

I want to argue that agreeing to teach Asian American studies for nothing can be the result of not only real material need, but also the *feeling* so many of us have towards the field: what it gave us, how we want to contribute, how we relate to senior scholars, and the students we see in the classroom. How it troubles the line between classroom and community in ways that we think explain the type of labor we do for the institution.

I hope you don't simply feel relief that this didn't happen to you; that you don't think what happened to me is the outcome of bad decisions or misfortune, or a lack of intelligence, talent, or drive. That I was too difficult or not disciplined or legible enough. I hope you don't think I was an exception.

If institutions could, they would do to you what they did to me.

I am the disposable future many of them hope for.

One last testimony, from Lawrence, who read his own at that plenary, voice shaking. As he reminded me before the session, what happened at UMD was not only my grief, or even only our shared grief. It was his too.

LAWRENCE-MINH BÙI DAVIS: I wrote this suffused with rage. I woke up in the middle of the night last night thinking about it.

For 11 years, as a grad student and adjunct, I taught for the Asian American Studies Program at the University of Maryland. I taught more classes for the Program than anyone in its history.

I also spent countless hours mentoring and advising students, building curricula, getting curricula formally approved by the university, helping ease directorial transitions including thru scandal, working with students on public programs, grant writing, boosting course enrollments, boosting minor numbers: all the rudiments of program building.

In 2017, contingent faculty for the Program received an email reminding us that per university policy our current contracts were no guarantee of future employment. And that none of our contracts would be renewed for the following spring term.

I was never hired again by the Program. I was simply asked to pick up my mail and pack up my personal belongings from the shared office. I was never given even a basic thank you for my years of service.

I'd had stability and relative security over my 11 years because of the good will of directors in that span and because I could teach classes, primarily Asian American literature, which drew consistent enrollments and that no one else in the Program's ecosystem could teach. But when a new director took over, that security evaporated.

I lost a very dear friend in the process, the outgoing director, someone I'd always admired as a good, decent human being. She refused to fight for me, for us, or rather, to put it more generously, found herself in a position where she felt a limited ability to fight for us. The point is that contingent exploitation is not the product of some distant set of bureaucratic relations. It is us. It is our friends. It is good people, who are suddenly not good on this particular civil rights issue when it feels dangerous, or maybe just inconvenient. Part of tenure privilege is the ability to opt out and look the other way when one's colleagues and friends are being disposed of.

I was openly critical of the decision and its handling. I was openly critical of a number of decisions leading up to that point, and surely that played a part in my disposability. I like to think that Asian American studies should be capacious enough to handle honest, good faith criticism, even if harsh, but on this point I was dead wrong. One of my central criticisms was illuminating a tension between models of governance. Here was unilateral decision-making without transparency or accountability to anyone other than the dean. But Maryland's Program, like many Asian American studies units, was founded by student protest. It was built by way of community investment and community governance. It had always depended upon a complex set of interrelations between not just dean and director, but faculty tenured and contingent, staff, students, student groups, student services, alumni, donors, invested community members. Its decisions of course impact all of those folks; why should they not have some say in those decisions and how they are made?

Which is to say: the exploitation and disposal of adjuncts is a departure from the founding of units, the founding of the field, and the spirit of Asian American studies, which exists in antagonistic relation to an academy that never wanted it and has made space for it only begrudgingly and ruthlessly takes it away when and where it can.

I've stayed on the listserv for the Program, painful as it is. I consider myself not former faculty but an exile. I predated the current administration, I predated the prior administration, and the one before that, and I'll postdate the current one and the one after that, and after that—and I'll still give a shit when they don't. Administrations come and go. Communities remember. The disposed remember.

A final note: Franklin Odo isn't here at this conference, and I'm missing him. He's a titan of our field, former AAAS President, editor of *Roots*, one of the first collections of Asian American studies materials, and founding director of my current workplace, the Smithsonian Asian Pacific American Center. Since leaving the Smithsonian he's become fungible. Traveling from VAP to VAP, high-end, fancied-up, contingent positions. He would definitely not like me talking about this, he and I have never talked about this, he is too proud to talk about this, but we need to hear it and face it. This is one of the founders of our field, and as a field and an association we have done nothing to ensure him the security he's surely earned, we look away as at 80 years old he continues to hold on where he can because he still wants, and needs, to work. At his most recent stop, at Amherst College, thankfully, he's been renewed repeatedly, and why?

Because students fought to keep him. Not us.

At that 2019 session, the grief built up in the room, undeniable, unbearable. I hope your reading was like our listening: breath caught in the throat, stomach clenched, body frozen in place. I want something to break inside you. The discussion that followed was the most careful and respectful on contingency I've been a part of. Tenured faculty did not tell us adjuncts to simply "keep trying" for those tenure-track jobs or that we should simply work within our contracts to minimize our exploitation or that tenured folks have it just as hard in these white neoliberal institutions. Instead, they sat with the horror. They acknowledged how dire things were. They expressed deep feeling, deep outrage. They asked what they should do. They brainstormed particular strategies for their own universities and departments. They centered adjunct feelings, experiences, and ideas, as they explored their own responsibilities.

This was a dwelling in unwellness. We don't do this at conferences. We don't put our unwellness on display. We don't ask each other to feel, collectively, in this way. Perhaps we should. Perhaps this kind of collective feeling work to hold our fields and ourselves accountable should be one of the central purposes of our academic conferences.

My argument, though, is not that we simply need to get individuals to care about adjuncts. Caring matters, but I already know from experience that individual caring is not enough. The point of the testimonies in the plenary was a larger affective intervention in the *structure of feeling* around contingency. And to create new structures of feeling. I share my personal story in this chapter not because it is representative or universal, but because as a good humanities scholar I want to close-read it for what it can tell us about the structural conditions of the work we do. My former friend failed me not because she didn't love me. She failed me because the structures of feeling in place told her it was more important, to herself and academia more broadly, to uphold institutional hierarchies, lines of power, and processes—and that it was *right* to do so. My former friend is a good person. Who became a bad person when faced with her own complicity and alliance with institutional power. Who cried tenured tears, which like white tears may be an indicator of real feelings but are fundamentally a reflexive deflection away from the grievances of the disempowered. She could not care enough for me to risk herself, because everything in place told her not to. She had been trained to respond that way, as all of us are actively trained, and, even more disturbingly, train one another.

I'm working on building spaces that tell everyone to feel differently. From there we can collectively create structures of care that don't depend on the goodwill of individuals but on the collective will for social justice. It must no longer be acceptable for the university and those empowered within it to refuse to care for us. Some of us shouldn't have to die so that others may live.

It remains to be seen how far the energy of that dwelling in 2019 will go. I have already noticed a shift, during the plenary itself and then afterward that year and at conferences in the years since then. Contingency has become a real (if not necessarily central) concern for AAAS. A concern now regularly reiterated publicly by senior scholars and association leadership, without prompting. But will this sustain, and how? What will the association actually do about this newfound concern? What care structures will it actually build? The pandemic has made these questions even harder to think through.

My presence on the AAAS board from 2018 to 2021 was extremely welcome, but I am unsure how much one contingent rep can do, even with a seat at the table. All the work was on me to come up with initiatives and execute them, on top of existing board duties, and while the rest of the board supported my ideas, there were and still are no structures in place to ensure anything beyond the goodwill of the current board members and the capacity of the current contingent rep. At the time of this writing, AAAS still charges its contingent members $100 to attend its conference—half the cost tenured members pay, when tenured members might make fifty times what a contingent member does. Charging the unemployed to attend is unconscionable, but the charge remains. AAAS continues to provide no travel or lodging support. That goodwill from AAAS leadership hasn't translated into real structural change yet. Plus, I've had good friends in high places before. I've had people who cared—until they didn't.

So dwell we must, and keep on dwelling, so that we change how we feel but also how we engage the structures around us. So that we cannot so easily choose to stop caring. So that we stay at the edge of the abyss with anyone who needs it, for as long as they need.

That same year I also worked with the Mentoring Committee of the AAAS board. Made up of one or two tenured board members, the graduate student rep, and, now, the contingent rep (and sometimes external members), that committee is tasked with organizing three to five mentoring sessions for each conference, highlighted in the program as official board-sponsored sessions. I served on the Mentoring Committee my first year and would continue as its chair for the remainder of my three-year term. I volunteered (which I rarely do—I hate doing more work!) because I was tired of what is traditionally offered to graduate students and junior faculty. (See all the job market advice above.) Yes, it can be helpful to have sessions on professionalization and publishing and navigating the job market and getting tenure. But what I had been hearing from graduate students and colleagues through my work on mental health was that we needed to figure out how to live in a system that dehumanizes us. We want to know that it's possible to do this work and feel happy and balanced and not overwhelmed all the time. We want to know how to be full human beings. We want this work not to cost us so much.

I structured my first mentoring session around academic hyperproductivity. I wanted to delve into the terrifying work of detaching ourselves from that object of misplaced faith.

I organized the session under the rubric of "slow professoring," a term popularized by Maggie Berg and Barbara K. Seeber's *The Slow Professor: Challenging the Culture of Speed in the Academy*. An analysis of the corporatization of the university and the culture of speed it induces, the book offers strategies for resisting that culture across structures of time management, teaching, research, and our relationships in the university. The authors rightly identify the idealization of hyperproductivity in academia and helpfully provide the language of corporatization to point to the dynamics of efficiency, speed, and quantifiable "excellence." But speaking to a seemingly universal academic experience, they make little room for differential experiences of vulnerability and exploitation by race, gender, sexuality, and academic rank. Not everyone experiences this culture of speed in the same way, nor are the consequences the same for "resisting." The book also does not engage disability studies and disability justice at all, which arguably would have been slow professoring's most useful conversation partners. Disability studies and disability justice have been thinking about our relationships to our bodies, to space, to time, for decades. Disabled writers and scholars have been thinking about slowness (to the point of not moving!), not as choice, but as ontology, a way of being in the world, the term *crip time* emerging out of disability culture.[32] Ellen Samuels popularized the term in her widely cited essay "Six Ways of Looking at Crip Time," and the special issue "Crip Temporalities" of *South Atlantic Quarterly* she and Elizabeth Freeman guest edited is an important example of academic explorations of disability and nonnormative temporality.[33] For me, any thinking about slowness in academia must draw on the insights of disability studies and disability justice—and it must also draw on ethnic studies to think through intersectionality and differential experiences of structures that enable or preclude slowness.

Enter Mel Y. Chen and Mana Hayakawa, two disabled Asian American disability studies scholars, also two people who have very consciously navigated their own bodies' and minds' capacities in relation to academia. Mel is a tenured professor; Mana is a relatively new PhD moving in and out of adjuncting and student affairs positions in universities. Then there's me, a permanent adjunct, one foot in and one foot out of academia, doing hybrid scholarly-arts work.

Here's the session we came up with together: "If You're Not Already Sick, You Will Be: A Workshop on Slow Professoring and Surviving Academia's Hyperproductivity." We wanted to highlight the stakes—we are all getting sick—and foreground a disability studies approach that both normalizes illness and examines structures of disablement. We wanted to encourage participants to engage with their own experiences of struggle and survival in academia. The last lines of our session abstract read:

> Let us share and reflect upon our anxieties that we are never doing "enough," our own attachments to productivity, and our secret feelings of failure, particularly as Asian Americans. Join us in generating more sustainable ways of "professoring" that do not ask us to leave our bodies and spirits, and the bodies and spirits of others, behind.

We developed the following discussion questions for participants to engage in small groups:

- Do you feel like you are doing "enough"? What is "enough" to you? Do you feel like you are "failing"? What do "success" and "failure" look like to you?
- Do you feel like you are balancing all of your priorities? What does balance look like to you? What do you feel like is "out of balance" in your life?
- What do we fear might happen if we slow down?

- What might it look like to "slow down" in our fragile body-minds, as graduate students, adjuncts, and tenure-track faculty, and resist academia's culture of hyperproductivity?
- How can we "professor" in ways that are loving and life-affirming to ourselves and others?

There were around thirty attendees for our session, ranging from undergraduates to senior professors. Mel, Mana, and I floated around to the different groups to listen to the conversations. People shared fears and struggles, foreclosures of personhood, illnesses, tears—and in response to just the first question! The groups never managed to move on to the next questions; there was too much to feel and say simply about the words *enough, success,* and *failure.* There had never been the time or space to feel and say these things, together. A shared crip time, for Asian American studies.

I have since moved away from "slowness" as antidote to academic hyperproductivity, even a complex version that takes a disability studies approach. Because it carries the implication of choice, that we all just need to choose to slow down. Yes, we should slow down. But some of us, many of us, maybe most of us, are already "too slow," drowning in an environment that penalizes slowness. Some of us are sloths, without choice. Being a sloth is a state of being and identity, like being disabled, racialized, contingent. What I have termed Sloth Professoring tells us to not be ashamed of these states and identities, to not feel like something is wrong with us, to acknowledge our unwellnesses so that we can move through academia and the world as our whole selves, asking that world to care for us in all our slothy glory.

As of this writing in early 2022, Mel, Mana, and I are in the process of creating another session for the 2022 AAAS conference in April. We've added an undergraduate student organizer, Sanzari Aranyak, whose work is on student activist burnout. Sanzari also knows deeply what it means to both choose and not choose to be slow. The four of us are being so slow and slothy, though, we've barely done anything at all beyond saying, "Hi! Let's do it!" and coming up with a title. We'll see what our capacities are as we draw closer to the conference. A sloth's gotta be okay with not knowing when they get to where they're going or if they'll ever get there at all. Also, a sloth is lazy. A sloth moves as slowly as possible to conserve as much energy as possible. A sloth figures out how to survive not despite this slowness but through it. Sloth Professoring asks you to be lazy.

Let's talk about laziness. *Lazy* is a very scary word, in the wider US culture and in academia in particular. We are so afraid of being called lazy. Laziness, not wanting to work or put effort into something, is a *moral* trait; it speaks to whether we are good or bad, deserving or undeserving. It is a measure of our personhood. It is also a measure of how we are in relation to others: to be lazy is to be a burden. It is to need too much and contribute too little. In a culture of meritocracy, laziness is one of the worst sins. (Asking for more than you deserve is the other.) Social psychologist Devon Price helpfully names this narrative the "Laziness Lie" and identifies its three main components:

1 Your worth is your productivity.
2 You cannot trust your own feelings and limits.
3 There is always more you could be doing.[34]

This is ableism. And I agree with Price: it is killing us.

Price tries to dismantle the tenets of the Laziness Lie, refusing a culture of hyperproductivity and affirming that our achievements are not our worth. (Read their work instead of *Slow Professoring*!) Their other major intervention: "laziness does not exist" (which is the title of both their 2021 book and a 2018 essay). Instead, there are situational factors that give context to "lazy" behaviors. This is a critically important reframing. So-called lazy behaviors are not moral failings but expressions of need. They are indicators not of bad personing but of unseen barriers to be identified and dismantled. This aligns exactly with a disability lens—indeed, disability studies and disability justice call these barriers *access issues*. Price's examples in the 2018 essay of student needs and struggles ring particularly true for me, as well as Price's insight that some universities, in their proud refusal to accommodate disabled students, "mistake cruelty for intellectual rigor." (Remember this line when we get to chapter 5!)[35]

Next, however, is where some of us might jump ship. Price argues that laziness should be understood as self-preservation: a healthy response to doing too much. In fact, we have a *right* to be lazy.[36] Reclaiming laziness as *good* might feel to some of us like a bridge too far. We might give ourselves (begrudging) permission to need supports to overcome barriers to our productivity, but ultimately we still gotta get our shit done. Because not getting our shit done remains terrifying. Failure is still bad personing.

Repeat after me, and Price: laziness is a right.

I often see colleagues reassure other colleagues that they are not lazy. They list out the other's accomplishments. They point to various barriers—parenthood!—to contextualize any supposed lack of productivity. Some even share Price's essay to introduce the idea that laziness doesn't exist. (This is actually how I first encountered Price's work.) But very few go as far as embracing laziness. They are willing to disconnect particular behaviors from that moral failing, but moral failing it still is. Laziness remains the terrible thing we must distance ourselves from. Productivity remains the ideal.

How many of us allow ourselves self-care, rest, support, *so that we can do more work*?

What about just resting to rest? What about simply not wanting to do work? Not wanting to do anything? Conserving energy, spoons, because you want to? Because you don't want to expend it in the ways you're being told to expend it?

When I say that laziness is a right and that I identify as lazy, and when I ask you to disrupt the stigma associated with laziness, what I'm trying to do is *reclaim the inherent value of the nonproductive body and mind*. You deserve to live, deserve to have love and joy and meaning, deserve safety, deserve to create things that you want and consume things that you want, whether or not you are productive and contribute to whatever it is you've been told you need to be accountable to. As I've written and said elsewhere, you deserve these things even if you never achieve another goddamn thing for the rest of your life.[37]

I don't know if I've convinced you that the lives, and pain, of our students and contingent colleagues matter, or even that your own do. Colleagues have been hard to convince because, well, meritocracy is a helluva drug—especially for those who have supposedly "made it." But even for those who have not. The most vulnerable of us at the bottom of academic stratification still often believe our unwellness is our own fault, proof of our inability to meet the standards of academia. Academia depends upon this belief.

I made *Open in Emergency* in large part because I was trying to make sense of my own unwellness. I wanted to know that my unwellness was not my own fault, that it was not proof of my inability to meet the standards of academia, of motherhood, of life. Adjuncting at UMD was a huge part of the backdrop of the making of the project: I was teaching at UMD all the years of its development, from 2013 to 2016. (I was pushed out in 2017, right after its publication.) *Open in Emergency* would not have been possible had I not been adjuncting at UMD. I would not have met my partner, taught with him, dreamed with him; AAST was fertile ground for our dreaming work (we were the geniuses, remember?). The conditions of adjunct labor had already begun to reveal themselves, the contradictions of meritocracy already begun to take their toll, reinforcing for me the stakes of the work I wanted to do. Any kind of care work has to engage the structures of uncare in which we are embedded. It must not be individual but collective. The ethic of community governance and community care we practiced in our teaching and program building we applied to *Open in Emergency*, developing it via community curation and prioritizing getting copies of it into the hands of those who needed it most, often those who could afford to pay for it the least. Having made *Open in Emergency* helped me to understand what was happening in 2017 as my institutional home unraveled, providing the foundation for an analysis of adjunctification through a lens of unwellness. *Open in Emergency* also opened a pathway to a new career, an intellectual and arts practice beyond adjunctification, in and outside the academy, working within and across higher ed but housed outside of it. I learned that Asian American studies is not a home. Our departments and universities are not homes. Believing so, placing your faith so, grants people institutionally situated above you the power to kick you out of that home and tell you you never belonged in the first place.

I intentionally left the story of UMD out of the first chapter of this book in my retelling of the origins of *Open in Emergency*. I waited until now to tell that part of the story because you needed to read the hundred-plus pages before this to get to a place to understand it. Our unwellness in the academy might be the hardest for us to face, the poison that runs deepest. I want us all to face this unwellness because all our lives depend on it. But I am not interested in trying to convince deans and tenured colleagues that I and other adjuncts have value, on their terms. What I am most interested in is unlearning this poison and crafting a life with others who want to revalue lives outside of meritocracy. There is little space for this kind of work in academia as it currently operates—and critical disability studies scholars, as well as other insurgents across ethnic studies, gender and women's studies, and queer studies have cracked open what space there currently is. But academia is not a place that nurtures the work of dreaming and building collective care. We have to think really hard about how to squeeze into those cracks, if the squeezing is worth it, and how to find balance between the parts of ourselves that must be squeezed and the parts that must find more fertile ground elsewhere.

Even with all the advice I've given here, I don't actually know how to fully be unwell in the university. My story is not a happy story of surviving and thriving in academia as a disabled Asian American/ist scholar. It is a mundane story of being unwell and figuring out how to get by, like so many others. It is a strange story of finding creative ways to do the work I want to do, within and outside of the academy, in order to live. It is a sad story of dying some in the process, at the hands of those I called colleague, friend, family, home. It is a stark story of discovering the contours of Asian American unwellness, as professor, as scholar, as teacher, as adjunct.

The Professor is ill. The Asian American Professor is ill. The Asian American Studies Professor is ill.

interlude 4
surveying access

Teaching in Pandemic Times--checking in about access needs

Welcome to our chapter on teaching in pandemic times! This is a wild time to be trying to do education. I want to make this chapter as responsive as possible to our individual and collective needs in this time, so please fill out this form to give me more information about your particular needs.

Thanks,
mimi

* Required

Email *

Your email

Name *

Your answer

Do you have a stable and safe place to live right now? *

Your answer

Will you be able to fulfill basic needs around housing, food, medical care, mental health? Will you have access to necessary support systems? *

Your answer

How are you feeling about in-person learning and remote learning right now? *

Your answer

Do you have easy access to this book? A copy that is accessible to you (print, digital, audio)? Time to read it? Spoons to think about it? Emotional capacity for the intense content? Emotional stability for dealing with discomfort and fragility as they arise? Structures in place to take care of yourself when things feel hard? The following chapter will have content that might be difficult for some, such as pandemic trauma, student trauma, teaching trauma. *

Your answer

Do you anticipate any access needs other than the ones I listed above? This may be a question that doesn't make sense if you haven't had much exposure to disability studies and disability justice. I approach access issues as anything that is an obstacle to you participating as much as possible in this space. You have a right to have needs and to ask for those needs to be met. You have a right to be believed and trusted when you say you have needs. Access is something we will negotiate as a community committed to each other's well-being and full participation. Think of what you can here, but if you don't have anything right now, feel free to communicate things to me in the future as they arise. No obstacle or struggle is too small to discuss. We will work together to find ways forward. *

Your answer

Do you have any questions or concerns you'd like to share with me, about this book or upcoming chapter or the awfulness of life right now? *

Your answer

Submit   Clear form

If you'd like to actually fill out and submit this form, you can do so here: https://tinyurl.com/dear-elia-access-form. Responses will go directly to me, and only I will be reading them.

5 teaching in pandemic times

Dear pandemic students and teachers,

I am writing in the early months of 2022. We are still in the COVID-19 pandemic, currently riding the alarming wave of the Omicron variant, case numbers reaching record highs across the country. I am frantically gathering (but not hoarding!) KF94 masks and rapid antigen tests. I'm teaching on Zoom again. I can hear my daughter in her bedroom in remote school, the tinny sounds of her teacher's and classmates' voices ringing from her crappy laptop speakers. I have five cats now.

    The pandemic has marked time in an indelible way. All writing now has to acknowledge it, witness it, make sense of life in its wake. But we are always behind. By the time this chapter is published, I'm sure life will have shifted drastically again, the pandemic taking on new form. We've gone from sheltering in place in early 2020 to mass vaccination of adults in early 2021 to a summer of tentative normality to two new variants in the fall and winter of 2021 that devastated us all over again, with incomprehensible antimasking and antivaxxing and anti-social-distancing sentiments metastasizing across the country. As of the beginning of this writing, 850,000 people have died from COVID in the United States; by the time I finish writing this chapter, the death toll will easily be over one million. I really have no fucking idea where we'll be in a year or two from now. But I will hazard a pandemic reflection here in this chapter anyway, knowing it may not be an exact blueprint once this book is in your hands. At very least, it will serve as a document of what it has meant to teach, and reconceptualize teaching, amid the worst health epidemic of our lifetimes.

In 2020, schooling took a wild left turn. The pandemic hit the United States in midspring, and most universities triaged by going remote in March. Faculty scrambled to revamp and finish their courses, and students flew "home," or someplace like it, to shelter in place. We all jumped on the Zoom bandwagon, a ride we can't get off now, no matter how much we want to. Public and private K–12 schools closed all across the country, and suddenly school-aged kids were home doing their own version of emergency remote schooling, while parents were left with no child care but continued work demands.

In my corner of Facebook (yes, I know this dates me because the youth don't use FB anymore—but academics disproportionately do for some reason!), groups on teaching and parenting proliferated in the first months of the pandemic. How do we teach remotely during a pandemic? we desperately asked each other. How do we survive with our children at home full time, doing their own remote learning? Each task, separately, felt herculean and, together, soul-crushingly impossible. Yet here we are, almost two years in and still trying to do it. I'm not really sure what it is we think we are trying to do at this point. Teaching and schooling and parenting have all shape-shifted beyond recognition. They are not the same things anymore. The structures have changed along with the terms and the stakes.

I currently teach disability studies at Georgetown University. Watching the changing shapes of teaching and student experience through disability studies and disability justice lenses has been fascinating and horrifying. I am assessing access and normativity, ableism and care, not only in my own classrooms and the wider space of Georgetown, but also across higher ed as colleagues from all over the country (and even globally) report on social media about their teaching experiences, what their universities are demanding of them, what they are demanding of themselves and their students, what their students are telling and not telling them. The picture slowly coming into focus is not pretty. Or rather, it's not good, or kind, or caring. We are finding creative new ways to be unwell.

Georgetown's mission and values, grounded in the Catholic Jesuit tradition, have fascinated me since I joined its faculty at the beginning of 2020, just two months before the pandemic. I'm thinking especially of the university's embrace of *cura personalis*, often translated via the shorthand "care of the whole person," defined at length on Georgetown's official Mission and Ministry page as follows:

> *Cura Personalis*—This Latin phrase translates as "Care of the Person," and originally was used to describe the responsibility of the Jesuit Superior to care for each man in the community with his unique gifts, challenges, needs and possibilities. Today this value applies broadly to our shared University life, to include the relationship between educators and students and professional relationships among all those who work in the University. *Cura Personalis* is a profound care and responsibility for one another, grounded in individualized attention to the needs of the other, attentive to their unique circumstances and concerns, and their particular gifts and limitations, to encourage each person's flourishing.[1]

Profound care and responsibility for one another. Individualized attention to needs, concerns, limitations, gifts. Each person's flourishing. This all sounds wondrous—and eyebrow raising. Collective care and collective responsibility for meeting each other's needs form the pillars of my own work in mental health and disability justice. Could a university embody these principles? What would that actually look like? During my mental health tour in the years after *Open in Emergency*'s publication, I asked students across the country if they felt their universities cared about them. I spent half a dozen years before that learning from my own students how they were dying, and trying to teach them, without much institutional support, how they might live. I have watched too many students crushed by the machinery that is higher education, and have myself been crushed too well, to naively believe a university wants—and knows how—to care.

I began teaching in January 2020 with an eye on *cura personalis*, which manifested as regular university-wide emails laced with the language of concern, plus a spate of new programs dedicated to care ranging from direct services to pedagogical development. I kept another eye on the students themselves, because who better to tell me if the university cares than the students to whom the care is given? As I've said previously, the university can say it cares all it wants, but if students don't *feel* cared for, this thing called caring is not actually happening.

When the pandemic hit in March, Georgetown was on spring break, many of its students away from campus. Georgetown decided to transition to full remote learning upon return the following week. I was in the middle of teaching Intro to Disability Studies for the first time, a core course for the Disability Studies Program that introduces students to key concepts and foundational texts in disability studies. My daughter's K–8 school announced its decision to go remote too. "Instructional continuity" became the new buzzword. While I understand the educational desire for little to no gap in learning, I was disturbed that how to ensure this was the main question we were asking during the beginning of a mysterious, out-of-control, global pandemic killing people all over the world in panic-inducing numbers. I threw my entire syllabus out the window. My daughter's teachers didn't, but I wish they had. Those first weeks of sheltering in place were some of the scariest of the pandemic so far (rivaled only by sending our children back to in-person schooling without vaccination during the Delta surge of fall 2021, and perhaps this moment of the Omicron surge of spring 2022, during which the United States breaks positivity and death records every day). What are teaching and learning in such a moment?

This is the question I want to ask in this chapter. In a moment of profound need for care—and the overwhelming failure of structures of care—how must we shift our approaches to the projects of teaching and learning to responsibly engage both that need and those failures? Universities and school systems all had to reckon with this question in 2020, and they have continued to grapple with what it means to do education in the context of an ever-changing and evolving public health crisis over the last two years. I want to reflect on some of these grapplings as part of my exploration of what a radical care project, one grounded in a pedagogy of unwellness, might look like *during a global pandemic*.

What does it mean for a class to be accessible? At the most basic level, universities and classrooms after 1990 had to comply with the Americans with Disabilities Act (ADA). We all include that standard "Accessibility" paragraph in our syllabi—you know, the one that tells students to go to whatever the disability services unit on our particular campus is called to get official approval for accommodations. I will venture that relatively few of us teachers outside disability studies have really thought about nurturing access in our classrooms. This was definitely not the case fifteen to twenty years ago, when the language of accessibility was still fairly siloed to disability rights advocacy and accommodations were narrowly thought of in terms of physical entrances to buildings. More recently, some of us may have heard of Universal Design for Learning (UDL), an educational framework developed from architectural principles of universal design in the 1990s, with its focus on multiple means of engagement, presentation, and expression.[2] Awareness of UDL and adoption of its guidelines have picked up steam in higher education in the past decade or so, and while I had very little disability-related professional development when I started teaching in the early 2000s, accessibility guidelines and resources are now readily available across higher ed spaces. Over the past half decade I've seen an explosion of concern about accessibility across a swath of social arenas—at academic conferences, community organizing spaces, museums, and so on—expanding access to include ASL interpretation, live transcription, audio description, lighting, scent and chemical sensitivity, and trigger warnings. I now regularly see disability justice writing shared on social media and as part of organizational trainings.[3] Disability justice language suffuses student organizing—again, students know what's up. We're witnessing a real, palpable transformation.

But access has always been a tension inherent to pedagogy, whether or not we've thought about it explicitly. How, we've always asked, do we create classroom policies, assignments, and assessments in "fair" ways, and how do we maintain things like integrity and rigor in education? These are actually questions of access—and care—even if we don't realize it. The pandemic has forced a reckoning with tensions of access we've historically overlooked. I know it has pushed me to more intentionally reflect on what accessible teaching really means. Is there something we might call a pandemic pedagogy, both in terms of what we might learn from the pandemic and the shape teaching has had to take during it? (Spoiler: yes, there is.) I wonder how a pandemic pedagogy might inform a pedagogy of unwellness, even when/if someday this pandemic ends.

What is *cura personalis*—of students, of teachers, of families—during a pandemic?

And when I say *pandemic*, I mean: illness, illness of loved ones, lockdowns, uncertainty, dread, isolation, loss of housing, living with family, not living with family, taking care of family members, remote schooling, remote working, not working, quarantining, not quarantining, not hugging another human for months, coming back in person whether you want to or not, not having a private space for Zoom, please keep your camera on, not having a mask, not having the right kind of mask, not being able to get tested, waiting in long lines for testing, waiting five days for test results, confusion about what mitigation measures are effective, confusion about the safety and efficacy of vaccines, not having access to vaccines, having small children or siblings without access to vaccines, afraid of needing to go to the hospital, not being able to go to the hospital when you need to because they are overloaded, long COVID, fear of long COVID, a variant, now another variant, being immunocompromised while everyone around you says, "Omicron is mild," quarantining for ten days no wait five days no wait until you test negative, hearing people call COVID the "Wuhan virus" or "Kung flu" and watching old Asian women get beaten on the street in viral videos while a white gunman goes on a killing spree of Asian and Asian American women in an Atlanta massage parlor, and people who look like you or your family are blamed for the lockdowns and unemployment and masking policies and school closures and economic shutdown, and you're wondering, when will this ever end, how can we keep living like this, why won't people just wear a fucking mask, why are we okay with almost a million dead, will we all just have to get COVID and let more of us die because an unconscionable portion of our population won't get the fucking vaccine or stop hanging out with others unmasked or change their lives at all because eugenics is all the rage again? All of this is what I mean when I say *pandemic*.

I've always eschewed lectures and multiple-choice exams, the rudiments of the traditional "banking" model of education. As a humanities scholar in ethnic studies, and one also trained in women/gender/feminist studies, I've often articulated my job as helping students "develop critical thinking skills"—which *everyone* in the humanities and even beyond says in that time-honored academic tradition called the Teaching Statement. It's a document required of almost all academic job applications but likely of least consequence to a hiring committee, in part because all teaching statements sound the same. We all articulate our pedagogical approaches in the interests of getting a job and satisfying departmental and university-level investments and agendas. We all learn the genre as part of academic professionalization while on the market; The Professor Is In even offers a template.[4] We know who the audience is; we learn what appeals most to that audience; we check off the boxes for the shape and scope and register, sometimes well, sometimes badly. Some of us love teaching and some of us don't, but we all end up writing more or less the same thing across the humanities. It might be an open secret that hiring committees sometimes (often?) don't even read teaching statements.

But articulate our teaching we must if we want a job in this profession. We say we want to develop students' critical thinking skills, and while there is some variation across the humanities, we share key ways of defining what that means. I don't think my articulation early in my teaching career differed all that much from my peers': I meant the ability to ask questions of one's social and cultural environment, to critically analyze these environments as text and subtext, to locate oneself as a social being in these environments, and, most importantly, to see the life of structural violence in one's own life. These lofty goals required that students be willing to be challenged in terms of what they think they know, because for me teaching was and is an epistemological and ontological project. I teach to shift students' relationships to knowledge production and their own personhood. Ultimately, I want to give them tools to reorient themselves as social and ethical beings in the world. This is fairly standard in the humanities. We all want to change our students' lives, make them more informed and skilled in their engagement with the world. Perhaps the only small differences between my teaching philosophy and those found across most of the humanities are my emphases on the life of violence and the cultivation of understanding and agency in the context of that violence, both of which come directly out of feminist and ethnic studies approaches. My peers in these fields would likely articulate similar goals.

These goals should sound very familiar to those influenced by, say, Paulo Freire's *Pedagogy of the Oppressed* or bell hooks's *Teaching to Transgress* or Audre Lorde's *Sister Outsider* or the classic women of color feminist collection *This Bridge Called My Back*. These texts and others in conversation with them have defined teacher training for a large portion of graduate students in the humanities, especially in ethnic studies, over roughly the last fifteen to twenty years. There is of course a much fuller body on pedagogy I'm not citing here, especially feminist pedagogy, but these texts help us begin to ground and connect certain pedagogical approaches of this period.

I started teaching my own courses in 2008 as a PhD candidate but really began teaching in earnest after earning the PhD in 2012, teaching mostly in UMD's Asian American Studies Program.[5] Even as my graduate work directly engaged Asian American studies (which I consider my main field, even though my degree was specifically in religious studies), at the time I joined UMD's program, I barely had any experience teaching in Asian American studies; most of my teaching in grad school had been in religious studies and feminist studies. I began teaching armed with my woman of color feminist pedagogy—but already beginning to adapt in light of Asian American studies concerns as well as what I saw as the particular needs of Asian American students taking these courses.

Yes, critical thinking. But not simply to better understand their social world, but also *survive* it. By 2013 I had just survived postpartum depression. By 2013 I had read erin Khuê Ninh's work on the Asian immigrant family and the debt bondage that strangles the second generation.[6] By 2013 I had read—and been haunted by—Eliza Noh's "A Letter to My Sister" and its stark claim that "the Asian model minority is not doing well." By 2013 I had begun to realize that our students are dying. The stakes of critical thinking had gotten much, much higher.

How could I teach Asian American studies to Asian American students in ways that recognized and addressed their struggles, what I would come to call their unwellness? At the time I had not yet encountered disability studies as field or disability justice as framework, and had not delved into mental health as project, but the need to center and make sense of pain was becoming clear to me. It would continue to become clearer as I taught more Asian American studies courses. Pain, struggle, and unwellness constituted a crucial dimension of my students' Asian American lives and thus needed to constitute a crucial dimension of my Asian American studies courses and, I came to realize, a crucial dimension of what one might call an Asian American studies pedagogy writ large.

I quickly learned that teaching Asian American students in Asian American studies classes is its own thing. The kinds of questions and commitments that my University of California, Santa Barbara (UCSB), students brought to feminist studies courses were not the same ones that my UMD students brought to Asian American studies courses, even as Asian American studies as a field grew out of similar commitments around representation and social justice. My UMD students often had never taken an Asian American studies class before, often had never encountered any framework for understanding Asian Americanness as political identity or strategic engagement with US racism. They often had never even encountered humanities approaches to thinking about race or gender or sexuality or any number of other vectors of social organization and violence. I should periodize this observation more precisely: my students in the early 2000s and 2010s often had little fluency or investment in these issues. In a post-Ferguson and post–George Floyd world in which Black Lives Matter has become part of the vernacular, and in a post-pandemic world in which anti-Asian hate has become visible to mainstream media, racial politics have suffused the cultural landscape in such a way that my current 2020s students have a shared, basic racial justice consciousness that was only sporadically manifest, if at all, in years past. It's kind of stunning. For my students a decade ago, I realized I could not create this kind of consciousness or vocabulary simply by lecturing them into antiracist commitments or solidarity politics. Nor could I simply tell them that the history of their community matters and demand they believe it. Most of all, I could not persuade students that Asian American studies classes reflect their lives and their communities if the classes didn't *feel* that way.

For years I've heard my colleagues in Asian American studies report that their Asian American students often resist the idea that the model minority is a myth imposed upon us. This resistance now makes a lot of sense to me. I have come to understand the model minority as *subject formation*, not simply myth (thank you, erin). If, as a student, your whole Asian American life is shaped by powerful forces molding you into various forms of the model minority, and if the ideology of the model minority tells a story of your life that makes sense, how can you believe professors who tell you it's just a myth? Calling it a myth, and framing the myth as a wedge used to divide and conquer BIPOC peoples, doesn't help students understand why it *feels* real or what it is doing to their personhoods. Teaching race means teaching racial subjectivity: how social and cultural forces shape us into being, including *what this feels like and what the costs are.*

We have to give students the tools they actually need, not just the tools we think they should have. Yes, students don't often know exactly what they need, in large part because education doesn't license them to know. Recognizing and asking for what you need is drilled out of all of us—by racism, by sexism, by meritocracy, by ableism, all endemic to our educational systems. If we want a class to be important to our students, if we want their commitment and investment, the class has to engage students in the work of identifying and naming their own needs—or else why would they care? I'm not talking about the dreaded word *relatable.* I'm definitely not talking about catering to student preferences. I'm not even talking about making a course "relevant" exactly. What I'm talking about is acknowledging the reality of Asian American student suffering, and giving students permission to make sense of that suffering. In other words, we must license them to ask, *What hurts? And how do we go on living while it hurts?* We say we need to "meet students where they are"; where most Asian American students are is at the edge of an abyss.

I reoriented my classes. I asked students to look directly into the abyss. Before I came to UMD, I was teaching students how to be critical thinkers and ethical people. At UMD I started teaching students those things in the context of the abyss, and in service of staying alive. In 2013 I also began working more closely with Lawrence, who would, over the course of that year, become my partner, romantic and intellectual and pedagogical. We had (and still have!) endless conversations about teaching. I would visit his classes and observe. We began cross-pollinating our classes, having our students discuss shared films and texts. We would mentor students, interns, and minors together. There is no story for me about teaching without Lawrence.

His teaching was student-centered in a different way. His model: trust students to collaborate in their own learning, and be willing to follow them in unexpected directions. Teach on the fly. Teach projects. Teach creating. Cut corners. Save time, save energy, because as a full-time PhD student teaching two of his own courses a semester (in order to maintain income and, most importantly, health insurance for his kids) who also cofounded and was co-directing a literary nonprofit while *also* freelancing for the Smithsonian and parenting and beginning the awful (and, we now know, endless) process of divorce, there was never enough time or energy for anything. Something, maybe everything, has got to give.

Watching Lawrence teach helped me to let go more, to trust students in their learning more, to see the classroom as a space for wrestling with concepts, sometimes in surprising ways, and not always requiring a clear end point. I learned to teach "cold." Walk in, no prep. Sometimes I would glance at the syllabus and come up with a couple questions to discuss just ten minutes before class. Sometimes I would walk in without even remembering the topic for the day, looking it up in the first few minutes of class. I gave myself grace, assumed the students might also be walking in cold (i.e., didn't do the reading!), and found ways on the fly to create a generative space for thinking and feeling together. This requires some talent and practice; it requires framing "less prep" as a fundamental graduate student and contingent faculty access need; and it requires shifting what you think teaching is and what it's supposed to achieve. Yes, critical thinking. But also *presence* and co-ownership of the learning process, including its directions and pacing. Sometimes one question can be enough to drive conversation for an hour. One concept can take several classes' worth of grappling. One text, even one page, can be enough to think about, to analyze, to close read—for an hour, a day, even a week. The work of wrestling with a concept, applying it to your life, bringing your own life to bear upon the concept, listening to others' ideas and grapplings, synthesizing others' experiences with your own, coming up with new questions and directions that grow from that concept—this is a lot of work! If the goal is the ability to put your life in complex context, then a lively discussion around one question, one concept, one text, can do that work, sometimes breathtakingly so. Why devote so much time? To make sure students understand, to stay in tune with student needs, because students should help shape how long the class as a collective entity needs to grapple with something.

I started trimming down my syllabi more and more, teaching fewer and shorter and more accessible texts—"accessible" in a popular sense but also in the sense of meeting the access needs of students constantly asked to work beyond their capacities. I shifted my assignments away from research or even analytical papers, and instead asked for brief reflections and projects that nurtured synthesis and application. I chucked a final exam and traditional final paper and shrank midterms down to a five-minute lightning oral exam. In other words, for access reasons and for nurturing deeper, communal engagement, I shifted away from time-consuming independent work, away from quantity and speed (covering as much as possible as fast as possible). I had students help to write the midterm questions, making it a collective and collaborative process. I had them prepare for the questions in advance. I told them the point is for you to learn and synthesize—there is no need to surprise you or trick you. At the end of the semester, I asked them to write a short final reflection paper in which they simply tell me what they've learned and what has been meaningful to them—instead of me evaluating and assessing them on what *I* think they should have learned. They get to tell me, on their own terms. They loved writing this reflection. I loved reading them. Nothing makes you feel more like a success as a teacher than to hear students tell you in their own words something they learned and why it mattered to them. Nothing makes a student feel more like a success than their teacher validating to them that how they've synthesized the material was important and worthwhile work, and that you are grateful for their bravery. Part of meeting students at the abyss is building care and reciprocity—or, interdependence—into the very assignments themselves.

Class time itself oriented around discussions. I rarely ever lectured. I would introduce or define concepts as they arose organically in the conversation. "Oooh, your comment reminds me of X!"—fill in the concept or framework or historical context. Or "I think this concept helps explain what you're talking about." Or "oh, but I think your classmate's comment helps us understand gender a bit differently." Or "remember how we talked about Y last week? Now we're getting another dimension of that."

Part of the reason that I could walk in cold was that I set very small goals for each class session: one idea/concept/question/text. Let students explore that one thing. Be okay with messiness, with loose ends, with explorations that go in multiple directions. Be okay with "wrong" ideas; pose questions to nudge them to reexamine those wrong ideas, and don't worry if they have all the "right" answers by the end of class. Be okay with process, not always product. I let go of what I thought teaching was supposed to accomplish, and for whom. I chose presence over prep. Presence versus prep is Lawrence's language. Students need us to be present in the classroom, to facilitate a conversation that is alive and sometimes unpredictable and surprising. We have to be in the moment in order to respond to them. While prep is not the opposite of presence, it can conflict with presence. Prepping a lot can mean rigidity, forcing a direction and pace that don't always align with where the students are. Prepping can be detrimental to presence, and students need presence more than they need prep. Being responsive, addressing need—creating access—requires presence.

I also learned to recognize students as authorities about their own lives. We want them to see their own lives as text, right? The ultimate goal is for them to go forward in their lives reading their social and professional environments with the knowledge and tools we provide them. But if their lives are text, then we need to trust that they are experts in their own experiences. We also need to license them to identify what is urgent and relevant in relation to those experiences, and why. What they say about their lives matters, and I learned to treat, and directly frame, their contributions to class discussion that way.

I cut corners too. As an adjunct, I had to find ways to reduce my workload. Again, this is a hack to meet a basic and largely unacknowledged access need. I am not paid enough to spend the number of hours and spoons people in power seem to think I should. No contingent faculty are. I reduced or eliminated prep. I shifted to grading that could be done on the spot: oral midterms, group presentations, project presentations. A final reflection paper that is joyful to read. Eventually, I stopped taking attendance. All of these hacks coincided with greater presence and collaboration, produced greater presence and collaboration. I started having students grade themselves and included self-evaluation forms on their presentations, projects, participation, and overall class performance. Students were sometimes harder on themselves than I was! I didn't just give them the grade they thought they earned, but I did heavily take their self-evaluations into account. My sense of them should closely align with their sense of themselves, and if there is a big difference, then that's something to meet and talk about and work through on an individual basis. That was rarely necessary.

By the time I left (ahem, was pushed violently out of) UMD, I was known for classes in which students felt heard, felt like their contributions were valued, and felt like they learned something that helped them with their lives. At least once a semester, a student would tell me that I saved their life. I was finding a balance in which teaching was fun, meaningful, and not exhausting, not martyrdom. I was addressing student need in very real ways, while also not overtaxing myself in the process. And I was validated by my students on a regular basis.

My success at creating these kinds of spaces at UMD hinged upon two underlying things: vulnerability and trust. Students have needed to trust me and my classroom space in order to put themselves into the ideas and texts and analyses. Really committing to deep engagement of the self requires being vulnerable—and feeling safe enough to be vulnerable. I see vulnerability as a crucial part of the learning process, and I've worked to nurture it. I model it: I talk about my struggles, I give examples from my own life, I share how things we're talking about make me feel and how these forces have affected me. I let students know when I am sick, and I cancel class when I am sick. I am flexible with myself and with them—if the course schedule needs to shift or change, we'll all figure it out together. I admit I am fallible; I make mistakes. I mix shit up, forget things, fumble with the tech, have a bad day. I offer them generosity, and they offer it in return.

I encourage vulnerability from students by acknowledging that their lives are hard. By believing them. Students always seem shocked by my insistence that I do not need documentation for anything. They really can't comprehend this kind of trust and respect. They are so used to the opposite. My students often submit documentation to me anyway, a kind of reflex because they can't fully accept that they won't get punished for lack of "proof." Margaret Price tells us the number one thing we can do to accommodate others: "The next time someone tells you they need something—anything, any accommodation for any reason—*believe them*."[7]

Students don't trust their professors. Nor should they. So many of us punish students for their needs. So many of us arbitrate what count as legitimate and acceptable forms of need and what count as "fair" forms of accommodation. We directly and indirectly tell students on a regular basis that they are not to be trusted, that they will lie and cheat—in our attendance policies, late-work policies, testing policies, and, now in Zoom University, digital proctoring/surveillance practices. Students have learned that their struggles and needs must come second, third, last, to our expectations in the classroom. They have learned that their needs don't matter, and that they will not be believed when they disclose them. They have learned that their needs actually create unfairness, demonstrate lack of integrity, and constitute cheating.

How many of us have joked about the number of dead grandmothers our students seem to have?

Students don't trust us because we are not trustworthy. We have not earned their trust. Nothing in the university really incentivizes us to. In fact, we are directly empowered to *do them harm*. It has taken me these past dozen or so years of teaching to really figure out how to build trust with students and how to overcome their (well-deserved) suspicion of us. The answer is both incredibly simple and incredibly complicated: students need us to care about them.

Cura personalis.

⸻

University of Maryland was where I began to directly face my students' unwellness. I wrote about that process late in my first year of teaching Asian American studies, a short essay called "Living Under Siege" for the Black feminist blog founded by Mia McKenzie, *Black Girl Dangerous.*[8] "I start the class with two days on suicide," I wrote, with Eliza's "A Letter to My Sister," because life and death were the stakes, and my job was to figure out with my students why and how that horizon haunts our communities. By 2017 I'd gathered my formulations on teaching about and through feeling into a TEDx talk, and I was starting to be invited to other campuses to lead pedagogy discussions and mental health workshops.[9]

Fast forward to January 2020. *Open in Emergency* had been out for three years, and I was "on sabbatical" (i.e., unemployed, or piecemeal employed, because no one pays an adjunct to rest or research or write), focusing my energy on following the life of *OiE* in the world, listening to students as I was invited to give talks and host workshops on mental health at college campuses across the country. I'd begun drawing on both *OiE* and disability justice to articulate what a pedagogy of unwellness might look like. That January I was about to step into my first disability studies classroom at Georgetown, an introductory course on the central interventions of disability studies as field and disability justice as project.

As I designed the course, I knew that I needed to deepen my implementation of access. How could I not only accommodate approved, documented disability but create a culture of access in which every student feels like they can participate in the course as much as possible? It was clear to me that such a culture begins with the assumption that all my students are unwell. They are all differentially unwell, navigating fluctuating capacities and limits and needs, as all humans do at any given moment. A course must be responsive to that differential unwellness in order to lower the bar to entry as much as possible. My training and experience so far had taught me that at any given moment students are dealing with trauma, racism, ableism, sexism, misogyny, toxic masculinity, queerphobia, transphobia, rape culture, financial instability, poverty, domestic violence, abusive relationships, health issues, car accidents, computer crashes, breakups, betrayals, abandonment, grief, loss, loneliness, depression, anxiety, PTSD, exhaustion, and perhaps most of all, institutional violence. A disability studies course teaching about access and care must design itself with these facts embedded in its foundation.

Looking back, however, at my January 2020 syllabus through pandemic-inflected eyes, I realize I didn't actually do this very well. As student-centered and flexible and caring as I had become, I was still holding on to pedagogical practices that I realize now are ultimately incompatible, even antithetical, to a pedagogy of unwellness—even as I was already writing about a pedagogy of unwellness! Let's take a closer look at what I was doing in January 2020.

Introduction to Disability Studies

INSTRUCTOR: MIMI KHÚC   Semester: Spring 2020

Office hours: MW 3:30–4:30pm (I am on campus only the days of our class)
Office: New North 330
Email: mimi.khuc@georgetown.edu

Introduction

This course explores major theoretical and political interventions from the fields of disability studies and disability justice, with a special focus on mental health and the arts and humanities. Topics covered include ableism, disability, intersectionality, interdependence, cure, access and accommodation, disability as metaphor, neurodivergence and autism, universal design, and structures of care. The course will culminate with a student-led mental health arts pop-up for the Georgetown community.

Texts

* *Brilliant Imperfection: Grappling with Cure*, by Eli Clare (purchase ASAP)
* *The Collected Schizophrenias*, by Esmé Weijun Wang (purchase by mid-March)
* *Open in Emergency 2.0* (purchase by mid-March—I will provide a purchase link. Please **put Georgetown in the first line of the shipping address**. I will bring the books and deliver them in class.)
* All other readings will be available online.

Learning Outcomes

* Students will learn core disability studies and disability justice concepts of ableism, disability, intersectionality, and access.

mimikhuc

See, this was my jam! Creative student-led projects. This iteration was the culmination of the approach: a collective creation the larger community could engage or, put another way, one that intervened in Georgetown's broader mental health landscape, growing a new model for mental health engagement. I was and still am very proud of this idea!

mimikhuc

These are some standard learning objectives, maybe with the exception of wanting the students to apply the concepts to their own lives. These objectives make a lot of sense and intentionally open space for personal reflection. But I don't say anything about creating a collaborative learning environment, about collective care and collective access, about a shared commitment to each other's well-being and learning. And nothing about collective and individual survival during the end times! Maybe we hadn't collectively named it the end times yet, but the ongoing pandemic has made it ever clearer to me that crisis is always happening, differentially, and a course must structure itself around that reality.

I don't actually articulate the goals of my classes via the genre of learning objectives anymore. The audience for learning objectives encoded in syllabi isn't really students but department chairs and curricula/gen ed supervisors and the general university panopticon, as James McMaster reminds me. We tailor our learning objectives toward these audiences as performances of competence and respectability. Sometimes this is because we believe in those things. Sometimes it's because those performances can be a "shield" behind which we can do whatever the fuck we want in the classroom. "Live performance is ephemeral," says James—not on record in the way syllabi-bound learning objectives are.

What would it look like to conceptualize learning objectives untethered to the genre requirement of academic respectability? What do we really want our students to learn, and how could we communicate those goals to our students in ways that make sense and matter to them? If students could choose to take classes solely based on the stated learning objectives—on evaluating how a class might be meaningful to them, how it might give them something they need—how would that change the way we shape and articulate the goals of our classes?

* Students will apply disability studies concepts to their own lives.
* Students will explore mental health through a disability studies lens and through the arts and humanities.
* Students will learn how to create and run a mental health arts pop-up drawing on arts+humanities interventions in mental health.
* Students will hone analytical, collaboration, and facilitation skills.

Requirements

Attendance, participation, readings	10%
Midterm	20%
Weekly journal	25%
Disability Studies Cluster events and reflections	10%
Pop-up creation and reflection paper	15%
Final reflection paper	20%

ATTENDANCE, PARTICIPATION, READINGS

Attendance is **strongly recommended** for every class but not mandated. I will not be taking attendance, though I will be noting who is actively participating in class discussion each day. Please use your own judgment and sense of accountability to decide how you will attend and participate in class. Much of the knowledge production will take place **during class**, so please prioritize attendance and participation. Please also treat class like a workplace: You are of course allowed sick days to be used at your discretion—and please do take care of yourselves—but you must handle them responsibly by catching up on your work. If you need to miss class, please contact a peer to see what you missed. Do not email me to ask "what did I miss"—I will not summarize class for you. I am always happy though to discuss accommodations based on your health needs.

mimikhuc

These percentages seem wild to me now. How are we allowed to so arbitrarily decide what are appropriate amounts and proportions of work for what values? I understand these kinds of decisions have always been located within the realm of academic freedom and professorial agency—but what pedagogical training gives us knowledge about how to do these calibrations in ethical ways? Shouldn't grading be context conscious to be responsible? What keeps professors and departments accountable? If work amounts and grading percentages are based on personal and/or departmental tradition, how and when do these traditions come under critical scrutiny? Per chapter 4, to whom do we think we are accountable when we are teaching? The dept? The university? Our promotional files? The field? What does accountability to the students look like?

mimikhuc

Good to see I had already gotten rid of mandatory attendance, wanting to allow students flexibility and the simple ability to be unwell without penalty, punishment, or the need to prove their unwellness to me. By 2020 I was firmly in the camp of "students' lives are hard; I will always assume their lives are hard; I will always believe them."

mimikhuc

What the fuck is this??? Class is a workplace?! I was allowing unlimited sick days, but I was still seeing the classroom space through a corporate lens. Handle your sick days "responsibly"??? This frames sick days as disruptions that need to be managed. I thought I was allowing students to be unwell, but this shows I was still on that wellness train, without even getting into how I was corporatizing education. I had already read and written about Johanna Hedva's "Sick Woman Theory," in which the artist-activist explains the temporality of our construction of sickness—that we assume wellness is the norm and sickness the occasional aberration to be managed; hence care is only occasionally necessary. I was already writing about a pedagogy of unwellness! Yet here I reinforce the idea of individual responsibility for managing sickness. There's no understanding of sickness as the norm, not an aberration, and no understanding of care as collective.

How come we don't ask people to handle their *wellness*—the privilege of enablement—responsibly?

mimikhuc

I was also still somewhat on the accommodations train, apparently. Even as I was teaching a class on disability justice, I still articulated access in terms of accommodations. Maybe I get a slight pass on this because I was speaking the institutional language that I knew would make sense to students at the beginning of the term.

Active participation is expected of every student. Active participation consists of completing the readings before class and contributing to class discussion in thoughtful ways that engage the readings, materials presented in class, and your classmates' contributions. You MUST participate in class regularly to receive a passing grade for participation. I am happy to discuss various modes of participation to accommodate your needs. Coming to office hours can count towards participation.

DISABILITY STUDIES CLUSTER EVENTS

This course is participating in the Disability Studies Cluster, a program that brings together core and elective courses in the DS Minor for lectures, performances, and interactive workshops with leading disability scholars and activists. Our mental health pop-up we are hosting as a class on **April 20th, 7 p.m.**, counts as one of the cluster events and is required for this course. You are required to **attend 2 additional events and** write a 2-page reflection on each. Reflections are due within one week of the event. Please choose from the following:

* **February 10th, 7 p.m. HFSC Herman Meeting Room: Institutions and People with Disabilities: An International Perspective**. Executive Director of Disability Rights International Eric Rosenthal discusses the findings of DRI's latest report on orphanages, group homes, and international human rights violations with the University Center for Excellence in Developmental Disabilities' Marisa Brown.

* **February 26th, 7 p.m., HFSC Social Room: Underbelly: Performance Making and Environmental Illness Exposed**: A Zoom Presentation by Artist Julie Laffin in conversation with Professor Jennifer Fink.

* **March 28th, time and location tba: Disability in an Age of Climate Change: Ethics and Activism from Puerto Rico, the Bay Area, and Beyond**, a conversation with Germán Parodi and Shaylin Sluzalis (Partnership for Inclusive Disaster Strategies), Jina Kim (Smith College), Stacey Park Milburn (#PowerToLive organizer), Alex Ghenis (World Institute on Disability), and Julia Watts Belser (Georgetown University).

* **April 14th, 7 p.m. HFSC Social Room: Dismantling Settler Colonialism and Ableism: Disability Justice and Decolonization**. A facilitated discussion with disability justice and indigenous peoples' advocates Dustin Gibson, Najma Johnson, Jen Deerinwater, and Lydia Brown.

mimikhuc

Y'all. Let's have a conversation about participation. Yes, participation is important, especially in a class that is discussion-based and uses reflection as its main form of engagement. We all want our students to participate actively (though what does "actively" even mean???). But let's be honest that our desire for this is not simply pedagogical— it's also ego and fragility. We think our courses—we—deserve the respect of participation. We take it very personally when our students don't participate in the ways we expect them to. Here I am demanding participation rather than thinking about how to enable it. I am treating participation as an act of individual willpower and not an ability circumscribed by structures and capacities. I am attaching punitive consequences for not applying this supposed willpower sufficiently. I should instead be asking, What am *I* doing to enable each student's participation? How do the structures of the course enable participation across needs that vary and change over time? How might I contextualize students' ability to participate within the structures they experience inside and outside of my class?—like a fucking pandemic and institutional failures of care and health issues and financial insecurities and trauma, and on and on.

mimikhuc

I am relieved and happy that past-me was willing to be somewhat flexible on what participation looked like. But I only offered two options: talk in class or talk to me in office hours. As I diagnosed above, I wasn't thinking very deeply about my own responsibility for enabling those (and other) forms of participation.

mimikhuc

While this is a reasonable assignment, I am not about this life anymore. Tell me that you went, and I will believe you, and that is enough. Honestly, if you couldn't go, that's fine too. We are all allowed to be sick and out of spoons at any time. I didn't have the spoons to attend any of them myself!

mimikhuc

Ah, my lightning oral exam. One of the crown jewels of my pedagogical developments at UMD. I treated midterms as a collaborative process by having students help create the questions. I then gave them the finalized questions in advance so they could prepare—if the goal is mastery, there's no need for surprises. In the exam itself, they could bring whatever notes they wanted (again, if the goal is mastery, why can't they bring what they prepared? The preparation is the process of learning). One at a time, in my office, each student would verbally answer one question for five minutes, with me giving the occasional nudge to help them if needed. Then I graded them on the spot and was done! The orals took a lot of energy as a whole—five minutes for twenty-five or thirty-five or forty-five students totals to a

MIDTERM

In-class "lightning" oral exam. Students will be given essay questions ahead of time in order to prepare. On the day of the midterm, each student will orally answer the essay questions for 5 minutes.

WEEKLY JOURNAL

Students are to keep a reflective journal throughout the semester, contributing one entry of 2-3 double-spaced pages per week. I will provide a prompt related to each week's readings/topics to respond to. The entire journal is due on Canvas on 4/8. Journals will be graded on depth and sophistication of reflection.

POP-UP CREATION AND REFLECTION PAPER

Students will work in groups to create and run our class-hosted mental health pop-up on 4/20. Afterwards, students are to write a 3-4 page (around 1000 words) reflection paper. Discuss the station that you helped to run as well as 1-2 other aspects of the pop-up. In your discussion, reflect upon what kinds of interventions in wellness the activities generated. Connect to at least 2 readings from the course in your analysis. Due at the beginning of class on the last day of class: 4/27.

FINAL REFLECTION PAPER

A 5-page (around 1500 words) reflection paper that will discuss what you've learned from this course, how you've been changed, what your takeaways from this course are, and why the topics of the course are important. Questions to consider: What were some of the assumptions you held before taking this course, and how have those changed (and through what readings/discussions/ assignments)? What are some course concepts that have become useful for you in analyzing your own life? What have you learned from your fellow classmates? This will be a personal reflection that must substantively engage course materials from throughout the semester (at least 5 texts). You may draw upon your weekly journals for ideas but do not use more than one or two sentences verbatim. Think of this as a chance to develop and synthesize ideas you started to reflect upon in your journals. Grading will be based on sophistication and depth of analysis. Due on Canvas at the time of our final exam: 5/5 2:30pm.

LOT of time being "on." But no reading and grading afterward was the reward for me. Students did well and felt good about the whole process: relatively low stress, with lots of structures in place to support and enable success, and some continued relationship and trust building to boot. A really great assessment tool.

But I am not about that life anymore. I don't need students to regurgitate ideas and theories back at me. I want to know how they are doing. And how the structures around them are shaping their lives. And what from the course so far has been meaningful. This is what I ask them now, conversationally in small groups, and they apply what we do in class directly to their lives and not to an arbitrary midterm question. They are able to tell me what ableism looks and feels like and are able to articulate their needs in these contexts. This is mastery of the material, with no studying, no rigid and pressurized performance, and no grades needed. This is also being human, together, which sounds simple but is *much* harder to do than you think. Humaning by itself is already hard work. Humaning with others in caring and ethical ways is possibly the hardest work of all.

mimikhuc

I discovered early in my teaching that students could and would engage with the material deeply if assigned a simple, short reflection assignment. I first developed the semester-long journal as an assignment for an Asian American Mental Health class at UMD in order to help students sustain that engagement throughout the term. Also to allow them (and me) to track the progression and trajectory of their learning. Weekly prompts connected to the respective topics and readings helped guide their reflections. At the end of the course, I found the journals were some of the most amazing things my students had ever written: deeply vulnerable and feeling-full, and rich with the hard work of grappling with new ideas and revelations. I wanted to replicate that in this DS class, which I don't think was a bad impulse at all. This was and is a great assignment. It's just that in the context of the pandemic and our drastically reduced capacities, I cannot imagine asking this of my students. I cannot imagine myself being able to write in a sustained way, each week, for four or five classes. We are that dog in the house on fire saying, "This is fine," and things are definitively not fine. How might we do thinking work together in our classes in ways that take that "not fine" into account by directly addressing it?

mimikhuc

Ha! Past-me thought we'd get to make it to the end of April 2020 with normality. Sweet summer child.

mimikhuc

This was my other crown jewel from my time at UMD. The final assignment of all final assignments, a way for students to synthesize the

You can earn extra credit throughout the semester by writing 2-page reflection/ ○——
response papers on outside materials/events related to the course. These can
boost your participation grade and help bump borderline grades. You can
write an infinite number of extra credit reflection papers. When choosing
something to write on, run your ideas by me first. These are due **hard-copy**
to me by the last class session, 4/27.

Grades

Grades are based on your level of mastery of the course concepts and skills.
Full effort is expected from every student; mastery of the materials will require
effort and hard work, but "hard work" in itself will not guarantee mastery and ○——
therefore a particular grade. You will receive the grade that you earn based on
your performance. Please know that grades are not up for negotiation. If you
have questions about your grades throughout the semester, feel free to come
talk to me so that we can be clear on the expectations and the standards of
assessment for the course. I am happy to go over any assignments and course
expectations, in office hours and not by email, both before due dates and
after grading.

Accessibility & Accommodations

I strive towards a classroom that is accessible as possible for all involved. I
recognize that everyone has access needs, and that these needs will change
over time. I also recognize that not everyone knows what their access needs
are. If you are aware of your access needs, please communicate them to me. ○——
I do not require documentation or working with any university support
services, and will work with you to generate structures to meet your needs
as much as possible. For instance, you may know already that you will need
extra time for in-class exams, or that a note-taker would be helpful for you
to process in-class information. Or you may not know until a particular crisis
arises that you are not in an emotional or cognitive or physical state to be
able to attend the next couple classes or complete the next assignment. Please
try to communicate your needs to me as soon as possible so we can figure out
together how to best meet them. I will be as flexible as I can to make all of our
experiences of this course as accessible—and even enjoyable!—as possible.

ideas from the course and tell me what they've learned in a reflective form that feels approachable and personally meaningful. Students have enjoyed writing this final. I have greatly enjoyed reading them. Reading a student tracking their own learning and articulating what is meaningful to them—this is a recipe for everyone to feel like a success. They feel good about what they've learned; I feel good about what they've learned. Everybody wins. I've iterated this assignment further during the pandemic, finding a form that allows even deeper reflection and letting go of some of the rigid requirements that I now realize hampered creativity. I experimented with the epistolary form early in the pandemic, and now I'm never going back. Writing a letter clarifies (and deepens) the purpose of the writing, and having a particular audience that is not simply me opens up new kinds of reflection. And vulnerability.

mimikhuc

Again, a fine sentiment—it allows students to apply course materials outside of the class, allows them an alternative mode of participation, is flexible and unlimited—but I'm just not about that life right now. I don't want to make them do this kind/amount of writing, and honestly, I don't want to read it!! Let's not kid ourselves—I wasn't even reading these in the beforetimes.

mimikhuc

Sigh. Past-me was so defensive, but I have feeling for this. I remember being questioned about grades, students demanding grade changes or the chance to do extra work to raise their grade last minute. I remember trying to explain to them that they are earning their grade—I'm not giving them their grade, and I'm definitely not giving it to them willy-nilly. I remember entitled students, racist students, sexist students—all of whom refused to recognize the authority of a young queer woman of color. I remember one (white, male) student even pulling a Karen, going to tenured faculty "bosses" to report me, an adjunct, for "inappropriate" behavior and unfair grading, all in the name of demanding a higher grade to which he felt entitled. I remember feeling under siege the moment I turned grades in each term. I remember. But I've learned two things (among many!) in the pandemic. Grades don't equal mastery or engagement or meaningfulness. And of course students are "grade grubbers," as we so derogatorily call them, if their entire sense of worth (and their ability to maintain scholarships, get scholarships, get into postcollege schools, get a job) relies upon grades—a pressurized conflation that we as their professors actually draw upon and encourage in the ways we structure our classes. We are the ones telling them, on the ground, in the trenches, that grades matter, that grades reflect their merit, their smarts, their hard work, their worth as students, their ability to comply with our rules which we conflate with their morality, their respect for us, and their status as "good students." The stakes are very high for them, and we help ensure it remains that way.

Communication

Email is my preferred communication for brief matters. I will not discuss lengthy matters via email, especially assignments and grades. If you have questions about the course material, assignments, or your grades, I am available in office hours and by appointment.

Academic Integrity

I expect academic integrity, which means honesty and accountability at all times when conducting yourselves as members of this classroom and university community. This means treating others with respect and being accountable for the ways your actions affect others. In terms of your assignments, please refer to the following list of prohibited behaviors: https://honorcouncil .georgetown.edu/system/policies/standards-of-conduct/. There is only one way to "cheat" in my courses, and that is to pass off others' work as your own. Please do not do that, as it misrepresents yourself and does harm to both yourself and others.

I'm not saying everyone has to throw grades out (well, maybe I am), but I do think we all need to question what we think grades mean, and how we conflate rigor with grades. Having grades does not ensure rigor. It does ensure stress. I threw grades out at the start of the pandemic and EVERYONE in my classes is much happier for it. Learning and engagement are happening in my courses, in some of the most meaningful ways I've seen. I took the pressure away and instead tried to think about how to create shared commitments, nurture shared responsibility and collective care, and enable engagement in breadth and depth. Grades might be able to be a part of those things (you'll have to convince me), but only if we prioritize those things over grades. How do we create those things, and how can we structure grades to help us create those things?

mimikhuc

Oh thank god I was already using the language of access instead of accommodations and was committed to believing students and not requiring documentation. I might've stopped writing this whole fucking chapter if I discovered my accessibility paragraph was shit. I acknowledge that needs change over time. I also reassure my students that I will work with them to generate structures to meet their needs. I give examples of needs and the structures that can be created to meet them. I mention emotional and cognitive states of being, so that they understand needs are not simply physical. This is a good foundation. I've deepened my approach to access and my language around it during the pandemic, but this version covers the important and necessary bases.

mimikhuc

What is academic integrity? I had already shifted away from worrying about "cheating"—I had intentionally created assignments that did not lend themselves to the kinds of cheating we worry about. The assignments were low stakes and mostly reflective or creative. Instead of focusing on cheating, I was defining integrity through interpersonal honesty and accountability, and I was defining accountability in terms of thinking about our relationship to others—which reflective/creative assignments can help develop. But I hadn't yet thought very deeply about my responsibility to nurture those things. I intuitively knew that if I treated the students with respect and made it safe for them to be honest, I would build the trust necessary for the kind of integrity and accountability I was looking for. I knew that believing them, and believing in them, would shift the culture of the classroom, and perhaps that was embedded in the structures I did create across my course policies and activities. It was a good beginning, and now, almost two years later, my teaching journey has taught me very clearly that integrity is nurtured not through punishment but through care. *Cura personalis*.

Well, that annotation was a wild ride. Both horrific and fun. Well, it started out horrific and then became fun. I was horrified and embarrassed when I first looked at my old syllabus. But as I annotated, I realized what I was doing is what we in disability studies call an access audit: an evaluation of an environment to see if it meets access needs *so that it can be improved*. I've never seen an audit done on a syllabus before, but why the fuck not? The goal is more access, and universal design tells us there are always new ways to move toward that aspiration of full accessibility, particularly as environments and needs evolve. Why shouldn't pedagogy engage a continuing appraisal process so that our teaching grows and adapts to meet new and more needs? We should all be doing this kind of audit on our own teaching regularly, without shame. As I moved through my annotation, I found the process easier and ultimately freeing. We are all works in progress; we can all always do better. I share my process here in a moment of vulnerability with you that I hope creates a kind of safety. It's much easier to admit you can do better when there are other people around you admitting it too.

As the pandemic hit in March 2020, I saw how useless and irrelevant my syllabus had become, even with all of its flexible policies and creative assignments. What students needed in March 2020 was not what I was offering—and I got my first glimpse that maybe that had always been true. I threw my whole syllabus out. I canceled classes for two weeks to allow students to figure out where the fuck they were going to "shelter in place." Then I made an entirely new syllabus for the last five weeks of the semester titled "Teaching and Learning in the Time of COVID 19," and I formulated my first course access survey.

I hope you took the access survey before this chapter. I hope it allowed you to reflect on your needs and capacities right now. I hope this chapter anticipated at least some of your needs and took them into account. If we were having this conversation in real time, I would likely have to recalibrate often with you as we navigate our collective needs. Actually I'd probably be taking a long break right now. Twenty-plus pages is too fucking long for one conversation. (If you need to take a break, please do!)

I made my first access survey because I recognized that I needed to check in with my students as Georgetown transitioned abruptly to remote learning. I didn't yet call it an access survey, simply a "check-in." I wanted to know: Since students couldn't return to campus after spring break, would they have safe places to go? Could they fulfill their basic needs? Did they have access to the course texts? Would they even have stable internet to attend synchronous classes online? What the fuck is Zoom, and can everyone access it? If I didn't know the answers to these questions, there was no way to move forward with the course at all.

Here's what I sent out (see figs. 5.1–5.3 on next pages).

Sometimes a revolution happens quietly, right under your nose. It felt so natural and right to send out this survey that it seems odd now that I never thought to send it before. It seems odd that none of us ever send one. That oddness was confirmed in the form of student surprise and appreciation—for the simple fact of the survey, and that it asked about basic needs first. Student well-being came first, over their ability to meet my desires as their instructor and the requirements of the course (which are really the same thing). Both the structure and tone of the form (as well as foundations I had built in the first two months of the course) communicated that (re)prioritization. *Cura personalis.*

Immediately afterwards I shared my Google form on social media, and colleagues from Georgetown and other institutions excitedly picked it up. My Disability Studies Program director shared the form with the rest of the program's faculty, and since my course was officially housed in the English Department at the time, she also encouraged me to share it to the English listserv. From there it made its way to the executive director of Georgetown's instructional development unit, the Center for New Designs in Learning and Scholarship (CNDLS), and went out in a campus-wide email blast of tips on making the transition to remote learning. The chair of English at the time suggested I share it with the college dean's office, and that office responded appreciatively. The form spoke to something that faculty and even admin intuitively recognized needed to happen but hadn't known how to enact. Many of us care about students. But there are few structures in place to incentivize this caring and few models to show us how this caring might be expressed most effectively—that is, in a way that actually addresses student needs, and in a way that makes students feel cared for. The model I provided in March 2020 was a simple and easy intervention, the best kind of revolution, legible to both those in charge of education and the students receiving it.

What if we just ask students what they need, in a holistic sense, to be safe(ish) and stable(ish), which is also, and always has been, of course, what they need in order to learn?

I'd invented what I think was higher ed's first course access survey, I realized later. (If there have been others, and I hope there have been, they've sadly never made their ways into public circulation.)

ENGL270: Intro to Disability Studies-- Checking in as we transition online

Please fill out this form so I can better understand how each of you are doing and what your needs will be as we transition our class online.

Thanks,
mimi

mimi.khuc@georgetown.edu

* Required

Email *

Your email

Name *

Your answer

GU is asking students not to return to campus. Do you have a safe place to go? *

Your answer

Do you have any concerns about fulfilling basic needs around housing, food, medical care, mental health? Will you have access to necessary support systems? *

Your answer

Will you have reliable internet and the ability to access Canvas to read and post stuff? *

○ Yes

○ No

○ Maybe

Will you be able to participate in video conferencing during our class time? *

○ Yes

○ No

○ Sometimes

Will you be able to do video conferencing at other days/times? *

○ Yes

○ No

○ Maybe

Do you anticipate any new access needs? Remember, we approach access issues as anything that is an obstacle to you participating as much as possible in the course. You have a right to have needs and to ask for those needs to be met. I will try to anticipate as much as I can, but please let me know if things arise. *

Your answer

I'll likely be shifting us to online discussions, online group-work, and some face-to-face Zoom discussions (once I learn how to use Zoom!). I don't lecture but I might also record a few short videos if I work up the nerve. Do you have any concerns about any of these formats? Do you have any suggestions for me about these formats or other formats that you've found helpful? *

Your answer

I will be posting the rest of the semester's readings online--except for Esme Wang's book, which hopefully you have already purchased. Will you have access to a copy of Esme Wang's book? *

○ Yes

○ No

Do you have any questions or concerns you'd like to share with me, about this course or other aspects of this overall situation?

Your answer

Submit   Clear form

[5.1–5.3] Google form check-in for transitioning course online.

Simple and easy, but it took a global pandemic.

That spring, Georgetown pivoted quickly, creating pandemic-inflected resources to support students, faculty, and staff. The collective crisis necessitated more access in terms of flexibility, remote options, emergency financial support, even therapy and self-care—and Georgetown made announcement after announcement about its new policies and resources designed to help. In missives and town halls, Georgetown encouraged its faculty to be as flexible and caring toward students as possible. Suddenly, everyone deserved help, more help than Georgetown had ever offered before. I was heartened to hear this messaging and hopeful that Georgetown's mission of *cura personalis* opened it to more compassionate approaches than what my colleagues at other institutions were reporting.

But as always, you gotta ask the students. Because care is not happening if students don't actually feel cared for, no matter the best of intentions. My students' intensely grateful responses to my Google form suggested their other classes were providing no such care. They directly confirmed this to me in that first week of transition: many of their other professors gave them no time to settle in, continuing classes remotely immediately with little to no change to course policies and assignments. Instructional continuity was not balanced with student well-being but prioritized over it. Some faculty even justified their business-as-usual approach by arguing that it was *helping* students by maintaining familiar structures and expectations for them. "Students need this sense of normalcy," I saw proclaimed in some spaces on social media. I found the cover of virtuousness particularly appalling for what it hides: ableism, attachment to productivity, fear of change, fear of not being a "rigorous" teacher, fear of students taking advantage of them, fear of students getting things they don't "deserve." Most of all for its appropriation of the language of care, especially care of students, in order to maintain not just instructional but *institutional* continuity. For many instructors, the two were the same, inextricable: instruction could only continue wrapped in the forces that historically shape it in our institutions—ableism, meritocracy, uneven access, differential punishment.

Students at Georgetown advocated immediately for the implementation of a "Double A" grading system across the board, de facto converting courses to pass/fail or complete/incomplete and granting students an A- or A for completion. Relieving pressure for students and taking into account the varying experiences of crisis and need across the student body, the call offered a new structure of support beyond Georgetown's ability to imagine but well within its capacity to implement. But Georgetown chose not to embrace the Double A system, instead adopting a less drastic option that simply extended the deadline for students to officially convert their courses to pass/fail should they want to.

I did embrace the Double A. Adopting it took nothing away from me or my course. Honestly, who gave a shit about grades at a time like that? Completing my course, any course, let alone four or five courses, seemed herculean at that point. Students deserved those As, because they deserved the decreased pressure, because they deserved a kind of care that could address the differential experiences of crisis they were going through. No one would have to explain to me, convince me, that their particular experience of struggle in the moment was deserving of exception, and no one would have to endure my arbitration of the validity of their pains. A simple and easy solution, but one that few professors at Georgetown adopted because it wasn't mandated by administration and, just as likely, because few professors keep abreast of student organizing.

I implemented many other changes to my syllabus. What was it we all needed in that moment? How could I really apply disability studies and disability justice principles of interdependence, recognition of needs, commitment to collective care, and especially rejection of ableism and its expectations around the "normal" bodymind and its denigration of need?[10] I looked at what was left to cover in the course. Thank the gods, old and new, that my last several weeks were on new approaches to mental health and care. How apropos. Here's what I did.

ENGL270

Introduction to Disability Studies

INSTRUCTOR: MIMI KHÚC   Semester: Spring 2020, part II

Office hours: MW 2–3:15pm by Zoom—I'll try to be available by the "Office Hours" link on Canvas, but let me know in advance that you plan to stop by. I'm also available at other times as necessary.

Teaching and Learning Disability Studies in the Time of COVID19
Welcome to the second half of our course, which is changing dramatically in some ways. We are revamping the course according to my and your needs

mimikhuc
I retitled the course because I wanted to clearly mark that we were entering a very different moment, necessitating a very different course. We would not be continuing business as usual.

during this unprecedented time and to make the class more responsive to the current crisis. I feel that it is my responsibility as your professor to pedagogically ensure that the course provides helpful tools for understanding—and surviving—this crisis, and to not add any burdens that will make life feel more unlivable for you. This kind of pedagogy—teaching in the context of crisis and teaching as a transformative care project—has always undergirded my choices in the classroom, so this doesn't feel that new or different for me, and it shouldn't for you either since you've been with me for almost 3 months now. But what is new is our shared and heightened sense of crisis and our inability to be physically in a classroom together at all anymore—which necessitate new and different forms of teaching/learning/care.

Class Priorities and Commitments

* Your mental health—and physical health—come first. Do not prioritize this course (or any other course) over your own health at this time. Self-care and care for loved ones are the most important things right now.

* The assignments are meant to help you through this time. Please engage them as much as you feel is helpful. They are meant to be self-care, as well as application of DS principles, frameworks, and methods.

* Remember that access needs are needs that when met enable participation in the course to the fullest—therefore they are wide-ranging and can be met in wide-ranging, creative ways. I continue to be committed to making participation as accessible as possible. Please let me know if anything comes up that makes participation feel hard. We are taught not to have needs, that needs mean we are "weak"; resist this impulse. That is the biggest lesson I want you to take away from this class.

* Fuck business as usual.

New Grading Policies

* You have already passed the class. Anyone who would like to take the course Pass/Fail will automatically get a Pass without having to do any additional work.

mimikhuc

I wanted to clearly explain why we were implementing changes—to address need and make sure the course made sense in that moment. We were tackling this crisis directly and not as an afterthought.

mimikhuc

I wanted to articulate—and assert—that this is how I understand professorial responsibility in times of crisis. Do no harm. Try to help. I'm not that kind of doctor, but the overlap in ideals became more apparent as education and health began crisis-ing together.

mimikhuc

As I was writing this, I realized that this was simply a deepening of a pedagogy of unwellness, and I tried to articulate here what made this moment different pedagogically than before.

mimikhuc

It was important to me to set and front-load a clear list of priorities, extending the work of the access survey. No more learning objectives as respectable academic performance. Instead, real commitments to well-being and the learning that derives from that.

mimikhuc

First and foremost. Health. Comes. First. Especially during a health crisis. (But maybe, actually, always?)

mimikhuc

This was my first reimagining of the work of course assignments. If the goal is to get through this shit together, then the work assigned must contribute to that goal. What does it look like to do assignments that care for the self?

mimikhuc

My clearer iteration of access needs. It's one thing to say I will accommodate your needs or please let me know if you have access needs; it's another to insist that everyone has needs and deserves for them to be met, and to locate that within the denigration of needs that we have all internalized. I wanted to very clearly depathologize need and give my students permission to need. This is disability justice in action.

mimikhuc

Because yes.

mimikhuc

This line alone did more immediate work to support my students than anything else I rewrote in the syllabus.

* I am also implementing the "Double A" system that GU students are advocating for. This means that if you complete the rest of the assignments (described below), you will get either an A- or A in the class.
* If you are unable to complete the assignments described below but still would like to get a letter grade instead of a Pass, come talk to me, and we can figure out alternatives.
* I will post midterm grades just so you can see what you got, but remember that they no longer "count" in the same way.

Assignments

SMALL GROUP DISCUSSIONS

I am assigning you to small groups of 5 on Canvas so you can have smaller discussions. Each week, I'd like you to create and participate in a discussion thread based on the reading/activity. Everyone should post at least twice (~100 words each, more if you want). **Please have these done by Thursdays 11pm.** I will comment on each of your discussions on Fridays.

JOURNAL

You should have completed 5 journal entries before the midterm. If you are behind on the journal, don't worry. Just move on to the new entries. Below I've included the journal prompt for each week already. Often they are related to your discussions, so you decide whether doing the journal entry before or after your group discussion is more helpful. Journal entries should be around 1 page (250–350 words, more if you want), with the exception of your final entry, which should be closer to 2 pages (500–600 words, or more if you want). Your entire journal (whatever you did before the midterm plus these 5 new entries) will be **due on the day of your final (5/5 2:30pm)**. This deadline can be extended if you need; just ask.

mimikhuc

To be as flexible as possible—and as humble as possible—I had to recognize that even my conception of *complete* may not work for all students. My conception of *complete* remained and remains arbitrary, something I decided on my own that may or may not reflect the real-world capacities of my students. So now I always offer the chance for a more "bespoke" set of accommodations to fit individual circumstance if needed.

mimikhuc

Ah, our attachments to the discussion board. No more discussion boards please. Students don't want to do them; professors don't want to read them. I have since nixed all discussion boards—there are more engaging mediums, and there is no need for me to surveil discussions so closely. Trust students to talk to each other. We don't have to see it all.

mimikhuc

The birth of the small-group discussion. Since I was getting rid of synchronous class completely for the rest of the term (because it felt unimaginable both for them and for me in the midst of all the instability), I wanted to create a new structure that would allow collective discussion. Small groups seemed the best way, and I have since iterated this assignment to make it more fulfilling and less work. Jim Lee shared with me his version: an assigned small group that meets each week in real time on any platform of their choosing, discussing what they *notice*, what they *know*, and what they *wonder* in relation to the week's readings. He told me how much students connected in their small groups and how they came to rely on these groups for friendship and care during virtual learning and isolation. So I adopted his approach, creating groups of three or four students who would meet each week on their own for twenty to sixty minutes on platforms of their choosing and on days and times of their choosing for maximum flexibility. I would not be attending any of these to surveil. I simply asked them to write a brief summary to post to a shared Google doc so I knew that they had met. No right or wrong answers, no high-stakes group work. Just discussing and connecting with each other through that discussion. More recently I've explicitly explained that our class depends on a collective commitment to each other's learning and well-being. Show up for each other. Do the reading and come to your discussion groups as acts of care, not because you will be penalized if you don't. We all do what we can, when we can, so that we all make it through to the end. My students have also reported that these small groups have been some of the most meaningful experiences in college, showing them how to be vulnerable, how to build trust and intimacy and care.

In future terms, I added a "midterm" to the syllabus, in which I would meet virtually with each of the small groups for twenty minutes to check in with them. No grades, no test. Just a conversation about how they're doing and what they have enjoyed in the course so far. And what their other midterms in other classes look like. This conversation stealthily accomplishes many things. I get to know the students a little better. I get to observe small-group dynamics. I get to check in on my students' well-being. They get to share something they've learned in the course so far, which makes them and me feel like successes. And they apply a disability studies/disability justice lens to their other classes, evaluating the kinds of ableism that frequently structure the assignments. Synthesis and application, once again, with little to no stakes or penalties and a whole lot of intimacy and care. This is the work. This is rigor, without all the trappings we think must accompany it. A+ for everybody.

I have created a class Instagram account: @DSinthetimeofCOVID19 (pw: ▮▮▮▮▮▮▮▮▮▮▮). Take one picture a week (or more if you want!) and **post to our class account by Sundays 11pm** with the following in the caption:

* your name
* how you're feeling/mood
* something you or a loved one needs right now
* any observation you've made this week relating to course concepts, like ableism, needs, distribution of resources, "normal," care, collective access, spoons
* an image description

Memes are welcome if you create or revise them (not just reposting one you saw). Make sure to follow the shared account with your own Instagram to see your classmates' posts. Feel free to comment on each other's posts (kind + supportive comments only!). If you don't have your own account, you're welcome to log into the shared account to read, though don't post comments from there unless you're the OP for that particular post and want to respond to classmates' comments. At the end of the semester, screenshot your posts and drop them into one doc to submit to me, **due on the day of your final (5/5 2:30pm).**

Schedule

We will not be having regular Zoom meetings—these feel too difficult logistically in terms of access. I would like to see as many of you as possible before the end of the term, though—because seeing your faces makes me happy!—so we'll aim for at least one during the last week of April.

The rest of the readings this semester are from Open in Emergency, the mental health project that I curated and published. Since not everyone has Esme Wang's book, I decided not to assign from it, though I do recommend reading it (especially the 3 chapters I was going to assign: "Diagnosis," "Yale Will Not Save You," "On the Ward").

WEEK 1: 3/30–4/3

* If you need a refresher, re-read my editor's note for Open in Emergency to get a sense of the framework+purpose of the project.

mimikhuc

Again, this is my attempt to question my own definitions of *complete*. If they were already behind on the journal entries, clearly they were already struggling, so why should I ask them to make it up now when their stress is surely even higher? Let's just figure out what we have the capacity for moving forward.

mimikhuc

This is the crown jewel of my pandemic-times syllabi: a shared Instagram account on which students post weekly reflections. It was inspired by two colleague-friends who shared their assignments on social media that spring: Jigna Desai, who had her University of Minnesota students photo-document their pandemic lives with a daily photo, to be shared as a slideshow at the end of the term; and Ronak Kapadia, who asked his University of Illinois Chicago graduate theory seminar students to create and share course-related memes on a shared Instagram account. I synthesized these two assignments into what I like to think of as a pandemic archive of feeling. "How are you doing?" I asked my students. "What are your needs right now? How are you encountering course concepts in daily pandemic life?" The form is flexible, with very few requirements, just an image, short reflection, and image description. Almost all my students were already using Instagram, and I was scrolling it regularly. The process is user-friendly: you can easily use your phone to post; high-contrast text and images make for easier viewing; photos break up text for much easier reading than on Canvas discussion boards; added image descriptions and/or alt text make for screen-reader friendliness. And Instagram is a platform on which students can be fairly anonymous and therefore more vulnerable, on which students can and will read each other's posts.

As usual, students surpassed my expectations. Their posts became weekly joys to "grade." It was the highlight of each of those early, stressful pandemic weeks to see heartfelt reflections pop up in my Instagram feed every few days, and to be able to know how each of my students was doing every week, without having to schedule virtual meetings or email check-ins. Intimacy over social media became the foundation of a structure of collective care that we all needed but hadn't known we needed.

I've kept the same Instagram account with each of my courses since that first term, each set of students adding to a living archive of hardship and connection and isolation. I've iterated the assignment slightly, asking them to reflect on their assigned weekly self-care (see below for more info on that), which has really deepened their engagement by giving them a focal point and shared "text" that changes and progresses throughout the term. Light load, not time consuming for them or for me, rich engagement, and powerful community building—everybody wins.

These posts, going on two-plus years now at the time of this writing (across five courses and two institutions!), remain my favorite things to "grade" and bright spots of joy and connection dotting each week.

* Watch the new documentary, *Crip Camp*, just out on Netflix last week. If you do not already have a Netflix account, Netflix is offering a 30-day free trial right now. Let me know if you have any trouble accessing Netflix. Discuss this film in your small groups.
* Choose a card from Erin O'Brien's Queer Self-Care cards (the corresponding image and text are mirror-imaged in the PDF). If possible, follow its instructions. If not possible (because of social distancing!) try to modify it for the current conditions, or choose a different one. Reflect on the experience in your journal (1 page).
* Post your weekly Instagram post.

WEEK 2: 4/6–4/10
* Read Kai Cheng Thom's essay, The Myth of Mental Health.
* What does productivity mean to you? Think about how we tie mental health to productivity—does this resonate? Can you think of an example? Think about this especially in relation to the current moment—are we still doing that? Is it different than how we usually tie productivity to mental health?
* Do you feel like you are allowed to take care of yourself right now? How about before the COVID19 crisis?
* Discuss these questions with your group and reflect on them in your journal (1+ page).
* Post your weekly Instagram post.

WEEK 3: 4/13–4/17
* Give yourself tarot readings using this set of Asian American Tarot Cards I created. Click on this random number generator and then read the corresponding card. Reflect on the text and image—what resonates? What is it telling you about your life, and how does it help to better understand something about your life? Do this with as many cards as you like; you don't have to read all the cards.
* In particular, be sure to read The Student, the final card in the deck. This was written collectively by students all across the country, curated by a team of student editors, and finalized by me and my partner-in-editing (and in life), Lawrence. I sincerely hope it does its job of capturing student life (and death).
* The Emergency may also feel particularly relevant in these times.
* The Crip is particularly related to our course frameworks and language.

mimikhuc

For the remaining five weeks of the term, I assigned short readings and corresponding activities and reflections for their journals each week. The activities here are the proto version of what would become a required weekly self-care assignment. In future semesters, I developed a self-care activity for each week, drawing on that week's themes and asking students to apply those to their lives. I call these activities self-care for several reasons. I want to normalize care for oneself—that we all deserve care, that we should take time to care for ourselves, that needing care is not pathological. I also want to expand my students' notions of what counts as self-care and what kind of work self-care is supposed to do. We're not talking about bubble baths and manicures here (though those are nice!). We're talking about self-work that is transformative and revelatory—and sometimes really hard to do. (More on self-care later in the chapter.) Engaging course materials can be care for yourself. Thinking and feeling deeply about new things can be care for yourself. Finding ways to apply what you learn can be care for yourself. Doing all of these things with others can be care for yourself. This is also a lesson that self-care doesn't always feel easy or good. But it should always be in support of full personhood, yours and others'.

Professors with a keen eye will also notice, though, that these self-care assignments are stealth reflection assignments, often doing the same work as more traditional assignments like

* Choose a tarot card to share with a friend/loved one who might find it helpful. (Don't share the link to the whole folder; download the card and attach it to your message.)
* Share in your discussion group one card that you picked for yourself and your experience of reflecting on that card. Comment on at least one other person's post about their card and experience. Feel free to share about the card you picked for a friend too.
* For your journal (1+ page), reflect more on the cards you read. Also reflect on the overall experience as a care practice. How did these tarot readings shift how you move through your day/week?
* Post your weekly Instagram post.

WEEK 4: 4/20–4/24
* Read Chad Shomura's Corner of Heart-to-Hearts and do one with a friend or family member: choose one word and take turns talking about it for 2 minutes each while the other person just listens. Do as many words as you like.
* The activity was designed to be done publicly, in part to reclaim the public space as one for intimacy and feelings—to disrupt the everyday experience (and rules) of feelings (i.e., what kinds of feelings we're allowed to have and when/where), but now you're doing it in the very intimate space of your home. Does it still break open something new? How does it feel to try to form intimacy over video chats? How does the current crisis inflect how you talked about the word(s) you chose? Was there a reason why you chose the word(s) you did (or did you choose at random)? Or perhaps your home doesn't feel private since there might be many people there all sharing space right now. If so, how does that shape the experience?
* Discuss in your small group what word(s) you chose and how it felt to talk about that word with your heart-to-heart partner, and reflect in your journal (1+ page).
* Post your weekly Instagram post.

WEEK 5: 4/27–5/1
* *Optional reading:* peruse these daughter-to-mother letters. (I recommend Raven Anand's and erin Ninh's in particular—content warning: sexual violence, abuse.) Consider writing a letter to your parents saying things you haven't said but wish you could. This may feel particularly fraught as

discussion posts, reflection papers, and short-answer essays. The key distinction is students will do these self-care assignments willingly, enthusiastically, engaging deeply in that reflective work because I've given it to them in a form that feels like it matters.

Over the last two years, my students have reported that the self-care assignments have been their favorite of all my assignments. They've looked forward to receiving my weekly announcement detailing the new thing they have to do, taking delight in being surprised by the unfamiliar and feeling hopeful for what it opens up for them. Many of them even share the activities with friends and family, having them follow along! Perhaps this is the real mark of this assignment's success: students finding such meaning in an assignment that they recruit others to do it with them and in that process develop an entire new dimension of learning and community-making.

some of you are living with your parents full-time right now, so don't do it if it feels too hard. But if it feels helpful, go for it!

* *Optional reading:* read the <u>postpartum depression pamphlet</u>. Originally, I was going to have you find info pamphlets/brochures from campus (like the health center and CAPS!) to bring to class and analyze together, which would've been very fun! But now, just reflect on the interventions that I (and my co-writers) tried to make in the postpartum pamphlet as survivors. What would it look like if you were allowed to intervene in something "experts" had written about you and your experience?

* There are no required readings for the final week. Focus on your final journal entry, which serves as your "final paper" for the course. For your final journal entry (2+ pages), just tell me some things you learned in the class. What was new, exciting, surprising? What has stuck with you the most? What might you want to teach others based on what you've learned? How have you been changed? And, finally, name at least one thing you will commit to doing regularly to take care of yourself in the weeks/months to come.

* Submit full journal and screenshots of your Instagram posts by 5/5.

Again, these assignments are supposed to be helpful and not too stressful. If at any time you start feeling overwhelmed, please reach out.

Wishing you all the best and sending care.

—mimi

mimikhuc

Here is a simplified version of my final reflection paper assignment. Only two or three pages sharing some things that have felt meaningful. No need to be comprehensive, no need to hit an arbitrary number of texts to prove you've been reading. Just tell me what has stuck with you and what you'd want to share with others. And last, tell me something you will do to care for yourself going forward—because that matters, because you matter, because I want you to make it through to the other side of this.

As the pandemic forced me to deepen my understanding and implementation of access, I would begin giving talks to guide others toward more access-centered teaching, both at Georgetown and in virtual spaces across the country.[11] I would even come back virtually to UMD (!) to contribute to resources on pandemic teaching.[12] As Georgetown shifted completely to remote learning that fall, faculty shifted out of the triage moment of March 2020 and more intentionally reconfigured their classes for the Zoom environment long term. But I should put both "triage" and "intentionally" in scare quotes—I'm not sure all of us have ever left triage, and I'm not sure how intentional and thoughtful course reconfigurations were across the board. Georgetown's instructional development unit CNDLS became an epicenter of faculty adaptation, pumping out resources and guidelines and how-tos. Faculty scrambled to find new ways to deliver lectures, create discussions, and proctor exams. Recording, breakout rooms, and Zoom proctoring became regular practices. Anecdotally, faculty were overwhelmed. Anecdotally, students were overwhelmed. I'm sure administrators were overwhelmed. But we all kept going because, you know, Instructional Continuity! Stopping was, and remains, unimaginable.

I couldn't stop either. I had a course to teach, a contract to fulfill, bills to pay. I also had a daughter at home doing fourth grade via remote learning, and I am feeling triggered just writing that. A child at home full time trying to do learning online while you are at home full time trying to do work online means, on top of child care, adding tech support to your daily workload, for her and yourself (and sometimes also your partner!)—I mean, we are rounding into year 3 of the pandemic, so maybe it is now universally understood that what happened to children and their caregivers was, is, unconscionable. Let's just say, shit. was. hard.

I tried to counter that hardness. What could I do to make life easier for myself? For my daughter? For my students? In other words, what could I do to enable access? Or in other other words, what structures of care could I lean on? What could I build?

I formalized that check-in survey into a preterm access form built into my pedagogy. I built out that first one and began using it at the beginning of every semester for every class; checking in with needs should be something we do all the time. There will always be someone somewhere in crisis, if not shared crisis. Shit is always hard. We are always differentially unwell, yes? I wrote those words in 2016, coining the term *differential unwellness* that would become the cornerstone of my work, yet it had never occurred to me to check in with my students about that unwellness and their limited capacities *before* a course started. It had also never occurred to me to use a Google form to do so, posing these questions to all my students, giving them all an opportunity to ask for what they need and contribute to shaping the course in ways to meet those needs—instead of just ad-hoc helping individual, struggling students if they were willing and able to come to me throughout a term. I should have been doing that all along.

I always end my access survey by asking if there's anything else students would like to share, about the course or the awfulness of life right now. I want to communicate to them that it is okay to share that life is awful, that it is actually important to me to know that something is feeling awful in their lives, that how they are feeling *matters*—in general, to our relationship, to their capacities to learn, to our shared learning work together. Six words can do so much work. In response to this question, students did sometimes share about awful things in their lives, but mostly they shared deep gratitude for the access form as a whole. Over the last two years, so many have told me that they'd never been asked any of these questions before, that they already felt cared for before the term even started, that they suddenly felt like a full human being and not "just a student." That they felt hopeful and excited and grateful for the course. I had barely even done anything yet! But a handful of questions can do all this care work. Set against a vast academic landscape of uncaring, a handful of questions can build enormous trust.

I would also continue to develop my accessibility statement. In a virtual "fireside chat" on access-centered pedagogy I had with scholar Aimi Hamraie for the Autistic Women and Nonbinary Network in early 2021, I learned the approach that "access is relational," not simply a transaction between teacher and individual student but a collective commitment and collective labor for everyone involved. I had already come to understand access as processual, a negotiation that is never complete because our needs are always changing. But I had yet to fully realize how this process was embedded in relationships. As Aimi so astutely outlined, the negotiation for access occurs in an ecosystem of needs and relations; we create access out of a set of continually renewable commitments to each other, enabling participation for everyone, as much as possible, on each of our own, ever-changing terms. Enablement is a complex, collective labor, and I now explain this explicitly to my students. (I also now add: the only way to fail this class is to treat others like shit. We commit to each other's well-being and learning, which is the only way this class [without grades, penalties, or hard deadlines] can really function. The number one rule: Don't be an asshole.) This is interdependence in action, a recognition that we depend on each other and have *always* depended on each other, and then leaning into it, building in accountability. Which actually raises both the stakes and the responsibility. A different kind of rigor—more on that later.

In fall 2020, I moved almost entirely to an asynchronous format. I tried Flipgrid videos as a way to communicate and share ideas—because I didn't have it in *me* to meet synchronously. Students didn't seem to either. Half a year into the pandemic, we had all grown increasingly anxious and exhausted. Many of my students were in home environments detrimental to their mental health, or had become caregivers to younger siblings also now at home, or had to help their families with domestic labor or income or health management. One student shared that not only did they not have a place to live, but that Georgetown in some wild mix-up threw out all of their belongings in their previous campus housing. I would learn about some of these hardships through my students' preterm access surveys, but mostly I would learn through their weekly Instagram posts about their lives. Life was *hard*, and my students and I were wondering what the fuck we were all doing trying to still do school in a time like this. Asynchronous engagement seemed the most flexible and least labor intensive (though Flipgrid was much more work than I realized, so never again!). I am not advocating that all learning should be asynchronous all the time. But I am saying that at *that* time asynchronous engagement was all we—I and my students—had the capacity for, so it made the most sense and was the most supportive of our stressed and exhausted states. I'm saying it's okay to do this when you need to. I'm saying you sometimes *should* do this. There is nothing inherently virtuous about synchronous learning.

Content warnings were another update for me, based on student request. Content warnings, or trigger warnings, have been a subject of debate for years in academia, and have become a flashpoint for conservative critiques of the supposedly liberal classroom—but they've also been criticized by those of us who don't want students to easily opt out of the challenging material we present in our classes. Some of us derogatorily call students who want trigger warnings "snowflakes." For years I've given impromptu content warnings in class discussions, but I'd never thought to do it systematically in the syllabus itself. But I teach about unwellness and trauma and suicide—of course students should get some warning of the contents of the material they are being assigned. I fall firmly in Angela M. Carter's camp, which understands that trauma suffuses our daily lives and thus also the classroom, requiring an approach that fully recognizes this and its ethical implications.[13] Trauma necessitates building care into the classroom, and I have come to realize it is our responsibility as teachers to create that care, especially if the course stages traumatic encounters. It is unethical to do otherwise. Content warnings are one easy way to begin this care work. I didn't think to include content warnings in *Open in Emergency*, and sometimes I haven't remembered to include them when sharing my first letter to Elia, like in my TEDx talk, and I wish I had. Currently my warnings on the syllabus are simple: "one asterisk (*) denotes mentions of suicide, trauma, and hospitalization; two asterisks (**) denote mentions of some of the above as well as sexual violence." I add verbal warnings for particular content as we move through the semester: "This week's reading is on forced institutionalization, next week's depicts self-harm. Take care of yourself while you engage," I tell my students. "Make sure you have the spoons. You can't learn without enough spoons."

I transformed my self-care assignment as well. Self-care seemed so obviously important in that moment—which made me realize it should have been a priority in the beforetimes as well. We all needed a structure that would enable us to commit to self-care, and specifically the kinds of self-care that could really address the manifestations of unwellness we were experiencing. Like I said, I'm not talking about bubble baths and mani-pedis—though no shade if that's your thing! I won't yuck your yum; I'm just asking you to consider self-care in a fuller context. My concern about popular forms of self-care, especially if they are your only recourse, is that they draw on the medical model of mental health, placing the responsibility on the individual to create wellness for themselves and directing them to do so through largely commodified forms that are about selling products and services (and apps!). These forms may address some level of our needs—I need my weekly aerial yoga class for sure!—but they also tend to distract us from the larger structures of unwellness shaping our lives. Bubble baths may help with the symptoms of anti-Asian racism, but they won't do anything for the root causes. In fact, popular forms of self-care can sometimes *complement* institutional harm—see the kinds of wellness universities promote that contribute directly to student unwellness discussed in chapter 2. So, yes, take your bubble baths and get your mani-pedis—but also let's do the hard thinking and feeling work, with a focus on structure, that is necessary to create lasting care for ourselves. In fall 2020, I came up with assignments that were a combination of reflection and interactivity, some done individually and some with others. All were short, not time or labor intensive; post-self-care reflection in student Instagram posts could be any length with very few content or form requirements. But what the assignments didn't require in time or writing labor they required in self-reflection and feeling work, vulnerability and interdependence. Again, rigor in a very different way.

In addition to the assignments I designed in March 2020 using Chad Shomura's Corner of Heart-to-Hearts, Erin O'Brien's Queer Self-Care cards, and my Asian American Tarot deck, over the last two years I've developed the following to accompany our weekly work:

- The semester has started! And it's likely already stressful! Take a moment to do something that is specifically UNproductive— meaning, not related to work or school or anything else you think you "should" be doing. Then reflect on what feelings came up for you when doing this unproductive activity! Was it hard? Or easy? Guilt-inducing? Relieving? Easier to do because it was an "assignment"?

- What structures and people do you rely on? Are there people who rely on you? Take a moment to reflect on your own interdependence. What feelings come up for you when you think about this reliance?

- How does ableism regularly manifest in your life? Think of the two definitions we discussed. How does "normal" get defined around you? What kinds of bodies and minds and experiences are valued? How/when/where are vulnerability and needs and care viewed contemptuously?

- Make a list of five things you appreciate about yourself that are NOT about achievement or productivity. Is this easy or difficult for you to do?

- Expanding on last week's self-care, make a list of five things you appreciate about someone you love and share it with them. Then ask this person to make a list for you and share it back with you. Was this different/easier/harder than doing the activity alone? Was it easier to not focus on achievement and productivity this time? Did anything surprise you?

- Something we discussed in class, drawing from Eli Clare's work, was how we tend to conflate healing with cure, thinking that healing must involve the elements of cure (pathology, eradication, restoration, overcoming, the natural). Can we imagine healing without the ideology of cure? What might that look like? Reflect on this, and then choose an activity that feels like it might do the work of "healing" in your life but not necessarily of cure. Think more process and transformation, less getting rid of or returning to some prior state. I'll be interested to see what kinds of activities you come up with!

- In class we shared things that our brains are "bad" at. There was such a wonderful range of "bad" things that helped demonstrate both neurodiversity and the ableism around neurodivergence. For your self-care, I'd like you to reflect some more on the things your brain is "bad" at. How has it felt to be labeled "bad" at those things? What kinds of structures could support you more to help you navigate being "bad" at those things?

- Take a few minutes this week to rearrange your space in a way that enables you better. Pick one or two things in your space that could be redesigned to better support your body and mind, and try to revise them. This could be your work space, your sleeping space, your food space, your access to the outdoors, etc. Think about how it might be also more accessible to others who share that space with you.

- Go through Jay Dolmage's suggestion list of UD (Universal Design) for learning. It's long—you don't have to go through all twenty-three pages! Just skim a few pages (feel free to skip around) and choose five that seem like they would be helpful to you. Reflect on how you might ask for these things as part of your access needs in your current classes or future classes. Do you feel comfortable asking for these, and why or why not? Think about what could help you ask for and get these things.

- What does mental health mean to you? Make a list of all the components/elements of mental health. Ask a friend to do the same and compare your lists.

- Tell a story about something that hurts in your life, something that is feeling hard. You can tell this story to yourself or to a friend, verbally or in writing. Then think about how your story exceeds the medicalized concept of "diagnosis," which we discussed in class as involving identifying a pathology and measuring its distance from "normal," and then eradicating it. Instead of trying to figure out what's wrong with you, use your story to "diagnose" your conditions. What does it tell you about structures around you? What does it tell you that you need? Reflect on whether what hurts might actually be a kind of normal that you don't want anymore.

- In class, we began exploring what a "good" student is. For your self-care activity, reflect more on Georgetown's definition. How has that definition shaped your experience as a student so far? In contrast, what do you think makes a good student for our class? Has our class shifted your experience as a student at all?

In spring 2021, I returned to my graduate alma mater of UCSB to remotely teach their first course on Asian American mental health. A chance to teach directly about Asian American mental health, during the pandemic, and to a class of almost entirely Asian American students? Fuck yeah. I let in every student on the wait list, ballooning a course of forty-five students to almost sixty, because I thought this was perhaps my one chance to help Asian American students there. (I knew remote learning wouldn't be forever. Georgetown's messaging throughout the remote year was that they were doing everything they could to bring us all back in person, whether we wanted to be or not.) I shifted to a once-a-week synchronous model to have more sustained live discussion but still with lots of flexibility—the second class session of the week would remain asynchronous, an opportunity to complete the other course assignments such as readings, small-group meetings, and self-care. This set of students would join my existing Instagram account to document Asian American life and unwellness in particular. They would do some of the self-care assignments I created for my disability studies course but also some designed specifically for them, such as this doozy:

- Write down all the things you think you owe and to whom. Reflect on what it would mean if you could wave a wand and have all that debt suddenly repaid—what would that feel like? How would your life look and feel differently?

I iterated the self-care assignments each term, clarifying or deepening here and there, as well as scrapping some entirely because of moments of collective crisis. A staff death and a student suicide at UCSB during my time there necessitated not the reflection on failure I had planned for that week but acts of connection, leaning into communities of grief. We can plan all we want, but the world goes to shit whenever it wants, and we have to figure out how to survive together.

This was the care I could build into my courses. Yes, some of this is individual affective labor (feminized, racialized in problematic ways, we know), but much of this is *structural*. The preterm access survey, the disability justice language of need and access, policies that put student needs first, and assignments all designed to build trust, engender vulnerability, create space for need, and build in time and labor for care: these are structures. They are structures that build care into every aspect of the course, and I have come to learn that the structures of my classes need to match what I'm saying I'm doing. Show, don't just tell. This is what Georgetown did not understand in that first year of the pandemic and continues to not understand in this second year and likely will not understand as we move into the third year and on. Yes, Georgetown created more lenient grading policies in spring 2020 that allowed more pass/fail options and more flexible deadlines at the level of the registrar—yes, these are structural. But I have seen little to incentivize care in the classroom. Emails from administration gently suggesting more leniency and lighter workloads on holidays *that the administration has canceled* are not structural interventions into ableism. As I've said over and over, students do not feel cared for. This is probably the most consistent thing students have told me throughout my teaching career and especially now during the pandemic, when we all recognize we're in a collective crisis of care. The university and even many faculty say they care, but if students don't feel cared for, then this thing called caring is not actually happening, no matter how hard you think you're caring. In preterm access surveys, in midterms, in weekly Instagram posts, in final reflection assignments, in course evals, students have shared what schooling (and home life) has looked like for them in the context of the pandemic, and it is devastating. If you want, you can check out my student Instagram account @DSinthetimeofCOVID19 to see some of what I've been seeing—the conditions of student lives but also their hard work of thinking and feeling and survival. This archive makes clear the stakes of what we do in the classroom.

I call the 2021–22 academic year the year of forced return. Come hell or high water, we were all going back in person. There were some structures built to enable this return—public health structures such as campus-wide vaccination requirements, masking requirements, accessible PCR testing, contact tracing—but many structures were actually *taken away*. The access gains we saw at the beginning of the pandemic that had made so many in disability justice both hopeful and bitter—remote learning, flexible modes of participation, flexible deadlines and grading, expansion of accommodations beyond the historical rigidity of campus disability services—were rapidly disappearing.[14] Access rollbacks, I call them, because universities, and faculty, were all trying desperately to get back to "normal": normative time, normative access, normative capacity and ability. We didn't learn that we all need and deserve access. We simply proclaimed the exceptionalism of that first pandemic year and reinscribed our ableist norms once we could "return" from that exceptional state.

This is a curative approach to crisis. Eli Clare delineates the ideology of cure and the violence it wreaks upon bodies, minds, and whole communities deemed pathological. To cure is to identify a pathology and then eradicate it so that one can return to some natural state of originary wholeness. To cure is to overcome the deviation from normal and be able to return. Let's extend Clare's model now to the pandemic as public health crisis: instead of the pandemic revealing the existing conditions of crisis that make us realize we need this kind of care all the time and even more forms of care, it is simply a deviation that must be contained and eradicated so that we can go back to a normal that is of course our collective natural, and good, state of being. Why hello there, compulsory wellness, terrible to see you again.[15] I'm reminded of how artist Sofía Gallisá Muriente thinks about disasters and relief funding: "Disasters have a special power to make economic inequality visible; suddenly governments approve unemployment benefits that surpass meagre minimum wages, and foundations find it in their hearts to give unrestricted grants." Muriente asks how we might "extend reactive 'disaster funding' techniques to ordinary times." I think also of Dean Spade's work on mutual aid as survival work at the community grassroots level, recognizing crises as ongoing and ever-evolving and requiring sustained structural responses. What would it look like to build collective care at universities that fully recognizes the ongoing and ever-evolving needs of the university's communities?[16]

As a lone, lowly adjunct, I can't affect the larger systems of an institution like Georgetown, but as I tell my students, I *can* affect the world of my classroom (at least until I'm fired/not rehired). I have tried to resist the manifestation of this compulsory wellness at Georgetown, this refusal to see unwellness and this assumption of wellness as our normal baseline, through continuing to build and iterate structures of care in the classroom. Hybrid has been the structure I've introduced this godforsaken academic year, an attempt to create the most flexibility for my students and to continue to prioritize their well-being (and encourage them to prioritize their well-being). Georgetown's classrooms are technologically equipped, for the most part, for relatively easy hybrid teaching, where with one click I can open a Zoom link to the classroom for students to join virtually. On this, I commend Georgetown. But offering hybrid is at the discretion of individual faculty, and so in the name of preserving academic freedom, we uphold ableism. I spoke on a virtual panel on how to do hybrid offered by Georgetown's instructional unit CNDLS, and the staff had to repeat the official party line that they are not telling faculty to do hybrid, and they are not even encouraging it; they are just there to explain how to do it if individual faculty want to. I on the other hand was not a spokesperson for the university and so chose to explain how hybrid is a necessary structure for basic access. *Do it*, I pressed. *Your students need it. Their lives depend on it.*

I'm telling you here as well. Your students' lives depend on the structures of access and care you build in your classes. Let go of your traditional policies and assignments. Be open to change. In the words of Jim Lee, "Break the genre of the syllabus, break the genre of the classroom."[17] Build in radical flexibility, and be ready to iterate again and again. The crisis is never over.

―――――

That last paragraph might have made you squirm.

Let's telescope outward from Georgetown to teaching across the country during the pandemic to explore why.

I started this chapter mentioning the proliferation of Facebook groups on teaching during the pandemic. I've watched colleagues post regularly on social media about teaching—venting or posing questions or giving advice. Pedagogical conversations have long been happening on academic social media, but they have increased in frequency and intensity during the pandemic as we all have had to adjust to Zoom University. And while new areas of concern have arisen—*How do I facilitate discussions over Zoom? Should I or should I not record my lectures? Synchronous or asynchronous? Cameras on required? How to best show a film on Zoom?*—pandemic teaching has actually made clearer to me many tensions that existed across the academy in the beforetimes that have been exacerbated in pandemic times. Some things I've noticed:[18]

» **We are more productive than ever.**

This is wild to me. In times of crisis, instead of slowing down, my colleagues are speeding up. A reason is many of us face increased responsibilities, especially if we are caregivers to school-aged children in remote learning, so the sheer amount of work has increased in absolute value. But what I'm also seeing is an increase in anxiety about productivity, and the compulsion to continue working even in the most dire of circumstances. I've seen colleagues show up in Zoom meetings while sick, sometimes even with COVID. I've seen colleagues refuse to cancel class when sick or even when a family member is sick or has *died*. Instructional continuity has taken on a kind of sacrality, conflated with good teaching and even goodness in general. We must continue working, continue achieving at all costs. It's like we have to prove that we can do it all in spite of the pandemic, perhaps *because* of the pandemic. Pandemic stresses drag at us and we have to show that we can overcome them. This is ableism on steroids. We have never been allowed to need; meritocracy has told us that we must show how hard we work to prove we have earned what we have and that we deserve to keep what we have, *so now when we need more than ever, we have to show that we need even less than ever.*

» **Professors hate students.**

Not all professors, you'll say, and of course not. But there is an alarming amount of hate and disdain for students that circulates on social media. I've written here and in previous chapters about how students don't trust us and how they shouldn't, because our own anxieties and insecurities—and our own investments in meritocracy—often manifest in ways that bear down violently on them. We have an intense fear of being undermined and disrespected. This makes a lot of sense for faculty of color, women, queer and trans folks: institutions and the people within those institutions have regularly undermined and disrespected us throughout our entire journeys through higher ed. Impostor syndrome fueled by constant microaggressions is central to our lived experience. Some of our students do directly disrespect us. But my worry is that our trauma and anxiety lead us to conflate many student behaviors with disrespect. We think students not doing the work is disrespect, to us, to our class, to their fellow classmates. We see disrespect in everything: not reading the syllabus carefully, not following policies, not doing the reading, not coming to class, turning things in late, asking for extensions/exceptions, emailing too much, emailing too little. Lying—that is possibly the biggest one. We are enraged about being lied to. We love to catalog all the lies we've heard over the years: the dead grandmothers, the computer glitches, the corrupted files. I've seen jokes on social media that claiming to have COVID is the new dead grandmother. (Who is disrespecting whom here?)

I want us to consider for a moment that students might not be doing the things we want (or doing things we don't want) for reasons outside of our classes. I want us to remember that students are whole people with whole lives that are just as shitty as ours, if not shittier. I want us to remember that students feel disrespected all the time too. I want us to remember that the stakes are actually much higher for the students than they are for us. And I want us to reframe lying not as moral transgression but as an indicator of a lack of trust. It is a response to unrecognized humanity, a response to being told some reasons are legitimate and some are not—and that others get to arbitrate the distinction, not the student, and often without transparency or consistency. If a student lies to me, it tells me that they do not trust me enough to tell me the real reasons. That lack of trust is *my* failure and the failure of the system.

There is *always* a reason for the "transgression"—the question is whether we are willing to listen and respect that reason. This doesn't mean it's totally fine for students to lie to us all the time! It means lying stems from a breakdown in trust, and that we should be asking what we can do to restore that trust. With some humility, perhaps we can ask what we as teachers can do to actually *earn* our students' trust.[19]

» **The crisis we fixate on is student cheating.**

Cheating is perhaps the biggest sin of all in academia. (I'm not sure why sexual harassment and gendered, racialized violence aren't, but that's another essay.) Cheating is also a sign of disrespect, not simply to the class and teacher but to the institution and the given field of study. As we have had to shift to remote learning and new technological platforms, I have seen colleagues fixate on the problem of cheating as the main crisis of concern. How do we find ways to prevent (and catch!) cheating on these new and unfamiliar platforms? Some colleagues proctor exams by Zoom, requiring all students to show up in the Zoom space and take their timed tests with their cameras on. Some colleagues have turned to automated proctoring: welcome, Proctorio, Skynet for academia, the program that requires students to show the computer camera the four walls of their rooms and the surface of their desks to make sure no "cheating" materials are present, requires students to provide digital access to their computers so that the program can make sure they're not opening browsers to google answers, and then *monitors their eye movements to track whether they might be looking offscreen for answers.* I italicize that last part as if it should be clear how horrifically ableist and dehumanizing that is, but apparently it's not that clear to faculty because so many—especially in STEM—are using this program. Let me break it down: in general, it is dehumanizing to be surveilled so thoroughly, and even more so for it to be by machines. It is ableist to track bodily movements because you are programming normativity directly into the code (what are "normal" eye movements?!) and then applying that code punitively. It is absurd—and gaslighting—to invade student privacy in the name of "integrity." It is draconian to take away student agency so drastically. Students have no say, no choice, no recourse. It is cruel to make students feel like the only thing that matters about them is their propensity toward immorality that needs to be firmly kept in check. During a global pandemic and a huge transition in the learning environment, this is the chief problem we have to ward against?

» **We think we know what fairness is.**

This is a tough one. We think fairness means everyone gets the same thing. All our students get the same policies, the same assignments, the same deadlines, the same grading rubrics. The only exceptions are those accommodations mandated by the ADA and approved by university disability services. This makes perfect sense; how can we ensure fairness unless we set and apply equal standards across our students? It's not fair to give some students preferential treatment over others. Definitely not fair to give some students negative differential treatment—we call this bias and discrimination and even harassment when it happens along axes of social difference. Official accommodations might even become "unfair" if students are somehow gaming the system. In the context of the pandemic, radical generosity needs to come to an end at some point; we're supposed to go back to normal—meaning sameness.

But ensuring sameness does not actually achieve the fairness we're hoping for. What is fair about a student who is suffering from panic attacks having to turn in an assignment at the same time as a student who is not? What is fair about grading a student down for not speaking in class when that BIPOC student feels they don't belong in the predominantly white space of their classroom? What is fair about asking a student to turn their cameras on and grading them down if they don't when that student's living situation is embarrassing or even dangerous? What is fair about expecting a survivor of sexual assault to come to class the next day, the next week, the next month, and complete all our course requirements? Sameness has historically assumed a universal white middle-class cis hetero able-bodiedness, with all the attendant privileges and insulations. But our students are not all white middle-class cis hetero able-bodied. Our students' lives are not all the same, nor are each of their lives consistent across the span of an academic term. Students are differentially unwell, going through unbearably difficult things at different moments of their lives in so many different ways, in some cases precisely because our universities do not make our campuses safe from racial violence, sexual violence, queerphobia, and so on, and in other cases, ones I've outlined, because our universities themselves directly cause students harm. Ensuring sameness is actually ensuring struggle. It actually ensures *unfairness. Sameness ensures ableism.* Some, if not all, of our students will find that sameness unbearable at some point. But they also have been taught that sameness is fairness, so they will endure, take the penalty, keep going, blame themselves. Or in extreme moments, ask for an accommodation or exception, filled with guilt and shame and self-loathing.

Fairness is not everyone getting the same thing; it is everyone getting what they need.[20] Fairness is the fewest obstacles for everyone. Fairness is everyone having the same opportunities for learning, not through the sameness of structures around them but through differential care specific to differential need. Sounds lofty, I know. Take this to its logical end point, and we realize that fairness is actually completely unachievable in an institution that already upholds, and exacerbates, differential unwellness. The university's framework of meritocracy *ensures* that differential unwellness will not be cared for. Students say they do not feel cared for *and this is why*.

We have all learned that fairness is sameness and therefore sameness is moral and good, so we hold tight to sameness, developing our pedagogy around it. But fairness here has been co-opted to bolster ableism (not to mention racism, sexism, etc.), this version telling us that there is a universal, ideal person/body/mind and that deviations from that ideal must be corrected back to the normative. Students who don't meet our expectations of student behavior and performance of course must be graded accordingly, right? Take points, grade down, show them how far they are from that standard. Then help them to improve. This is learning.

But what is fair and moral and good about punishing students for being nonnormal and, worse, unwell, and then telling them it's their fault?

You are probably thinking now, but what about standards?! Learning objectives? There are things we want to teach, things we want our students to learn, specific knowledges and skills we want them to develop. We are tasked with the responsibility of teaching; we have to have some kind of baseline standard for performance and a way to evaluate performance in order to gauge if and what they are actually learning.

It's not all or nothing. It's not rigid expectations versus no expectations at all. What I'm asking us all to reflect on is how our ideas about fairness intersect with ableism and therefore fuel particular pedagogical choices that are harmful—and ultimately unfair.

I am also not saying that we as individual professors need to somehow create complete fairness in our classes. We cannot. We cannot fix the unfairness embedded in the university and the education system more broadly. But this doesn't mean that we don't try, at least in the space of our classrooms, to make learning a little less awful, a little less punitive, a little less unfair. Because there is nothing fair or just about the ways many of us have learned to teach. We need to unlearn that "exceptions" should be rare, that giving one student something is somehow taking something away from other students— I hear this all the time! This framing pits students against each other and makes education a zero-sum system. Giving a student the care they need in that moment takes nothing away from other students, especially when you give care to those other students when they need it too. Embrace the "shit happens" philosophy: something(s) will inevitably go wrong in each person's life, and we can collectively roll with it so that no one gets left behind. Because fairness is no one getting left behind.

For those of us in charge of producing knowledge and evaluating academic achievement, fairness as sameness might be one of the hardest ideas to dismantle, so naturalized and embedded it is in education. Fairness is what undergirds meritocracy; it's what makes meritocracy "work." Dismantling fairness would mean that meritocracy is and has always been a lie, and then where would all of us high achievers be?

» **We have an intense attachment to rigor.**

Rigor defines achievement and excellence for academics. Thinking, writing, research must be rigorous in order to be good. The opposite is lazy, rushed, imprecise, not thought through, not fully developed, not valid: nobody wants to be those things. To be the opposite of rigorous is to fail as an academic. This construction—and anxiety—manifests in our teaching too. We want our classes to be rigorous; we equate difficult and demanding classes with rigor and goodness. Nobody wants to be that easy A! Good teachers challenge students, have high expectations, lift up the high achievers and weed out the duds. We also equate good teaching with hard work. Good teachers commit the time and labor that is needed to do good teaching and to get students to develop the skills they need. Good teachers are not unorganized or lazy. Good teachers have their shit together, show up prepared and on time, never cancel class "unnecessarily," get grading done on time, give students lots of feedback and support, and answer emails quickly.

Being a good teacher seems fucking exhausting.

By these standards, I am a bad teacher. I'm lazy. I often don't prepare for class. I sometimes lose track of where we are in the semester. I cancel class several times a term, every term. I assign little reading and few assignments. When I used to have grading, it would take me forever. Since the pandemic, I've become awful on email. Yet I'm writing this chapter on teaching! (Maybe you shouldn't be listening to me?!) I'm writing this chapter because I have shifted my relationship to rigor over the years, especially during the pandemic. I no longer fear (as much!) being "unrigorous" or "lazy" or "an easy A." Those attributes no longer speak to my worth as a teacher, scholar, or person. What do you think rigor says about you as a teacher, scholar, person? Why is being called unrigorous or lazy so scary? What kind of failure do those words encapsulate?

Our attachment to rigor manifests in an attachment to grades. We spend so much energy and labor parsing out the minute differences between A and A–, B and B+. We give and take a point here, a point there. We create elaborate point systems that are meant to tell the students and ourselves the numerical equivalent of their achievement. We do this because we need to believe there is a universal standard of excellence and we are in charge of maintaining it, evaluating others against it, and arbitrating who gets to be excellent and who doesn't. Grades undergird meritocracy, and meritocracy makes our places as professors—authorities—make sense.[21]

Indulge me for a moment: What is actually wrong with giving all As? We think it means we don't have standards and that our students aren't being asked to do any work. But standards and workload and grades are not inherently related. Grades do not inherently create rigor. What would it look like to decouple grades from rigor? Jesse Stommel and others have written about "ungrading," a movement to chuck traditional grading practices and replace them with processes of feedback, reflection, and self-evaluation for "a pedagogy that is less algorithmic and more human, more subjective, more compassionate." Grades can actually undermine the work we are trying to do, argues Stommel, and while a final grade may still be part of a course within the ungrading framework, assignments themselves are built to give feedback and make room for self-directed and self-reflective growth, something grades alone do not do. "Spec grading" is another approach, in which assignments are graded pass/fail based on "specs" that must be met for those assignments. Assignments are further bundled to correspond with particular final grades: completing this set of assignments is an A, while this other pared-down set is a B, and so forth. As Linda Nilson explains, spec grading recognizes that students may only be able to—or want to—partially complete a course; assignments and bundles are designed with that explicitly in mind. Both ungrading and spec grading decouple rigor from elaborate point systems and letter-graded assignments: it is not the one-time, high-stakes assessments that measure rigor here but the process of work that spans an entire term.[22]

"Hard work" doesn't have to look the way we've thought. Our attachments to rigor (and fairness!) also manifest in our attachments to particular kinds of policies and assignments: strict and punitive attendance, hard deadlines, rigid forms of participation, pop quizzes, required documentation for exceptions, high-stakes exams, long essays, and so forth. I have seen colleagues revel in their rigor on social media, luxuriating in their refusal of late work, for example, sometimes framing this position as reclaiming their time, creating healthy boundaries, and demanding respect from students. Boundaries and respect are crucially important, yes—but refusing late work of any kind is not the only way to keep boundaries, nor does late work necessarily indicate disrespect. Hard deadlines and other forms of rigidity don't necessarily engender respect either.

But what about the sciences? you say. And math! These are classes in which skill acquisition must be ensured and precisely evaluated. Get the math and science wrong, and you can't move on to the next course or, even worse, perform the real-world application that you're training for. One might argue that writing classes function similarly in the humanities: there are real consequences for not developing our abilities to think critically, write clearly and persuasively, and cite responsibly.[23] How do we ensure rigor across these kinds of classes if we chuck out exams or papers or precise numerical grading? The honest answer is I don't know. But there are many other people who do! Ungrading conversations are popping up everywhere, collaborative pedagogical think tanks forming to continually develop new kinds of assignments and processes of evaluation.[24] If you want to rethink rigor in your particular field's classes, I'm sure you can find someone who's already begun that work. Here I'll offer a few general suggestions to start you off:

- *Think process.* Do you need high-stakes assignments and grades for your students to acquire the skills you want them to? How might you support that skill development over time? What kinds of lower-stakes, cumulative assignments and structures create scaffolding and support for students to build skill? How might you make learning processual—if they don't get it right the first time, where's the space to keep trying? How can you change "failure" from being a devastating end point to being a normal midpoint in the learning process?
- *Less is more.* This goes for every class across every discipline. Whittle down the materials. There is nothing necessary or virtuous about cramming in as much as possible in a term—this does not make the course more rigorous or more successful or even more advanced. It just makes the course more ableist. Do less, so that you actually have the time and space and spoons to support students through the process.
- *Be open to new shapes.* Ungraders suggest iterative assignments and self-evaluation as potential new shapes for assessment. What this looks like in STEM may be hard to imagine, but luckily some folks have already started! Stommel suggests:

Project-based learning with self-assessment, process notebooks (like a lab notebook but with an emphasis on metacognition), and collaborative exams. Exams, in particular, are at their best when they are formative tools for learning, not just standardized mechanisms for summative (or end-of-learning) assessment. Collaborative exams allow students the opportunities to learn from and teach each other. Open-book and self-graded exams are not as good at sorting or ranking students, but they are often just as good (if not better) tools for learning.[25]

- When you focus on process, different shapes not only are possible but become quite necessary.

But don't the traditional policies—required attendance, hard deadlines, high-stakes assessment, and so on—work to prepare our students for "the real world"? some of you will ask. High expectations and clear consequences "treat students like adults." Does this mean that care, flexibility, generosity are . . . babying? Adults don't have needs? Adults shouldn't desire structures that meet their particular needs? This is ableism, hiding in the language of human growth. I treat my students like adults, too, in my own way: I believe them instead of invalidating them and telling them that their experiences don't matter. I take their perspectives into account. I build structures to try to meet their needs because students are equal members of the community of my classroom. Yes, "the real world" can be rigid and harsh and deeply ableist. It can also be flexible. Plenty of people don't face arbitrary fixed deadlines in their work; plenty of people rely on others to help them do their work; plenty of people can *take time off*. There is something called sick days in the so-called real world, not for every job, but for many. But even if the institutions students encounter upon leaving the university aren't flexible and generous, why are we teaching them to accept the ableism of "the real world" as normal and moral? We are retrofitting that ableism into education in the name of preparation. Why aren't we teaching our students to critically engage that ableism instead, to advocate for themselves and to build spaces of their own choosing, in academia and beyond?

Our attachments to productivity, respect, fairness, and rigor are all understandable responses to the way the neoliberal university has been structured in the late twentieth and early twenty-first centuries. Reproducing them, worrying about them, and enforcing them are natural responses. We are not bad people (well, some of us might be), intentionally doing harm with our pedagogical choices. But the fact is we *are* doing harm, not only to our students but also ourselves. It's time to ask what it is we really want our classroom spaces to be, and whether those shapes are truly humane and just and liberatory.

Let's not forget to ask the students, too.

———————

A confession, from my class in spring 2022:

This semester I've had the lowest attendance, participation, and assignment completion of all time—and I freaked the fuck out.

Are the students taking advantage of my generosity?

Do they not respect me, taking my flexibility as an invitation to walk all over me?

Do they think I'm an easy A, so they can do whatever the fuck they want?

One particularly dismal week midsemester, I scanned my course Instagram account to discover that in a class of twenty-five, a whopping six students had never posted at all, and six more had posted only a few times. In a fit of anxiety and anger, I emailed each of these twelve students to remind them that while the course was pass/fail, it did indeed require engagement, and I was not seeing enough engagement on my end so please schedule an appointment to meet with me in office hours. Cue student panic: responses rolled in full of fear and shame and remorse—and stories of intense hardship. Stories they shouldn't have been forced to share with me to prove that they were struggling. On day three of this very class, I'd taught about "forced intimacy," the disclosures that disabled folks must make to convince others of their needs, and here I was extracting those kinds of disclosures from my own students.[26] I felt awful.

But I made it up to them! As teachers we all make mistakes, but we don't have to double down. I figured out how to shift our communication and relational process back to a pedagogy of unwellness: individual check-ins to see how students were doing but also make individualized plans. I began the meetings by saying "No shame!" because the point was not to shame or scare them (as my email surely had!) but to reassure them—and me!—by making a plan to get through the semester we both felt good about. I reminded myself and students that the point of the course is engagement; the shapes of that engagement could be flexible. If they needed more flexibility than I had already offered, we could talk through possibilities. And I asked them quite frankly: "What grade do you need in this class?" Once we knew that, we could work our way backward and figure out together what kind of engagement, and in what forms, would make that grade possible in the remaining time of the term. Going into these meetings, I had to be reminded (by Lawrence!) to check my own anxieties and remember that student (lack of) engagement was not a reflection upon me (though easy for Lawrence to say, when he wasn't the one teaching). Students will get from a class what they want to get from it. If they can't or don't want to engage deeply, instead of being angry, I can figure out with them what level of engagement they can manage, and to what grade that level of engagement translates. For teacher and student, the meetings were necessary expectation management. We all left feeling so much better about ourselves, about the course, about the learning process, even about grades.

The meetings reconfirmed for me that students are good people, that their lives are really hard, and that they feel deep anxiety and shame about dropping the ball. Most students do not want to be irresponsible. Most do not want to fail expectations. I had to remind myself and allow the students to remind me of these things. I had to remember that my job is to see their struggle and honor it, and meet my responsibility to *do no harm*.

I'm sure some students do take advantage of me. I'm sure there are some who lie, who don't respect me. But I don't want to spend time and anxiety trying to discern who these students are, because care matters more than being right. I would rather let a few students take advantage of my classes than a whole lot of students be harmed by them. As I continue to evolve my courses to deepen structures of access and care, my goal is always to be responsive to the needs and capacities of the moment. I will make mistakes along the way—and so will the students. But as long as I keep to that goal, I'll know we're headed in the right direction.

Applying this to your own pedagogy: What might it look like to be responsive to the needs and capacities of the moment with your courses and students? Here's a starter access audit for your teaching:

- *On trust:* What are you doing to build trust with your students?
  - How is that trust reflected affectively *and* structurally in the syllabus? (I.e., does your syllabus still communicate somehow that your desires trump their needs?)
  - How are you showing that you respect your students' time, capacities, and needs?
  - How are you signaling that you are on their side—and not the university's? I'm not saying it's inherently students versus university; it doesn't have to be that way. But we need to listen to students and recognize that it currently feels that way to many if not most of

them. Students are in direct tension with the university and often see professors as the university's functionaries—because we often are. Telling them the university is actually on their side or that you are actually on their side is not reassurance—it is gaslighting, unless you show you are really aware of their experiences of betrayal, abandonment, and uncaring, and unless you can demonstrably enact your alignment with students. Are you willing to be openly critical of the university? Does the syllabus indicate you care more about the university than the students? Students are well aware of what cover-your-ass language looks like; they know when a person cares more about liability than harm being done. They know when policies uphold the unconditional authority of the institution. *Are you the warden—and do you communicate the impression that the inmates can't and shouldn't run the prison?*[27] To build trust with students—to become trustworthy to students—you will need to explicitly locate yourself in ethical relation to the university, and do so in a way that shows your priority is them and not the institution.

- *On vulnerability:* How are you normalizing vulnerability in your class? How are you giving permission for students to share about their lives, admit they are struggling, make mistakes, and ask for things they need, without shame? How are you normalizing struggle and need?

- *On structures of care:* What structures are there to cultivate collective care, between students, between you and students? What structures demonstrate and nurture a commitment to collective well-being?

- *For assignments:*

  - What are the goals of this assignment? Does the assignment actually achieve the goals? Are there alternative ways of achieving the goals?

  - Is the assignment within student capacity at the moment? Could they do this assignment across four or five classes at the same time? *Should* they? (Could you yourself do this assignment four or five times this term?) And do *you* want to read it? Is it within your capacity to grade? Ask the students if it's within their capacity. "Does this feel manageable?" is one of the most caring things you can say to your students. If they say no, restructure. It is not a failing on anyone's part to change or even scrap an assignment.

  - What are you doing to support and enable students to do your assignments, instead of simply penalizing students for not doing them?

- If reading and writing are key to your class, what are you doing to enable these activities? Build in structures that support students in these labors. Something as simple as giving class time over to them can be so helpful. There is nothing that says the bulk of the coursework has to happen outside of class.
- *For participation:*
  - Are there multiple modes of participation? Are there nonpunitive participation policies? A colleague of mine at Georgetown implemented a creative nonpunitive participation policy: attendance and participation will boost your grade, but absences and lack of participation will not harm your grade.
  - If participation is key to the functioning of your class, what are you doing to nurture participation, instead of simply penalizing for the lack of it?

I want to take a moment to reflect on *enablement* versus *punishment* some more. So many traditional course policies use a penalty system to produce the things we want. But a penalty system assumes two things: that what it takes to do work is willpower and effort, and that people not doing the work are unwilling, or irresponsible, or, to take it more personally, not prioritizing our class—as opposed to being unwell, which a penalty can't fix or overcome. Disability studies and disability justice and my own mental health struggles have taught me that everything has to be actively enabled. Care must happen all the time, in all the ways we need. The default is not wellness or productivity. The default is differential unwellness, brokenness in countless ways, obstacle after obstacle to moving through the world in livable ways. Our students are not simply lazy or willful or irresponsible or disrespectful. Some may be these things, but *all* are definitely exhausted and stressed and traumatized and feeling like they are failing all the fucking time—just like us. That is the reason most are unable to meet our rigid expectations. So rather than punishing students, build structures to support the work you want them to do. Not because you are generous or lenient or accommodating, but because that is the only way work can and should happen.

A final question: Can a student be ill—short term, long term, depressed, anxious, exhausted, in crisis, disabled—and still do well in your class?

"I didn't feel like I mattered."

A student said this to me in office hours about another class she was taking. It probably shouldn't have felt so revelatory to me—I've known for years that students don't feel cared for in many of their classes, and in the university as a whole. But that moment, and that particular phrasing, clarified for me both the dehumanization inherent to many of our pedagogical practices and the reason students respond so strongly to my teaching. In my classes, they feel like they matter. Strip away all the fancy access language and creative assignments and particular policies I've developed over the years, and it boils down to this one thing, perhaps the simplest and best definition of *cura personalis.*

When students feel like they matter, they invest. Most of my students come to class even when it's not technically required. They usually do the readings. They think really hard about the concepts and the hard work of applying them to their lives because they have a reason to beyond grades: everything we are doing in the class is to help them in ways they have collectively decided they need. They feel like I care, so they care, about the class but also about me and each other.

When students don't feel like they matter, when they feel like the professor makes little to no space for their humanity, when they feel like the professor's rules are there to punish them, when they feel like the professor cares more about upholding the institution than about their well-being, they don't care about the class. Why should they? Because they paid tuition? Because enrollment is a "contract"? Contracts are based in consent. Consent is a never-ending process—one doesn't give consent once but over and over; otherwise it's not really consent. (Basic consent culture and sexual justice, hello.) Students have been socialized their whole lives to respect institutions of learning—no matter how ableist and racist and sexist and oppressive they might be. The respect we are demanding from our students is unearned. It is one that comes out of power's entitlement to obedience and the related structures of feeling. It is not one that comes out of mutual recognition of each other's humanity and commitments to each other's well-being. It is not one born of trust.

Education is not zero-sum, where students mattering means profs don't matter or vice versa. Providing care—in the form of flexibility, leniency, compassion, generosity, and even vulnerability—does not diminish us as teachers. It doesn't take away from us. It creates access. For all of us. It moves us closer to what teaching could look like if all of us felt like we mattered. What teaching could look like if we all felt the collective responsibility to care and willingly, lovingly, bore it. If we all demonstrated a commitment to each other's survival, and if we all allowed each other to fall apart, to be unwell.[28]

This is disability justice. It is collective access and collective care. It is allowing ourselves to need, and working to meet everyone's needs. It is a radical commitment to the life chances of every person. The pandemic has helped me better realize these principles: a pandemic pedagogy aligns and overlaps with disability justice pedagogy, or a pedagogy of interdependence, and it aligns and overlaps with a pedagogy of unwellness. It is a pedagogy of recognizing we are always in crisis. It is a pedagogy that sees teaching and learning as processes that happen not *despite* unwellness (i.e., when we are well enough, or when we pretend we are well enough, or when we force ourselves to be well enough) but *with* unwellness and *through* it. The pandemic has shown me that education is a transformative care project, not a system of achievement, which may be the hardest pedagogical lesson to learn. Many of us can agree that we need to be caring and compassionate toward our students. Most will have trouble if that means divesting from meritocracy, going against everything we've been taught and think we know about education, about how the world works, about our very selves. What are professors if not achievement personified, tasked with safekeeping and gatekeeping that project?

Maybe, counterintuitively, my pedagogical journey has been easier as an adjunct. As an adjunct, my only investment is in the students. I have no other investments in the institutions that keep me fungible. I now firmly believe the tenure track actually forces us to *not* care about students by actively reorienting our investments elsewhere. The tenure track incentivizes not-caring. It predicates survival on not-caring. *Not all tenure-track faculty*, you insist? I'm not saying that all tenure-track faculty don't care about students or that being tenure track doesn't allow for any care of students. I'm pointing out the multiple and conflicting investments that are part and parcel of the tenure track.[29] I'm saying that truly aligning with students, where care is the rule, not the exception, requires intentional divestment from what the tenure track confers: stability inside an engine of harm. As a permanent adjunct (who now pays the bills in other ways because I have to), I am embittered and jaded. I divest from the university because it has already divested from me. I see myself as directly at odds with it. Perhaps adjuncts aren't different in degree from tenure-track faculty—meaning less of everything (less stability, less pay, less power). Perhaps we're different in kind. I'm reminded of Kai Cheng Thom's essay in the second edition of *Open in Emergency*, "Drinking from Your Tears: Re-framing Psychotherapy," in which she contrasts being a therapist with being a queer house mother. Being a therapist limited the kinds of care she could give because she was always an arm of the state. The model of the queer house mother allows a different kind of care, made possible through different kinds of relationships and structures. Being tenure track makes one an arm of the university and thus limits the kind of care one can give. Being an adjunct is a lot less cool than being a queer house mother, but it gives me freedom to nurture my orientation toward students and develop new forms of care. Obviously not all adjuncts feel they can do this safely, or even want to, but structurally the position of adjunct allows for it in ways the tenure track doesn't, even as the tenure track ostensibly gives more "freedom" because of the security of tenure. My freedom actually comes *from* my precarious relationship to the university: I do not depend on it (because I'm financially secure and career secure in other ways—this is key) and so can divest and bear the risk of being divested from.

I started my pedagogical journey centering students, and Asian American students in particular, because I wanted to and because I could. And because the stakes of education as care have been extraordinarily high for them. I say I teach students how to live, and nowhere is that clearer than among Asian American students navigating the university, especially as that university doubles and triples down on its ableism and meritocracy during a global health crisis. The university was already a death trap before the pandemic; it has only become more so. But even as I say I teach students how to live, I don't actually know how to ensure their survival as structures of care collapse all around them. Students remain, as they have always been, the canaries in the coal mine, the ones who are most vulnerable and yet most able (and willing) to help us all realize what is happening. The imperative to listen to students isn't for just students' sakes, but all of ours.

_____

I realize this letter is addressed to both students and teachers, but mostly I've been talking to teachers. Apparently teachers need the most talking to! I hope that in between the lines, you students feel seen, too, and can pull what you need to craft a different vision for your education, one in which your humanity comes first and isn't at odds with your learning. An education in which learning is enabled *through* your humanity, and you no longer feel like a failure all the time. The failure is all of ours, not yours. The pandemic has made that clear, and has shown that education in the beforetimes was not just insufficient but unconscionable. I have been part of that failure, and for that, I am deeply sorry. I will do better. I will keep listening.

cura personalis

In the early months of 2022, I was nominated by my Georgetown students to become an honorary member of the university's chapter of the Jesuit honor society, Alpha Sigma Nu, and invited to give the keynote at a ceremony in which I, another faculty member, and seventy-four students would be inducted and celebrated. I include the speech here in its entirety—it's a fitting coda to the book. That the speech made some Georgetown administrators and faculty intensely uncomfortable—for both its (very mild!) profanity and its message—and made my students in attendance extremely happy tells me I'm still moving in the right direction. It's perhaps a distillation of the central argument of this book and my entire oeuvre over the last decade, crafted into a loving message to students—because who better to receive it than those who taught me what it means to be unwell and create care? If you're able to read nothing else in this book, read this. The message is for you, too.

Cura Personalis
in Pandemic Times

DR. MIMI KHÚC

Lecturer, *Disability Studies Program*

FEBRUARY 13, 2022
Georgetown University

Thank you to the students who invited me to speak today and who nominated me to be an honorary member of Alpha Sigma Nu. It is deeply meaningful to me to be recognized by students because that is who I feel I serve first and foremost in my work as a teacher, scholar, and artist. My commitments are to students, above all, above any institution or peers, so my remarks today will be directed to you, the students here.

We are here today to celebrate all of you for your excellence. I admit I did not know much about Alpha Sigma Nu before this invitation—I'm fairly new to Georgetown, joining as the Scholar/Artist/Activist in Residence in Disability Studies in January 2020 and then staying on as a part-time lecturer since—so I took some time to do a little research. On Georgetown's chapter's website: "The purpose of the Society shall be to honor students of Jesuit institutions of higher education who distinguish themselves in scholarship, loyalty and service.... Of the competitive and highly accomplished pool of ambitious Georgetown students, only about 1.2% are ultimately invited to join the Georgetown chapter of Alpha Sigma Nu."

This is prestigious. You are being recognized for your achievements in multiple realms. Not just your academics but also your character, as expressed in the values of loyalty and service. You are the top 1 percent among students here, exemplars for how much you've done and how much you've given. There is real calculable achievement here. And real hard work and sacrifice. I am sure you have made an enormous impact on the lives around you through your dedication to these values. Y'all are the shit.

I believe y'all are the shit, and I am not here to take that away from you. But I *am* here to tell you that you are more than what you achieve. You are more than even what Georgetown celebrates in you. Excellence is not and should not be the measure of your personhood.

We talk a lot about care here at Georgetown. *Cura personalis*, students have told me, means "care of the whole person." I've been fascinated by that part of Georgetown's mission since I joined its contingent faculty. It's the first time

I've seen care as part of a university's central commitments. My work is in mental health, in thinking about care (and need) in terms of structures, in terms of the collective, in terms of the contexts of uncaring we all differentially encounter. I want to know what kinds of care we need and how to build it, together. I want to teach students, you, that you deserve the care you need, that you do not have to make yourself smaller, make your needs nonexistent, make your pain invisible, in order to be seen as excellent and therefore worthy. You do not have to be excellent to deserve care. This is what I teach in my classes here at Georgetown, in my talks and workshops at universities across the country, in my writing and curatorial work. The simplest of lessons but for some reason one of the hardest to learn.

I have found that my students at Georgetown have welcomed this lesson enthusiastically, sometimes with a kind of desperation, though, that makes my heart ache—and tells me they are learning something else in many places outside my classroom.

What does care look like at Georgetown?

When I came here at the beginning of 2020, that was one of my questions, because, as I said, I had never encountered an institution whose mission centralized care. But before I could even begin to investigate that, I knew it was important to first check in with the real experts here at Georgetown: the students. A university can say it cares all it wants, but if students say they don't feel cared for, this thing called caring is not actually happening. Or at least, it's not happening very effectively.

I've asked every student I've encountered at Georgetown over the last two years if they feel that Georgetown cares about them. Parents and administrators here today will probably not like hearing this, but the answer I've gotten is a definitive, reverberating "no." Individual faculty may show care, both affectively and structurally, in their courses. Peers show care. Students feel cared for intermittently, at the micro and macro levels, by individual people, maybe even departments and programs, maybe even particular university policies and initiatives. But the feeling is not sustained across Georgetown, nor is it sustained across their years here in any holistic sense. There is a major disconnect happening, because Georgetown is not lying when it says it cares and wants to build care for students. I've gotten email after email during the pandemic about ways the university cares, policies and structures being created to try to support students *and* faculty and staff, and these feel for the most part sincere, often involving real labor and effort.

In fact, the pandemic has ushered all of us into an unprecedented crisis of care. There are new needs, overwhelming in scope and scale, emerging constantly, necessitating the constant creation of structures of care, both collective and individual. We have to think about taking care of ourselves and each other in new, heightened ways, and the stakes have never felt higher. They are literally life and death.

But what I've learned in my mental health work over the last decade is that it has always been a matter of life and death for so many of us. We just might not have realized it. I won't quote you statistics about suicidal ideation among students, queer and trans folks, BIPOC peoples, but they are scary. We all have always needed care, for all the spectacularly awful ways we experience unwellness and suffering. We have always needed differential care—meaning, care that takes into account the different and very specific ways we experience unwellness in relation to the structures we encounter.

We just pretend we don't. Because we don't think we are supposed to need and receive care.

We are now approaching year three of the pandemic. Over the course of the last two years, I've watched policies come and go, structures of support wax and wane, access expanded and collapsed across universities all over the country. Perhaps there have been moments in which some students felt holistically cared for, but so many students have continued to tell me throughout the pandemic that they do not feel cared for. This past week, I visited a course here as a guest speaker, and I asked students whether they feel Georgetown cares about them, and they actually laughed. That is probably very hard for those in charge of caring to hear. But hear they must—otherwise they will keep missing the mark and failing the only litmus test that really matters.

I'm not here today to tell Georgetown or any university how to do better. (Don't worry—I do that a lot on other days, and sometimes even get paid for it.) I'm here to tell you, students, that you deserve the care you have not been getting. I'm here to tell you that you are allowed to ask for it, to demand it. You deserve to feel cared for as whole people, and only *you* get to say what *cura personalis* looks like and if it has been achieved. I will hazard an attempt, though, to outline what I think are its main elements, based on what I've heard from students here and across the country, and based on my own scholarly work in disability studies and mental health.

I think that *cura personalis* means you deserve care, at all times, not because you are excellent, not because of your achievements, but because you are human. That means you are allowed to hurt. Allowed to say life is hard, too hard. Allowed to need things, to ask for what we sometimes call accommodations, without shame. Allowed to let go of what we in disability justice call "the myth of independence," or the idea that we all can and should function independently, that it is *moral* to be independent, immoral to be dependent. That something is wrong with you if you can't get your shit together and do all the things you think you're supposed to do. You are allowed to *not* have your shit together.

To me, *cura personalis* means you are allowed to fail. Not fail as in fall through the cracks and be abandoned. Fail as in not meet the ableist standards of so-called excellence and still feel like a good, deserving, whole person. You do not have to be perfect. You will not be abandoned, no matter what.

You have been told, probably every step of the way through all the institutions you've grown up in, that you must be productive and extraordinarily so in order to deserve good things in this life. You will continue to be told this in all the institutions you move through once you leave here. I want you to resist this message. I want you to know that this is what ableism looks and feels like—a strangling of personhood down to normative perfection that leaves all of us dying in its wake. Some of us more quickly or intensely than others, but none of us are left unmarked. Ableism tells us there is an ideal person, body, mind that we have to aspire towards, and any deviation from that renders us less-than, maybe even worthless. Ableism tells us to need is to be weak, to be weak is to be a failure, to fail is to be undeserving. I want you to know it is possible to reject this system of valuation and find different ways to value yourself and others, different ways to be in the world. I want you to know it is possible to build care with others, interdependently, leaning into our needs and limits to do the collective work of care we all deserve. Think of all the forms of mutual aid that have sprung up during the pandemic, to distribute masks and diapers and food and vaccines to those without. We can have that all the time, and not just for our basic needs but also for our mental health needs, our access needs, our social needs, our needs for stability and support and the knowledge that we are not alone and we will not be left behind.

We all deserve belonging, safety, happiness, nourishment, joy, meaning, comfort, love, rest—whether or not we achieve or produce another goddamn thing for the rest of our lives.

Thank you.

Wait—I can't let you go without one last set of activities!

This is a book of letters you've been reading. Now it's your turn to write a few.

Start with one to yourself, past or present or future. Now that you've read this book, what do you want to remind yourself or teach yourself in this moment? What are things you wish you had known before, or things you hope for yourself for the future? What have you learned about your own unwellness, and what do you want to say about it, and to it? How will you care for what hurts?

_____

_____

_____

_____

_____

_____

_____

_____

_____

_____

_____

_____

_____

_____

_____

_____

_____

_____

_____

_____

_____

_____

_____

Now write a letter to a loved one, asking them what hurts. Make it safe for them to answer. See what happens.

_____

_____

_____

_____

_____

_____

_____

_____

_____

_____

_____

_____

_____

_____

_____

_____

_____

_____

_____

_____

_____

_____

_____

Thank you for joining me and engaging so deeply in this collective care project. I hope I've brought you into it in a way that nurtures the fullest possibility for our humanities, yours and mine. I hope I've given you something of a blueprint for building collective care across the spaces in which you live and love and hurt.

I don't know where we all will be by the time this book is published, if the pandemic will be over, what the world will look like, how many of us will still be here. But I hope somewhere along the way we will have listened more to our unwell, our wounded, our hurting, our dying, our dead. I hope we will more easily say what hurts, to ourselves and to each other and with each other, and do the work of figuring out together how to go on living while it hurts. I hope we can be gloriously and awfully unwell together.

But no matter where we all are now, I want to remind you again that you are not alone. I will stay by your side at the edge of the abyss, and I will not leave you. You and I, we deserve no less.

acknowledgments

A book takes a village that inspires, supports, protects, nourishes, comforts, and cares. It also takes a village that rages, mourns, despairs, and burns shit down. Most of all, it takes a village that believes in you. My path has been so strange and devastating that believing in myself has at times felt impossible. Following Jim Lee's wisdom, I have leaned heavily on the faith of others, trying to trust that they know something I don't. Apparently they do, because somehow I created the project of love and hope that is this book. I wrote this book held by a community whose far edges I can't even see—there are people who believe in me and this book whom I don't even know. How is that possible?

I try not to think about what is impossible anymore. The journey of me and Lawrence, of *Open in Emergency* and its ripples, of the writing of this book have all taught me that my dreams can always be bigger, the horizon can always be higher, the vision can always reach for more. Lawrence showed me how to dream impossibilities into being and for that he gets the very first, and deepest, thank you. But we'll come back to him later.

Elizabeth Ault gets the next thank you. I wasn't writing a book until she planted the seed, and she supported me in nurturing this wild plant in whatever directions it wanted. I was able to write the book I wanted to write, and that is no small feat in academia. Thank you, Elizabeth and Duke, for believing in a book that I hadn't even conceived of yet and then ushering it into the world with such care. Thank you to my two reviewers who read the manuscript with immense generosity and thoughtfulness; you helped me see the project with new eyes and expand my hopes for it even further. Thank you to my copyeditor, who moved me to tears by treating this wild prose with such respect.

To all the contributors of *OiE*: it's still hard for me to believe that everyone in the project trusted me and Lawrence enough to follow all our bizarre instructions. We ask people to do things they've never done before, and the fact that they actually do it never ceases to amaze me. I feel unendingly honored by that trust. Collaborators, thank you all for your brilliance. *OiE* could not have done the work it has in the world without it.

Deepest gratitude to all the people who supported our Kickstarters (and waited an ungodly amount of time for their rewards!), and those who have bought *OiE*, gifted *OiE*, taught *OiE*, and brought me out to their campuses and communities. You honor the work and all the unwellness it holds. Thank you to all the students whom I've met on the road—your vulnerability and bravery form the cornerstone of this book. Thank you for sharing your hearts with me.

To *OiE*'s and AALR's laborers: Deanna, you are the best. John, thank you for being our tireless mailboy. Aria, Jenna, Maggie, Ai Binh, Eileen: thank you for your belief in our work and all your generous (unpaid!) labor.

To my students at UMD. Thank you for teaching me how to teach. Thank you for fighting for me.

Asian American studies, you are an intellectual community suffused with friendship and care, and I am grateful to call you "home," even with all the baggage that word entails. You are a home that is often a haven; you are a home that at times needs to be called lovingly into account. You make me laugh. SO. MUCH. My community is far-flung, but almost every April I get to run around squealing and hugging so many of my beloveds. Thank you for this joy.

My fellow adjuncts: this one's for us. To those entrusting me with their words in this book, I hope I've done your heartbreaks justice. We will not let them look away.

To the Asian American literary community, thank you for your welcome. Somewhere along the way in the last decade, I became a writer. It was like coming into a self I didn't know could exist. Lawrence held my hand and introduced me to a community of weirdo dreamers, and there really is no turning back after that.

Disability studies knew I was doing disability studies before I did, and that recognition changed the trajectory of my career. Thank you to those who welcomed me into the field with such encouragement. I have learned from disability studies and disability justice the important lesson that care isn't just something you feel, it's also something you do; I owe so much of my thinking and praxis to the models of collective care I've been privileged to witness.

Thank you to the U.S. Disability Rights Program at the Ford Foundation for its support of the publication of this book. As an adjunct with little to no access to institutional funding, I am deeply grateful to co-conspirators who reach across the structural divide.

The Disability Studies Program at Georgetown gave me a much-needed place to explore my ideas and deepen my work with students. So much of this book was dreamed and written during my time there. The Disability Cultural Initiative at Georgetown has also supported this book—thank you for your commitment to those of us laboring at the margins. Georgetown students, thank you for teaching me some of the most important lessons I've learned on what it means to be accountable to students. I am so grateful we were able to weather the early pandemic together.

The FLOURISH Collective: Community-Engaged Arts and Social Wellness at University of Toronto Scarborough surprised me with a residency as this book was wrapping up, inviting me into a like-hearted community of scholars and artists and community organizers I had no idea existed. There is something breathtaking about this collective and how care manifests in every aspect of its life. Universities and departments aren't homes, I now know, but FLOURISH has been such an inspiring space of ethical community. Thank you for your generous welcome and spirit of collaboration. Here's to more collaborations to come!

To everyone who has supported me and Lawrence through the never-ending terror of our family life: your messages of outrage, heartache, horror, rage, disgust, bewilderment, admiration, and love have been a lifeline. You stay with us at the edge of this hellscape, and that has made the unbearable more bearable.

I cannot forget to thank our therapists, especially in a book about mental health. I like to joke that Lawrence and I have a whole team of therapists trying to keep us from falling apart, but that's not actually far off. Thank you, team, for caring for us and rooting for us. You are committed to our survival, as individuals and as a couple, above and beyond what the job calls for, and that has been an incredible gift. Also, your uncontrollable facial responses to the horrors we describe are an utter delight.

To CLAMM (or CALMM, as some insist!): Care, Leah, Audrey, Mai-Linh, I wrote the very first words of this book while with you all on our Easton's Nook writing retreat in the beforetimes. Thank you for always being a Slack message away and for cheering me on throughout this project. My skin also thanks you for introducing me to the amazing world of skin care!

To my writing buddies, Simi and James, who saw the majority of this project unfold over weekly sessions where we sometimes wrote and more often talked shit. Thank you for the care and community and all that queer life. Simi, thank you for loving me and Lawrence and our family, and thank you for always being ready to mourn with us. Thank you for Lou. I believe in you like you believe in me.

Jim and erin. You two are threaded throughout this book, woven thoroughly into its ideas (and footnotes!) but also its commitments and hopes. Thank you for your faith and love and savage humor. Thank you for staying steadfastly, enthusiastically, by my side at the abyss no matter how dark and deep it goes. Please don't ever show anyone our texts. You two are the best haters I could ever ask for as BFFs. Insert gif of ugly-crying.

To all my parents, who have worked hard to love a child that both resembles them and is totally alien to them. Thank you for the space for me to be different.

To John and Mazan, who had to learn very quickly how to love the strange and fierce woman suddenly loving their son—thank you for your unconditional acceptance. And thank you for your son.

Hugs to all my siblings, both the ones I love from far away on social media and the ones who build basement Airbnbs for me and laugh—loudly—at all my jokes. Love you, big sister.

To the kitties, whose wildness and weirdness bring me such delight and whose litter boxes bring me such despair, thank you for loving me. I wrote most of this book with at least one of you on my lap.

To my children. Elia, you already know this book is for you. Gabe and Sebastian, you don't know it yet, but there's another book coming for you. You two have taught me, and are still teaching me, how to love and parent under siege, a lesson that has grown my heart in ways I didn't know were possible. Being your stepmom is one of the hardest and most amazing things I've ever had to do. My dearest Elia, you are a star child, hurtling from the sky and transforming everything with your light. It is my greatest honor to be your mother. Mothering you is no fucking joke, and I hope I do the work justice. I hope I'm burning enough shit down and imagining enough new possibility into being to make space for your fullest personhood. And no, we can't have any more cats.

To Lawrence-Minh Bùi Davis, the love of my life: we found each other and chose each other, against the odds. We keep choosing each other, against the odds. Your faith has been the foundation for everything I've done in the last decade, your brilliance and love and magic embedded in every work. Thank you for letting me jabber ideas at you every day, and thank you for reading every word of this book, multiple times. Being loved by you has been the most transformative experience of my life. My anh, you are a gift, to me, to our children, to the world. May we keep making magic together for ourselves and all our beloveds for the rest of our lives. Let's get another cat.

notes

1. A Pedagogy of Unwellness

This chapter began as an essay I wrote while on a writing retreat in 2019 at Easton's Nook with members of my writing group, Caroline Kyungah Hong, Audrey Wu Clark, and Leah Milne. Our final member, Mai-Linh Hong, couldn't attend but was there in spirit and virtually. That essay would not have been possible without each member and without the exquisite hospitality and care offered by Nadine of Easton's Nook. That essay was further shepherded by the incredibly thoughtful and generous editors Ellen Samuels and Elizabeth Freeman and published as "Making Mental Health: A Journey in Love Letters" in their special issue of *South Atlantic Quarterly*, "Crip Temporalities." Writing takes a village.

1 See the Asian American Tarot in *Open in Emergency*, the AALR *Book of Curses*, the *DSM: Asian American Edition* in *Open in Emergency*, and interactive one-day arts-based pop-ups I've organized with universities and community orgs such as Harvard University's History and Literature program, the New York City chapter of the National Asian Pacific American Women's Forum (NAPAWF), and Richmond Area Multi-Services (RAMS) and Kearny Street Workshop in the Bay Area.

2 I employ *dwell* here as a mode—and temporality—of being and knowing. What can we learn when we stay in a time/feeling/experience that we are usually encouraged to flee from? In thinking about Asian American settler relation to indigenous sovereignty, I want to differentiate my use of *dwelling* from one of belonging by way of ownership. This dwelling is not about land and property but about time and affect, a kind of relational staying that I hope

can be aligned with indigenous sovereignty. I also want to point to the work of Crystal Baik, Vivian Truong, Amita Manghnani, Diane Wong, Lena Sze, Minju Bae, and Preeti Sharma, who developed the concept and language of "dwelling in unwellness" as a mode of collective writing about grief and pain during the pandemic. Their creative-critical essay by the same name beautifully outlines the theoretical, affective, literary, relational, and care work that their dwelling engages—and kicks us all in the gut with both their vulnerability and their invitation to the reader into vulnerability. Like this book, their essay leaves spaces for the reader to write in the text! And while they draw on my work for the language of unwellness, I'm pretty sure we each came up with the language of dwelling independently but simultaneously somehow! See Baik et al., "Dwelling in Unwellness."

3 Jim Lee's term "pedagogies of woundedness" resonates deeply with my concept of a pedagogy of unwellness. Jim asks what we can learn when we look at our and others' woundedness—illness, death, suffering—and the ways we narrate these wounds. In fact, Jim's commitment to looking at woundedness has greatly informed my own; he has always given permission to those around him to feel and hurt as much as they need to. For that space, and for his friendship, I am eternally grateful. Lee, *Pedagogies of Woundedness*.

4 Ninh, *Ingratitude*.

5 AALR was dreamed into being in 2009 over a homey meal at a small Chinese restaurant in Wheaton, Maryland, by two not-quite-of-this-world graduate students: Lawrence-Minh Bùi Davis and Gerald Maa. The story of Lawrence and Gerald may be just as fun as this story.

6 See Clare, *Brilliant Imperfection*, for a sustained exploration of the violence of cure, the dangerous implications of narratives of restoration and eradication, and Kafer, *Feminist Queer Crip*, for a helpful political model of disability that names and deconstructs ableism's ways of generating normativity.

7 For a definition and exploration of "crip time," or how disability shifts the experience of time, see Samuels, "Six Ways of Looking at Crip Time."

8 I would eventually be pushed out by tenured colleagues in 2017—but that is another story for another time. For now: fuck UMD.

9 I have been heartened to see some teachers moving toward more student-centered, compassionate teaching. The popularity of Becky Thompson's *Teaching with Tenderness* points to this. A critical disability studies and disability justice approach would deepen this kind of teaching, with its eye on ableism and its commitment to access. The work of Jay T. Dolmage and Aimi Hamraie on universal design as well as the kinds of community resources each of them has created (UD checklists, podcasts, Google doc resources) are inspiring examples. The pandemic has propelled even more innovation in teaching with and as care; see chapter 5 for an exploration of this.

10 See Asian American Psychological Association, "Suicide among Asian Americans"; and Noh, "Asian American Women and Suicide."

11 Thank you to Simi Kang for introducing me to Rob Nixon's term "slow vio-

lence" in conversations and in her essay "What Is Refugee Resilience?" See also Jina B. Kim's disability studies engagement with Nixon's concept to make visible the disabling environments created by colonialism and globalization. For deeper examinations into death by model minoritization, see erin Khuê Ninh's works, *Ingratitude* and *Passing for Perfect*.

12 Jim Lee is the mentor who said to me long ago that sometimes we need to have faith in others' faith in us. I have leaned on Jim's faith in me for over a decade now. *Open in Emergency* could not have happened without it.

13 Thank you to Ellen Samuels and Elizabeth Freeman for reminding me of the dance at the Society for Disability Studies conference as an example of bodily and affective disruption in a scholarly conference, which Simi Linton and Sami Schalk have both reflected on and theorized.

14 This letter to Elia appears as the editor's note in both editions of *Open in Emergency*.

15 Here, I think of "classical" thinkers from women of color feminism such as Audre Lorde, as well some of our most public and impactful contemporary theorizers of race, such as essayist Ta-Nehisi Coates, literary scholar and writer Viet Thanh Nguyen, geographer and prison scholar Ruth Wilson Gilmore, feminist theorist Sara Ahmed, poet and performance studies scholar Fred Moten, and literary scholar Christina Sharpe.

16 Email to editors at AALR, December 2016, my emphasis.

17 I include the response here to show readers what it looks like to do not only close-reading of mental health shenanigans, but also careful, thoughtful communication work (and relationship work) in and about our editorial practice.

18 Kai Cheng quotes the World Health Organization's definition of mental health as "a state of well-being in which every individual realizes his or her own potential, can cope with the normal stresses of life, can work productively and fruitfully, and is able to make a contribution to her or his community." Slight variations appear online. Currently the World Health Organization's web page offers the following: "Mental health is a state of mental well-being that enables people to cope with the stresses of life, realize their abilities, learn well and work well, and contribute to their community." See World Health Organization, "Mental Health."

19 Chapter 2 reflects more deeply on these discussions about this definition of mental health with students, faculty, administrators, and counselors across the country.

2. Touring the Abyss

1 As I mentioned before, I was pushed out in 2017. It was one of the most traumatic and humiliating experiences of my life. Such is adjunct precarity. Such is tenured privilege and tenured fragility. Again, that is a story for another time. For now: fuck UMD.

2 As quoted in Kai Cheng Thom's essay "The Myth of Mental Health." Again,

slight variations appear online. See World Health Organization, "Mental Health."

3 Here, I'm thinking of Georgetown, where I hold a part-time contract. A unit called Health Education Services "supports student well-being and creates healthy learning environments for individuals and the community by providing health education and caring for the WHOLE Hoya—body, mind, and soul. HES seeks to empower students to take responsibility for decisions regarding their health" (Georgetown University, "Georgetown University Health Education Services"). Additionally, the Engelhard Project, a grant-supported initiative to explore how classrooms might support student well-being, began organizing a "wellness workshop series" in collaboration with HES and Georgetown's counseling center in fall 2020 as a response to the pandemic. "Tolerating distress" and "emotional regulation" were two of the topics offered in spring 2021. While Engelhard is an interesting departure from locating well-being solely in the counseling center, their program still relies heavily on partnerships with the counseling center. Faculty who wish to be a part of their project and develop wellness in their courses must partner with a "professional" from the counseling center to do so. They also rely on faculty voluntary participation in their efforts.

4 Counselors at UMD actually received a grant to make these promotional videos during the time I was there in the mid-2010s; outreach and "demystification" were where the energy, and funding, went. These videos were the solution to the crisis in Asian American student mental health.

5 This has been and remains the only time I've been invited to work directly with a counseling center and its staff. While campus counseling centers have sometimes cosponsored my talks at various universities, this college remains the only higher ed institution that has asked me to do a workshop specifically for its counselors.

6 See chapter 5 for a reflection on how the university provides care to students beyond the counseling center in terms of access and pandemic supports—and how professors do and don't provide care in their classrooms.

7 Noh, "A Letter to My Sister," 67.

8 But archived here: Teotico and Yang, "Managing Anti-Asian Racism and Xenophobia."

9 Ninh, "Harvard's Bad Counsel."

10 See Ninh, *Ingratitude*; Ninh, *Passing for Perfect*.

11 See chapter 5 for a more in-depth discussion on Georgetown's mission as well as its, and other universities', responses during the pandemic.

12 Wang, *The Collected Schizophrenias*.

13 Thank you to Leanna Pham and Y-Binh Nguyen (and of course Lydia!) for your invitation, your organizing work, and your very warm welcome.

14 Again, chapter 5 explores our differential relationships to the classroom and the institution.

15 University of Chicago, "2019 Conference."

16 Alex Joh-Jung and conspirators were lovely hosts, and not just because I'm friends/colleagues with his mom! And I have to note that Emily Shen, the coordinator for the event, was absolutely masterful in her management of logistics and communication with me—an act of access and care that I truly appreciate.

17 Thank you to James Zhang for his invitation, but even more for his inspiring leadership and example. James's own talk at "Break the Silence" on the graduate student panel was incredibly smart and brave—and James's contribution to my discussion on filial debt has stayed with me all these years, so much so that he is quoted directly in The Student card published in the second edition of the Asian American Tarot: "We are finishing our parents' immigration stories." I wish you the best on your medical journey, James. I hope you are getting to finish your own story.

18 Asian American Psychological Association, "Suicide among Asian Americans."

19 Noor-Oshiro, "Asian American Young Adults"; Centers for Disease Control and Prevention, "Deaths, Percent of Total Deaths, and Death Rates."

20 Again, chapter 3 explores these issues directly.

21 A quote included in the APA fact sheet on Asian American suicide by psychologist Joel Wong: "By seeking professional help, many individuals who have suicidal thoughts are able to resist suicide." Asian American Psychological Association, "Suicide among Asian Americans."

22 Again, chapter 4 explores how meritocracy functions in the university and how that shapes unwellness in the academy more directly, and chapter 5 follows how this plays out in the classroom in particular.

23 I want to note here, at the helpful suggestion of a reviewer, that we should differentiate between faculty and staff—they occupy different positionalities in the university and face different vulnerabilities. I have seen enough verbal abuse of departmental administrative staff to know there are complex power differentials as well. Then there's the work of student services, which is its own world, sometimes aligned with the university's prerogatives and sometimes consciously at odds. Lumping faculty and staff together here is playing a little fast and loose. But I want to include staff here because they are literally the university's bureaucrats, carrying out policy and procedure on a daily basis, and with that bureaucracy comes the power to adjudicate, enforce punitive policies, deny access, and, ultimately, dehumanize, even as their power takes different shapes from the faculty's, even as they face their own pressures and perils, even if it's possible to say, "Not all staff."

24 See chapters 4 and 5 for a deeper dive into these dynamics—how we imbibe meritocracy and how this shows up in the stories we tell about ourselves, our relationships to our institutions, our relationships along the academic hierarchy, and our pedagogical choices.

25 Jenna Peng, Aria Pahari, Alex Joh-Jung—thank you for your heart-full and brilliant work on this card!

26 Jim Lee first introduced me to his language of "the abyss" in 2018 at the conference for the Association for Asian American Studies in a session on teaching *Open in Emergency*. He described his own teaching as "taking students to the edge of the abyss and standing there with them"—and telling them he would stay with them there as long as they needed. This image, and feeling, restructured my own approaches to teaching, helping me recognize what care can and should look like in and beyond the classroom. "The abyss" and our relationships to it have become woven into the fabric of my thinking and language around unwellness, and I am endlessly grateful to Jim for this.

Interlude 2. The Suicide Tarot

1 Siagatonu, "Queer Check-Ins: Nine Heavens."

3. How to Save Your Asian American Life in an Hour

1 Again: fuck UMD. See chapter 4 for the fuller recounting.
2 And it is the second leading cause of death for Asian Americans ages ten to fourteen. Centers for Disease Control and Prevention, "Deaths, Percent of Total Deaths, and Death Rates."
3 Noh, "A Letter to My Sister," 65–67.
4 David Eng and Shinhee Han, in *Racial Melancholia, Racial Dissociation*, posit a frame of racial melancholia for understanding Asian American depression, particularly among Gen X, drawing on psychoanalytic theory to point to the psychic loss of "suspended assimilation," or Asian American inability to fully assimilate. To Eng and Han, intergenerational conflict is immigrant melancholia, or grief over loss of cultures of origin and inability to achieve the American Dream, passed down to the second generation. While I agree that it is crucial to place Asian American mental health in the context of Asian American exclusion and other forms of structural violence, I am not convinced that failed assimilation should be our central concern. I am more interested in the model minority as racial project and subject formation in its own right, and not simply as mode of assimilation, not reducible to white aspirationalism. Along the lines of erin Khuê Ninh's work, I'm interested in how model minoritization manifests in the Asian immigrant family and the psychic lives of the second generation. I think erin's approach to examine "what it feels like to be the model minority" gets at the structures of feeling of my students' experiences in the most powerful ways, evident in their fervent, even desperate, responses in my classrooms and workshops, which I outline over the course of this chapter. And as I began to lay out in chapter 2, we have to look at the university as the other major site, and the major institutional site, for model minority subject formation and constructions of wellness—and thus for Asian American unwellness.
5 I'm referencing student responses about marriage from roughly 2013 to

2022, over which time notions of gender and sexuality in the United States had already begun to shift drastically, but not so much as to change student responses. Perhaps these continuing shifts will create more flexibility in the model minority frame around gendered expectations for romantic relationships.

6 See Edward Said, *Orientalism*, for the original formulation of this concept. There has been a vast body of work developing it since, expanding it through the lenses of geopolitical relations, colonialism and imperialism, US wars in Asia, religion and religious appropriation, technology and imagined futures, anti-Asian violence in the United States, all the way to the current moment of the COVID-19 pandemic and discourses of disease and contagion. Orientalism pervades how we understand the world—including in Asian immigrant families. Which brings us back to Eng and Han's (*Racial Melancholia, Racial Dissociation*) psychoanalytic model for Asian American mental health. One of my concerns is that a failed assimilation model comes uncomfortably close to this Orientalist construction of "Asian" versus "American," flattening an impossibly complex—and ever-shifting—spectrum of identifications and dynamics in much the same fashion as Asian Cultural Values. While aspirational whiteness is a constitutive element of white supremacy, framing the desire to assimilate as central to the psychic lives of Asian Americans is reductive in more ways than one.

7 See Sins Invalid, "10 Principles of Disability Justice"; and Mingus, "Changing the Framework."

8 Ninh, *Ingratitude*, 22.

9 Ninh, *Ingratitude*, 34.

10 Chapman, *The Five Love Languages*. Chapman's term "love languages" has become so mainstream as to be ubiquitous for describing varying expressions of love. Here I draw upon the ubiquity of this pop-psych language for its ability to quickly communicate, but I recognize—and argue—that we need to push the framework beyond its flattening essentialism and place it in historical and structural contexts. Only then does it become truly helpful for understanding Asian American experiences.

11 Ninh, "Ingratitude: A Cultural Theory of Power," 45.

12 Coates, *Between the World and Me*, 1:55:00.

13 Perry, *Breathe*; Dungy, *Guidebook to Relative Strangers*.

14 Noh, "Letter to My Sister," 70.

15 Ninh, "Ingratitude: A Cultural Theory of Power," 186–87.

16 See erin's recent book, Ninh, *Passing for Perfect*, for a deep dive into processes of model minoritization and the racial performance required in the "success frame"—and the toll all of it takes.

17 Lee et al., "An Insurgent Manual."

18 See again Harvard's counseling center's advice in response to rising anti-Asian violence during the pandemic: Ninh, "Harvard's Bad Counsel."

4. The Professor Is Ill

1 I want to point again to the work of Crystal Baik, Vivian Truong, Amita Manghnani, Diane Wong, Lena Sze, Minju Bae, and Preeti Sharma in theorizing "dwelling in unwellness" during pandemic times. Baik et al., "Dwelling in Unwellness."

2 See Price, *Mad at School*; Price, "Time Harms"; Dolmage, *Academic Ableism*; Brown and Leigh, *Ableism in Academia*; Kerschbaum, Eisenman, and Jones, *Negotiating Disability*.

3 For a large collection of the experiences of women of color in the academy, see Gutiérrez y Muhs et al., *Presumed Incompetent*; and Gutiérrez y Muhs et al., *Presumed Incompetent II*; and for women more broadly, see Garvis and Black, *Lived Experiences of Women in Academia*. A quick search about just Black women's experiences in the academy will render hundreds of articles. Academic hostility to motherhood is well documented, generating books such as Evans and Grant, *Mama PhD*; and Connelly and Ghodsee, *Professor Mommy*, both part testimonial, part survival guide. See Valverde and Dariotis, *Fight the Tower*, for a recent collection documenting Asian American women's experiences in particular; and see Ferguson, *The Reorder of Things*; Ahmed, *On Being Included*; and Ahmed, *Complaint!*, for how universities have incorporated diversity and "disruption" and the cost of these processes for the most vulnerable.

4 See the plethora of op-eds and essays in news outlets about the plight of particular adjuncts, "The Death of an Adjunct" from 2019 possibly garnering the most attention recently. In fact, adjunct death is so prominent that there's actually *another* essay titled "Death of an Adjunct," this one from 2013. Harris, "The Death of an Adjunct"; Kovalik, "Death of an Adjunct." A quick Google search shows an alarming number of pieces on adjuncts living in tents, living in cars, turning to sex work, and relying on public assistance. I'm aware of some tenure-track scholars writing and thinking about adjunctification and exploitative labor in academia; for example, Nick Mitchell's essay "Summertime Selves (On Professionalization)." Poet Truong Tran has published a searing book of prose poetry in response to his years of exploitation and mistreatment as a Vietnamese American creative writing adjunct at San Francisco State University—to significant backlash by those in power at SFSU. Tran, *The Book of Other*. For analyses and advocacy, see Keith Hoeller's collection of proposals for addressing adjunct exploitation, *Equality for Contingent Faculty*, and the organization New Faculty Majority, which advocates for equity and academic freedom for contingent faculty (http://www.newfacultymajority.info/). The stories and ideas are out there, but I have yet to encounter an analysis of adjunctification through the lens of mental health and the structural and differential unwellness of the university—and the lens of ethnic studies in particular. More on this later in this chapter.

5 The Professor Is In, home page, accessed November 2021, https://theprofessorisin.com/.

6 This one I remember comes directly from one of The Professor Is In's posts from when I was finishing grad school in the early 2010s, though I cannot find the particular post now.

7 The Professor Is In, "Unstuck."

8 National Center for Faculty Diversity and Development, home page, accessed October 2021, https://www.facultydiversity.org/; National Center for Faculty Diversity and Development, "Institutional Membership"; and National Center for Faculty Diversity and Development, "NCFDD Core Curriculum."

9 In another essay, I reflect more on a model of enablement for writing that allows for—even expects—unwellness; see Khúc, "Writing While Adjunct."

10 See Ninh, *Ingratitude*; and my discussion of the Good Child in chapter 3.

11 Again, see Ninh, *Passing for Perfect*, for our collective orientation toward the success frame and model minoritization.

12 Okay, it's time for the full story. But to paraphrase dear friend Mark Padoongpatt, who introduced me to the lovely phrase "motherfuck you," I'll say here as I begin: motherfuck UMD.

13 See Ahmed, *Complaint!*, for a deep dive into the bureaucratic world of claiming institutional harm: how complaints are institutionally managed and the kinds of discursive violence deployed against "complainers."

14 The essay I'm referring to here is also where the beginnings of my story about UMD were crafted—parts of this chapter appear there in earlier form. I want to thank my collaborators as well as the editors of the anthology for their deep generosity, kindness, and support while I explored how to begin telling my story. The space they all created is really what a true manifestation of the spirit of Asian American studies looks like. Kevin, Linda, Amber—you rock. Diane and Mark, your kindness is beyond words. Lee et al., "Insurgent Manual."

15 Again, see Ahmed, *Complaint!*, for various ways institutional critiques are often reframed and disdainfully dismissed.

16 Thank you, Simi, for this helpful observation.

17 With the extraordinary exception of Phil Nash, who stayed by us, supported us, and even helped students better understand what was happening. Phil faces his own precarity in this program as a fellow adjunct, relegated to the margins by the tenure-track faculty hired in over the years—faculty whose jobs would not exist had it not been for Phil's dedicated advocacy and organizing work with students over *decades*. Oh, did I not mention that Phil is a cofounder of the program? Yes. The fucking contingent cofounder of this program on whose labor and local community connections the program was built has little to no say over its workings, its directions, its accountability. Not when there are tenured faculty parachuted in.

18 In the earlier version of this story in that collaborative essay with student organizers, I wrote that institutional magistrates cannot care for those they manage—if they are cowards. I took that out of this version because I thought it important in this telling to dwell in the grief of these revelations instead of

the outrage. But betrayal is always both grief and outrage. And I stand fully behind pointing to cowardice where I see it, so I wanted to preserve that here in the notes.

19 More on this in chapter 5, on teaching.

20 Nguyen, *The Gift of Freedom*; and Nguyen, "The Refugee."

21 For reflections on transformative justice principles and models, see Thom, *I Hope We Choose Love*; and Dixon and Piepzna-Samarasinha, *Beyond Survival Strategies*.

22 I recognize that West Coast program building has looked different from East Coast program building, and in well-established departments in California, tenure-stream faculty outnumber the adjuncts. But I know of no departments that didn't at some point hire adjuncts or that don't currently hire adjuncts. There are always sabbaticals and leaves that require courses to be covered. There are always curricular gaps. There is always desire to grow and put more butts in seats, as affordably as possible.

23 And sometimes, maybe often, maybe as a rule, teaching their classes better because adjuncts are evaluated solely on teaching and are also structurally positioned to better align themselves with students. This is a separate line of argument I won't explore more here, but it's one well worth engaging, tracing some of the lines I've outlined earlier: tenured relationships to research versus teaching, investments in community governance versus a top-down model, adjuncts teaching intro classes and filling curricular gaps, adjuncts teaching more classes and having more teaching experience, and so on.

24 The exception among traditional fields is of course English departments, which have historically relied upon adjuncts (and graduate students) to teach their slew of introductory writing classes. The Asian American literature PhD knows, though, that English's reliance on adjuncts can intersect directly with that of Asian American studies—case in point, Lawrence's first years of teaching at UMD were not at AAST but in the English Department for freshman comp.

25 Nguyen, *The Gift of Freedom*; and Nguyen, "The Refugee."

26 See Chiang, *The Cultural Capital of Asian American Studies*; and Schlund-Vials's edited collection *Flashpoints for Asian American Studies*, especially essays by Amy Uyematsu, Timothy Yu, Cathy Schlund-Vials, Anita Mannur, and Nitasha Sharma.

27 Thank you so much to Laura Sachiko Fugikawa, Jean-Paul deGuzman, Kelly Fong, and Linta Varghese for all your contributions and care work. I have so much admiration and gratitude for each of you.

28 A risk I am aware this chapter runs because of my decision to reveal details and close-read those details for my analysis—and one I'm willing to take because I have come to the conclusion that not doing so serves only to continue obfuscating power. As I said, the ugly, the unseemly, the excessive, the uncomfortable are important here. There is no full accounting without them.

29 This approach might sound familiar as one employed by couples therapists

everywhere. Lawrence and I work on mirroring in our communication all the time! I point out the echo to help us see the scaled-up versions at Clark and AAAS as relationship work too—which is not to ignore the structural and reduce the dynamic to the interpersonal, but to frame the intervention as fundamentally a mental health one as well.

30 These testimonies have been included here with permission from each person.

31 An earlier, longer version of this account was published in Valverde and Dariotis, *Fight the Tower*.

32 In *Mad at School*, Margaret Price attributes the documentation of this term to two social science articles in the 1990s: Zola, "Self, Identity and the Naming Question"; and Gill, "A Psychological View of Disability Culture."

33 Samuels, "Six Ways of Looking at Crip Time"; Samuels and Freeman, "Crip Temporalities." An early version of my first chapter was published in Samuels and Freeman's issue.

34 Price, *Laziness Does Not Exist*, chap. 3, 10:27–10:42.

35 Price, "Laziness Does Not Exist."

36 Price, *Laziness Does Not Exist*, chap. 2, 20:58–21:39.

37 See my speech at the 2022 induction ceremony for Georgetown's chapter of the Jesuit honor society Alpha Sigma Nu, reproduced at the end of this book. See also Khúc, "Writing While Adjunct."

5. Teaching in Pandemic Times

1 Georgetown University, "Spirit of Georgetown."

2 See Hamraie, *Building Access*, for a critical history of universal design; see the org CAST and its website for detailed descriptions of UDL principles, guidelines, and applications as developed by their org: CAST: Until Learning Has No Limits, accessed February 2022, https://cast.org/.

3 Some examples we have been part of: I participated in a day long symposium on disability justice and the arts for the Ford Foundation's internal development in 2019; Lawrence organized a disability justice training by activist-scholar-artist Lydia X. Z. Brown for curators and artists at the Asian American Literature Festival in 2019.

4 The Professor Is In's blog post on the pitfalls of the teaching statement tells us both what PhDs on the market tend to write and what the genre prescriptively demands—especially along the lines of gender and the two-tiered academic hierarchy. The blog reinscribes the gendered and hierarchical expectations of the teaching statement, though, in the name of "helping" the job applicant be more "professional." Language that conveys passion and joy, according to The Professor Is In, is "overly-emotional and highly feminized in ways that, again, are self-sabotaging on the tenure track job market. Women in particular must beware of their tendency to over-invest in a 'nice' persona in their teaching statements. Teaching at the tenure track level is not

about being nice. It is about being a professional. Realize that the 'nicer' and 'sweeter' you sound, the more you are characterizing yourself as the classic female perennial one-year replacement adjunct." Kelsky, "The Dreaded Teaching Statement." See chapter 4 for a fuller discussion on The Professor Is In and other professionalization resources and their complicated participation in ableist meritocracy as well as adjunct denigration.

5 See chapter 4 for the sordid tale of my time in that godforsaken program, and again: fuck UMD.

6 See chapter 3 for a fuller rendition of erin's brilliant work and how it has impacted me, my teaching, and my students.

7 Price, "Time Harms."

8 Khúc, "Living Under Siege."

9 Khúc, "The Revolution Is in the Heart."

10 See Sins Invalid, *Skin, Tooth, and Bone*, for their articulation of disability justice principles. See Talila A. Lewis's definition of ableism in "January 2021 Working Definition of Ableism"; as well as Jina B. Kim's definition in "Love in the Time of Sickness."

11 Hamraie and Khúc, "Disability Justice and Access-Centered Pedagogy in the Pandemic"; Georgetown University, "From Accommodations to Access."

12 Wheeler, "Pedagogies of Care, Access, and Vulnerability." Lest you think I was welcomed back to UMD, please note that it was *not* the Asian American Studies Program that invited me to speak but the ODI unit. I doubt AAST has any interest in viewing me as a teaching resource.

13 Carter, "Teaching with Trauma."

14 Hopeful that perhaps able-bodied and able-minded people would finally understand what it is like to need—see Ellen Samuels and Elizabeth Freeman's reflection in summer 2020 about how the pandemic has ushered us all into a kind of crip time—and bitter because so many accommodations denied to disabled folks over the years (remote learning, supportive technology, flexibility, etc.) were becoming so easily available now that those more normatively bodied needed them. Samuels and Freeman, "Introduction," in "Crip Temporalities."

15 Clare, *Brilliant Imperfection*.

16 Muriente, "Sofía Gallisá Muriente on Community as the Basic Unit of Survival"; Quart, "Really Giving"; Spade, *Mutual Aid*.

17 Jim said this in a virtual book talk in early March 2022 in response to a question about how we as scholars can enact care in our research and teaching when caring is not encouraged or often modeled. To paraphrase him further: the point is not to simply virtue signal by saying one cares but to actually try to bring into being the world that we want, if even just for a few moments— by being vulnerable, being radically generous, being willing to try doing the things we are hoping for. Lee, "Pedagogies of Woundedness."

18 I want to explicitly engage here the ethics of discussing things shared on social media. I realize and respect that there are agreements, direct or tacit, that we do not publicly share things meant to be private or semiprivate. I used to

moderate a secret academic Facebook group in which sharing outside of the group was the highest infraction because of the potential professional consequences. But what I have been seeing across social media constitutes a text that tracks academic trends and contains revealing subtexts about the academy, and so I think it important to engage. I will, however, not divulge any individual names or even quote individual posts that may be recognizable. I am mostly engaging patterns across my social media circles, not looking at specific posts or particular individuals. I hope this respects the anonymity and privacy of people sufficiently—but I understand that this may feel like I'm pulling back a curtain that exposes too much and betrays confidences. I hope that the ethical work I'm trying to engage regarding faculty self-reflection and reflection on students' well-being justifies what may feel like a trespass. I want to balance the ethics of social media privacy with my allegiance to students and the damage that I think these kinds of posts, taken for granted, uncritically made and received, do. Privacy cannot and should not function to shield unethical practices from scrutiny.

19 Remember that we as faculty aren't always perfectly transparent or honest with, say, university administration, whom we don't always trust, because administrators don't always act in our best interests or recognize our humanity or arbitrate our professional lives transparently and consistently. We often must maneuver around administration; it makes sense our students would feel they need to maneuver around us.

20 I want to thank my first academic mentor and longtime friend Max Grossman for this simple and brilliant formulation. She said it to me one day when we were casually talking teaching, before I was even aware of disability studies and disability justice, and it has stayed with me, and undergirded so much of my work, since.

21 Colleague and friend James McMaster reminded me in a conversation on teaching that we often project onto students our own academic desires and goals and therefore believe they need to learn all the things we think they need to learn, instead of seeing them as having their own educational goals and us as eminently *unqualified* to teach them about how to do anything other than what we do!

22 Stommel, "Ungrading: A Bibliography"; Stommel, "Ungrading: An Introduction"; Stommel, "Ungrading: An FAQ"; Blum, *Ungrading*; Nilson, *Specifications Grading*; Nilson, "Yes, Virginia."

23 As some disability justice folks have noted in the ableism of writing norms that make little room for neurodivergence and reading and writing disabilities, norms that also, of course, have very classed and racialized roots. See Ladau, "Emily Ladau on Supported Storytelling."

24 Georgetown's instructional development unit offers alternative grading systems on its website and additional resources such as "teaching circles," faculty small groups for discussing pedagogical approaches such as ungrading. CNDLS, "Alternative Modes of Grading"; CNDLS, "Teaching Circles."

25 Stommel, "Ungrading: An FAQ."

26 Mingus, "Forced Intimacy."

27 Thank you to Lawrence for this line and its framing.

28 Ungrading and spec grading, as well as experimental educational projects like Dark Study (https://www.darkstudy.net/), all creatively try to nurture more fairness, equity, and care in the learning process. Some folks have rethought teaching specifically in terms of the pandemic, recognizing students' cumulative exhaustion and intentionally creating structures to "mitigate fatigue rather than contribute to it." Aimi Hamraie reminds us that we are bodies in the classroom and that learning is an embodied process. Becky Thompson, *Teaching with Tenderness*, also explores a body-based pedagogy, though less through disability justice approaches and more through holistic, ritual, and movement approaches. Blinne, *Grading Justice*; Helms, Kirby, and Merrill, "Designing for Fatigue"; Roberts, "Hamraie, Aimi."

29 See chapter 4 for an exploration into the investments of the professoriate and the tenure track's ties to university agendas—and academic meritocracy as an object of misplaced faith.

bibliography

Ahmed, Sara. *Complaint!* Durham, NC: Duke University Press, 2021.

Ahmed, Sara. *On Being Included: Racism and Diversity in Institutional Life.* Durham, NC: Duke University Press, 2012.

Anzaldúa, Gloria, and Cherríe Moraga, eds. *This Bridge Called My Back: Writings by Radical Women of Color.* Albany: State University of New York Press, 1981.

Asian American Psychological Association. "Suicide among Asian Americans." May 2012. http://www.apa.org/pi/oema/resources/ethnicity-health/asian -american/suicide-fact-sheet.pdf.

Baik, Crystal, Vivian Truong, Amita Manghnani, Diane Wong, Lena Sze, Minju Bae, and Preeti Sharma. "Dwelling in Unwellness: A/P/A Voices." *Journal of Asian American Studies* 25, no. 3 (fall 2022): 493–515.

Berg, Maggie, and Barbara K. Seeber. *The Slow Professor: Challenging the Culture of Speed in the Academy.* Toronto: University of Toronto Press, 2016.

Berlant, Lauren. *Cruel Optimism.* Durham, NC: Duke University Press, 2011.

Blinne, Kristen C. *Grading Justice: Teacher-Activist Approaches to Assessment.* Lanham, MD: Lexington, 2021.

Blum, Susan D., ed. *Ungrading: Why Rating Students Undermines Learning (and What to Do Instead).* Morgantown: West Virginia University Press, 2020.

Brown, Nicole, and Jennifer Leigh, eds. *Ableism in Academia: Theorising Experiences of Disabilities and Chronic Illnesses in Higher Education.* London: UCL Press, 2020.

Carter, Angela M. "Teaching with Trauma: Trigger Warnings, Feminism, and Disability Pedagogy." *Disability Studies Quarterly* 35, no. 2 (2015). https://dsq-sds .org/article/view/4652/3935.

Centers for Disease Control and Prevention. "Deaths, Percent of Total Deaths, and Death Rates for the 15 Leading Causes of Death in 5-Year Age Groups, by Race and Hispanic Origin, and Sex: United States, 2017." December 31, 2018. https://www.cdc.gov/nchs/data/dvs/lcwk/lcwk1_hr_2017-a.pdf.

Chapman, Gary. *The Five Love Languages: How to Express Heartfelt Commitment to Your Mate*. Chicago: Northfield Publishing, 1992.

Chiang, Mark. *The Cultural Capital of Asian American Studies: Autonomy and Representation in the University*. New York: New York University Press, 2009.

Clare, Eli. *Brilliant Imperfection: Grappling with Cure*. Durham, NC: Duke University Press, 2017.

CNDLS. "Alternative Modes of Grading." Georgetown University. Accessed March 2022. https://cndls.georgetown.edu/alternative-modes-of-grading/.

CNDLS. "Teaching Circles." Georgetown University. Accessed March 2022. https://cndls.georgetown.edu/teaching-communities/.

Coates, Ta-Nehisi. *Between the World and Me*. New York: Penguin Random House Audio, 2015.

Connelly, Rachel, and Kristen Ghodsee. *Professor Mommy: Finding Work-Family Balance in Academia*. Lanham, MD: Rowman and Littlefield, 2011.

Dixon, Ejeris, and Leah Lakshmi Piepzna-Samarasinha, eds. *Beyond Survival Strategies and Stories from the Transformative Justice Movement*. Chico, CA: AK Press, 2020.

Dolmage, Jay T. *Academic Ableism: Disability and Higher Education*. Ann Arbor: University of Michigan Press, 2017.

Dolmage, Jay T. "Universal Design: Places to Start." *Disability Studies Quarterly* 35, no. 2 (2015). https://dsq-sds.org/article/view/4632/3946.

Dungy, Camille T. *Guidebook to Relative Strangers: Journeys into Race, Motherhood, and History*. New York: Norton, 2017.

Eng, David, and Shinhee Han. *Racial Melancholia, Racial Dissociation: On the Social and Psychic Lives of Asian Americans*. Durham, NC: Duke University Press, 2019.

Evans, Elrena, and Caroline Grant, eds. *Mama PhD: Women Write about Motherhood and Academic Life*. New Brunswick, NJ: Rutgers University Press, 2008.

Fazackerley, Anna. "'My Students Never Knew': The Lecturer Who Lived in a Tent." *Guardian*, October 30, 2021. https://www.theguardian.com/education/2021/oct/30/my-students-never-knew-the-lecturer-who-lived-in-a-tent.

Ferguson, Roderick A. *The Reorder of Things: The University and Its Pedagogies of Minority Difference*. Minneapolis: University of Minnesota Press, 2012.

Freire, Paulo. *Pedagogy of the Oppressed*. Translated by Myra Bergman Ramos. New York: Herder and Herder, 1970.

Garvis, Susanne, and Alison L. Black, eds. *Lived Experiences of Women in Academia: Metaphors, Manifestos and Memoir*. New York: Taylor and Francis, 2018.

Georgetown University. "From Accommodations to Access." *What We Are Learning about Learning*. Podcast, season 2, episode 2, October 2021. Center for New Designs in Learning and Scholarship. https://instructionalcontinuity.georgetown.edu/resources/cndls-podcast/cndls-podcast-season-two-episode-two/.

Georgetown University. "Georgetown University Health Education Services." Accessed March 29, 2022. https://studenthealth.georgetown.edu/health -promotion/.

Georgetown University. "Spirit of Georgetown." Accessed January 2022. https:// missionandministry.georgetown.edu/mission/spirit-of-georgetown.

Gill, Carol J. "A Psychological View of Disability Culture." *Disability Studies Quarterly* 15, no. 4 (1995): 16–19.

Gutiérrez y Muhs, Gabriella, Yolanda Flores Niemann, Carmen G. González, and Angela P. Harris, eds. *Presumed Incompetent: The Intersections of Race and Class for Women in Academia*. Denver: Utah State University Press, 2012.

Gutiérrez y Muhs, Gabriella, Yolanda Flores Niemann, Carmen G. González, and Angela P. Harris, eds. *Presumed Incompetent II: Race, Class, Power, and Resistance of Women in Academia*. Denver: Utah State University Press, 2020.

Hamraie, Aimi. *Building Access: Universal Design and the Politics of Disability*. 3rd ed. Minneapolis: University of Minnesota Press, 2017.

Hamraie, Aimi, and Mimi Khúc. "Disability Justice and Access-Centered Pedagogy in the Pandemic." Autistic Women and Non-binary Network, February 28, 2021. https://awnnetwork.org/webinars/disability-justice-access -centered-pedagogy-in-the-pandemic/.

Harney, Stefano, and Fred Moten. *The Undercommons: Fugitive Planning and Black Study*. Wivenhoe, UK: Minor Compositions, 2013.

Harris, Adam. "The Death of an Adjunct." *Atlantic*, April 8, 2019. https://www .theatlantic.com/education/archive/2019/04/adjunct-professors-higher -education-thea-hunter/586168/.

Hedva, Johanna. "Sick Woman Theory." *The Asian American Literary Review* 7, no. 2 (fall/winter 2016); 10, no. 2 (fall/winter 2019).

Helms, Nic, Cait Kirby, and Asia Merrill. "Designing for Fatigue." Hybrid Pedagogy, January 27, 2022. https://hybridpedagogy.org/designing-for -fatigue/.

Hoeller, Keith, ed. *Equality for Contingent Faculty: Overcoming the Two-Tier System*. Nashville, TN: Vanderbilt University Press, 2014.

hooks, bell. *Teaching to Transgress: Education as the Practice of Freedom*. New York: Routledge, 1994.

Kafer, Alison. *Feminist Queer Crip*. Bloomington: Indiana University Press, 2013.

Kang, Simi. "What Is Refugee Resilience? Reframing Survival under Environmental Sacrifice." *American Studies (AMSJ)* 61, no. 3 (2022): 43–76.

Kelsky, Karen. "The Dreaded Teaching Statement: Eight Pitfalls." The Professor Is In blog, September 12, 2016. https://theprofessorisin.com/2016/09/12 /thedreadedteachingstatement/.

Kerschbaum, Stephanie L., Laura T. Eisenman, and James M. Jones, eds. *Negotiating Disability: Disclosure and Higher Education*. Ann Arbor: University of Michigan Press, 2017.

Khúc, Mimi. "Living Under Siege." *Black Girl Dangerous* (blog), September 23, 2013. https://www.bgdblog.org/2013/09/living-under-siege/.

Khúc, Mimi. "Making Mental Health: A Journey in Love Letters." *South Atlantic Quarterly* 120, no. 2 (April 2021): 369–88.

Khúc, Mimi, ed. "Open in Emergency: A Special Issue on Asian American Mental Health." Special issue, *The Asian American Literary Review* 7, no. 2 (fall/winter 2016).

Khúc, Mimi, ed. "Open in Emergency: A Special Issue on Asian American Mental Health, Second Edition." Special issue, *The Asian American Literary Review* 10, no. 2 (fall/winter 2019).

Khúc, Mimi. "The Revolution Is in the Heart." TEDxUMD, March 9, 2017. https://www.youtube.com/watch?v=3mBRcSH5IHY.

Khúc, Mimi. "Writing While Adjunct: A Contingent Pedagogy of Unwellness." In *Crip Authorship: Disability as Method*, edited by Rebecca Sanchez and Mara Mills. New York: New York University Press, 2023.

Kim, Jina B. "Love in the Time of Sickness: On Disability, Race, and Intimate Partner Violence." *The Asian American Literary Review* 10, no. 2 (fall/winter 2019).

Kim, Jina B. "'People of the Apokalis': Spatial Disability and the Bhopal Disaster." *Disability Studies Quarterly* 34, no. 3 (2014). https://dsq-sds.org/article/view/3795/3271.

Kovalik, Daniel. "Death of an Adjunct." *Pittsburgh Post-Gazette*, September 18, 2013. https://www.post-gazette.com/opinion/Op-Ed/2013/09/18/Death-of-an-adjunct/stories/201309180224.

Ladau, Emily. "Emily Ladau on Supported Storytelling." The Money, Creative Futures, Ford Foundation. Accessed April 6, 2022. https://www.ford foundation.org/news-and-stories/big-ideas/creative-futures/?popup=emily-ladau.

Lee, Amber, Linda Luu, Kevin Park, Mimi Khúc, and Lawrence-Minh Bùi Davis. "An Insurgent Manual on Organizing for Asian American Studies." Unpublished typescript, September 5, 2022.

Lee, James Kyung-Jin. *Pedagogies of Woundedness: Illness, Memoir, and the Ends of the Model Minority.* Philadelphia: Temple University Press, 2022.

Lee, James Kyung-Jin. "Pedagogies of Woundedness: Illness, Memoir, and the Ends of the Model Minority." Invited talk, Health Humanities Research Seminar, University of Texas at Austin, Zoom, March 8, 2022.

Lewis, Talila A. "January 2021 Working Definition of Ableism." *Talila A. Lewis* (blog), January 1, 2021. https://www.talilalewis.com/blog/january-2021-working-definition-of-ableism.

Linton, Simi. *My Body Politic: A Memoir.* Ann Arbor: University of Michigan Press, 2005.

Lorde, Audre. *Sister Outsider.* Trumansburg, NY: Crossing Press, 1984.

Mingus, Mia. "Changing the Framework: Disability Justice." *Leaving Evidence* (blog), February 12, 2011. https://leavingevidence.wordpress.com/2011/02/12/changing-the-framework-disability-justice/.

Mingus, Mia. "Forced Intimacy: An Ableist Norm." *Leaving Evidence* (blog), August

6, 2017. https://leavingevidence.wordpress.com/2017/08/06/forced
-intimacy-an-ableist-norm/.

Mitchell, Nick. "Summertime Selves (On Professionalization)." *New Inquiry*,
October 4, 2019. https://thenewinquiry.com/summertime-selves-on
-professionalization/.

Muriente, Sofía Gallisá. "Sofía Gallisá Muriente on Community as the Basic Unit
of Survival." The Money, Creative Futures, Ford Foundation. Accessed April
6, 2022. https://www.fordfoundation.org/news-and-stories/big-ideas
/creative-futures/?popup=sofia-gallisa-muriente.

National Center for Faculty Diversity and Development. "Institutional
Membership." Accessed October 2021. https://www.facultydiversity.org
/membership/.

National Center for Faculty Diversity and Development. "NCFDD Core Curriculum." Accessed October 2021. https://www.facultydiversity.org/curriculum/.

Nguyen, Mimi Thi. *The Gift of Freedom: Debt, and Other Refugee Passages*. Durham,
NC: Duke University Press, 2012.

Nguyen, Mimi Thi. "The Refugee." *The Asian American Literary Review* 7, no. 2 (fall/
winter 2016); 10, no. 2 (fall/winter 2019).

Nilson, Linda. *Specifications Grading: Restoring Rigor, Motivating Students, and Saving
Faculty Time*. Sterling, VA: Stylus, 2014.

Nilson, Linda. "Yes, Virginia, There's a Better Way to Grade." *Inside Higher Ed*,
January 19, 2016. https://www.insidehighered.com/views/2016/01/19/new
-ways-grade-more-effectively-essay.

Ninh, erin Khuê. "Harvard's Bad Counsel." *Reappropriate* (blog), May 1, 2021.
http://reappropriate.co/2021/05/harvards-bad-counsel/.

Ninh, erin Khuê. "Ingratitude: A Cultural Theory of Power in Asian American
Women's Literature." PhD diss., University of California, Berkeley, 2005.

Ninh, erin Khuê. *Ingratitude: The Debt-Bound Daughter in Asian American Literature*.
New York: New York University Press, 2011.

Ninh, erin Khuê. *Passing for Perfect: College Impostors and Other Model Minorities*.
Philadelphia: Temple University Press, 2021.

Noh, Eliza. "Asian American Women and Suicide: Problems of Responsibility and
Healing." *Women and Therapy* 30, no. 3/4 (2007): 87–107.

Noh, Eliza (Lisa Park). "A Letter to My Sister." In *Making More Waves: New Writing
by Asian American Women*, edited by Elaine H. Kim, Lilia V. Villanueva, and
Asian Women United of California, 65–71. Boston: Beacon, 1997.

Noor-Oshiro, Amelia. "Asian American Young Adults Are the Only Racial Group
with Suicide as Their Leading Cause of Death, So Why Is No One Talking
about This?" *The Conversation*, April 23, 2021. https://theconversation.com
/asian-american-young-adults-are-the-only-racial-group-with-suicide-as-
their-leading-cause-of-death-so-why-is-no-one-talking-about-this-158030.

Perry, Imani. *Breathe: A Letter to My Sons*. Boston: Beacon Press, 2019.

Piepzna-Samarasinha, Leah Lakshmi. *Care Work: Dreaming Disability Justice*. Vancouver: Arsenal Pulp Press, 2018.

Price, Devon. *Laziness Does Not Exist*. New York: Simon and Schuster Audio, 2022.

Price, Devon. "Laziness Does Not Exist, but Unseen Barriers Do." *Human Parts*, March 23, 2018. https://humanparts.medium.com/laziness-does-not-exist -3af27e312d01.

Price, Margaret. *Mad at School: Rhetorics of Mental Disability and Academic Life*. Ann Arbor: University of Michigan Press, 2011.

Price, Margaret. "Time Harms: Disabled Faculty Navigating the Accommodations Loop." *South Atlantic Quarterly* 120, no. 2 (spring 2021): 257–77.

The Professor Is In. "Unstuck: The Art of Productivity." Accessed November 2021. https://theprofessorisin.com/unstuck-the-art-of-productivity/.

Quart, Alissa. "Really Giving: Four Ways to Democratize Philanthropy." *Inside Philanthropy*, February 18, 2021. https://www.insidephilanthropy.com/home /2021/2/18/really-giving-four-ways-to-democratize-philanthropy.

Roberts, Leah Marion. "Hamraie, Aimi." *Leading Lines*. Podcast, episode 105, February 2021. https://soundcloud.com/leadinglines/episode-105-aimi-hamraie.

Said, Edward. *Orientalism*. New York: Pantheon, 1978.

Samuels, Ellen. "Six Ways of Looking at Crip Time." *Disability Studies Quarterly* 37, no. 3 (2017). https://dsq-sds.org/article/view/5824/4684.

Samuels, Ellen, and Elizabeth Freeman, eds. "Crip Temporalities." Special issue, *South Atlantic Quarterly* 120, no. 2 (April 2021).

Schalk, Sami. "Coming to Claim Crip: Disidentification with/in Disability Studies." *Disability Studies Quarterly* 33, no. 2 (2013). https://dsq-sds.org/article /view/3705/3240.

Schlund-Vials, Cathy, ed. *Flashpoints for Asian American Studies*. New York: Fordham University Press, 2018.

Shomura, Chad. "ChadCat's Corner of Heart-to-Hearts: A Public Feelings Project." *The Asian American Literary Review* 7, no. 2 (fall/winter 2016); 10, no. 2 (fall/winter 2019).

Siagatonu, Terisa. "Queer Check-Ins: Nine Heavens." Smithsonian Asian Pacific American Center. 2019. https://vimeo.com/331825899.

Sins Invalid. *Skin, Tooth, and Bone: The Basis of Movement Is Our People: A Disability Justice Primer*. 2nd ed. Sins Invalid, 2019.

Sins Invalid. "10 Principles of Disability Justice." September 17, 2015. https://www .sinsinvalid.org/blog/10-principles-of-disability-justice.

Spade, Dean. *Mutual Aid: Building Solidarity during This Crisis (and the Next)*. New York: Verso, 2020.

Stommel, Jesse. "Ungrading: A Bibliography." *Jesse Stommel* (blog), March 3, 2020. https://www.jessestommel.com/ungrading-a-bibliography/.

Stommel, Jesse. "Ungrading: An FAQ." *Jesse Stommel* (blog), February 6, 2020. https://www.jessestommel.com/ungrading-an-faq/.

Stommel, Jesse. "Ungrading: An Introduction." *Jesse Stommel* (blog), June 11, 2021. https://www.jessestommel.com/ungrading-an-introduction/.

Teotico, Catherine, and Wenhui Yang. "Managing Anti-Asian Racism and Xenophobia during the COVID-19 Pandemic." Harvard University, March 2021.

https://web.archive.org/web/20210331123255/https:/camhs.huhs.harvard.edu /files/camhs/files/anti-asian_racism_flyer.pdf?m=1590165422.

Thom, Kai Cheng. "Drinking from Your Tears: Re-framing Psychotherapy." *The Asian American Literary Review* 10, no. 2 (fall/winter 2019).

Thom, Kai Cheng. *I Hope We Choose Love: A Trans Girl's Notes from the End of the World*. Vancouver: Arsenal Pulp Press, 2019.

Thom, Kai Cheng. "The Myth of Mental Health." *The Asian American Literary Review* 7, no. 2 (fall/winter 2016); 10, no. 2 (fall/winter 2019).

Thompson, Becky. *Teaching with Tenderness: Toward an Embodied Practice*. Champaign: University of Illinois Press, 2017.

Tran, Truong. *The Book of Other: Small in Comparison*. Los Angeles: Kaya Press, 2021.

University of Chicago. "2019 Conference: Break the Silence." Accessed March 2021. https://www.uchicagobreakthesilence.com/2019-conference.

Valverde, Kieu Linh Caroline, and Wei Ming Dariotis, eds. *Fight the Tower: Asian American Women Scholars' Resistance and Renewal in the Academy*. New Brunswick, NJ: Rutgers University Press, 2019.

Wang, Esmé Weijun. *The Collected Schizophrenias*. Minneapolis: Graywolf Press, 2019.

Wheeler, Sika. "Pedagogies of Care, Access, and Vulnerability: A Conversation with Mimi Khúc, Ph.D." Office of Diversity and Inclusion, University of Maryland, April 29, 2020. https://youtu.be/LT3NruQ8GVU.

World Health Organization. "Mental Health." June 2022. https://www.who.int /news-room/fact-sheets/detail/mental-health-strengthening-our-response.

Zola, Irving Kenneth. "Self, Identity and the Naming Question: Reflections on the Language of Disability." *Social Science and Medicine* 36, no. 2 (1993): 167–73.

index

Note: *Page numbers in italics refer to figures.*

Americans with Disabilities Act (ADA), 152, 208

Amherst College, 29, 33, 137

Anand, Raven, 192

ancestral pain, 40, 79

anti-Asian violence, 7, 23, 31, 40–41, 53, 154, 156, 199, 241n6

anti-Blackness, 23

anti-racism, 7, 156

Aranyak, Sanzari, 141

Asian American Literary Review, The (AALR), 6, 19, 22, 26, 236n5

Asian American Literature Festival, 245n3

Asian American Movement, 51

Asian American studies, 4–5, 9, 66, 69, 77, 141, 144, 162, 243n14; and accountability, 112, 116–17, 120–24, 136–37, 243n17; contingent faculty in, 108–38; and mental health, 29, 46, 49, 85–86; and *Open in Emergency*, 15–16, 22; and racism, 156–57; at UMD, 10–11, 63, 108–20, 124, 134–36, 143, 155–56, 244n24, 246n12; and unwellness, 9, 126–27. *See also* Association for Asian American Studies (AAAS)

Asian American Tarot, 7, 9, 15, 45, 89–90, 235n1; The Hangman, 16–17, *plates 1–2*; The Mongrel, 22; The Pandemic, 56–58, *plates 5–6*; and pedagogy, 190, 192, 200; The Student, 22, 50–55, 58, 239n17, *plates 3–4*; Suicide, 60, 61–62, *plates 7–8*; The Village, 22

"Asian Cultural Values" discourse, 48, 68–71, 241n6

aspirational wellness, 8

aspirational whiteness, 240n4, 241n6

assimilation, 9, 65, 70, 240n4, 241n6

Association for Asian American Studies (AAAS), 10–12, 127, 139, 141, 240n26, 244n29; "Our Institutions Don't Care about Us, but Maybe AAAS Can," 128–38

asynchronous teaching and learning, 198, 202, 205

Atlanta mass shooting (2021), 40–41, 154

Ault, Elizabeth, 4

autism, 44, 164, 197

Autistic Women and Nonbinary Network, 197

Bae, Minju, 235n2, 242n1

Baik, Crystal, 235n2, 242n1

Belser, Julia Watts, 168

Berg, Maggie, 139

Berlant, Lauren, 123

BIPOC students, 23, 28, 49, 157, 224

Black Lives Matter, 23, 156

Brown, Lydia X. Z., 43–44, 168, 245n3

Brown, Marisa, 168

Brown, Michael, 128

Bùi, Long, 15

Canvas, 170, 182, 186, 189

capitalism, 7, 26, 48, 71; racial, 14, 47, 103

Carter, Angela M., 198

Chapman, Gary, 73, 79, 241n10

cheating, 161, 174–75, 207

Chen, Mel Y., 140–41

Chew, Camille: The Hangman (Asian American Tarot), 16–17, *plates 1–2*

child care, 52, 103, 150, 197

Chinese colonialism, 68

Christianity, 16

Clare, Eli, 164, 200, 203–4, 236n6

Clark, Audrey Wu, 235

Clark University, 128, 244n29

Coates, Ta-Nehisi, 74, 237n15

colonialism, 62, 68, 168, 236n11, 241n6. *See also* imperialism/empire

commitment to injury, 75–76, 81

community curation, 12, 51, 144

community organizing, 34

community pain, 12, 121

complex personhood, 31, 50

compulsory wellness, 9, 12, 42, 56, 204

conditional belonging, 11, 41, 49, 80

Confucianism, 68–70

consent, 218

content/trigger warnings, 13, 153, 192, 198–99

contingent scholars/faculty, 3, 46, 101, 141, 143, 222, 242n4; and AAAS, 127–39; and pedagogy, 44, 158–60; and UMD, 107–24, 135–37, 243n17. *See also* adjuncts counseling centers, 30–37, 40–42, 46–47, 85–86, 238n3, 238nn5–6, 241n18

COVID-19 pandemic, 7, 63, 81, 103, 106, 138, 225, 228, 235n2, 236n9, 238n6, 242n1, 246n14; and anti-Asian violence, 23, 40, 241n6, 241n18; deaths from, 23, 58, 149, 152; events during, 28, 53–59; and pedagogy, 6, 53, 149–220, 248n28; university responses, 31, 40–42, 52–53, 86–87, 150–54, 223–24, 238n3, 238n11

Crip Camp, 190

crip time, 9, 21, 140–41, 236n7, 246n14. *See also* nonnormative time

critical arts practices, 7, 55, 58, 111–12

critical race studies, 49–50

critical university studies, 4, 24, 108

CTRL+ALT: A Culture Lab on Imagined Futures, 26

cura personalis, 150–53, 162, 175, 177, 218, 221–28

cure ideology, 31, 37, 48, 164, 200, 203–4, 236n6

Dao-Shah, Anh Thang, 130

Dark Study, 248n28

Daus, Gem P., 115

Davis, Lawrence-Minh Bùi, 6, 11, 66, 190, 244n29, 245n3, 248n27; and AALR, 6, 236n5; and *Open in Emergency*, 6, 8–10, 22, 50–51, 54; The Pandemic (Asian American Tarot), 56–58, *plates 5–6*; and pedagogy, 157–59, 214–15; and UMD, 107, 109–18, 121, 135–37, 244n24

debt, 126, 202; filial, 45, 66–68, 71–77, 79–84, 86, 155, 239n17; student, 51

debt-bound daughter, 14, 66

decolonization, 4, 7, 168

Deerinwater, Jen, 168

defiance, 76, 83

deGuzman, Jean-Paul, 244n27

Desai, Jigna, 189

designated failure, 71

diagnosis, 7, 37, 169, 201

Diagnostic and Statistical Manual of Mental Disorders (DSM), 3, 17, 22. See also *DSM: Asian American Edition*

differential unwellness, 5, 12, 14, 21, 48, 105, 121, 162, 196, 209, 217, 242n4

disability justice, 4–5, 70, 123–24, 150–56, 202, 224, 245n3, 246n10, 247n20, 247n23; approach to mental health, 20, 24, 43–44, 248n28; approach to pedagogy, 150–220; and Sloth Professoring, 139–42

disability studies, 7, 16, 49–50, 156, 217, 224, 236n11, 237n13, 247n20; approach to mental health, 4–5, 20, 24, 45, 236n9; approach to pedagogy, 152, 162–202, 236n9; courses in, 43, 63, 150, 152, 162–202; critical, 7–8, 20, 144, 236n9; and meritocracy, 144; and *Open in Emergency*, 8, 22; programs for, 52, 54, 152; and Sloth Professoring, 139–42

Dolmage, Jay, 9, 201, 236n9

domestic violence, 45

@DSinthetimeofCOVID19, 188, 203

DSM: Asian American Edition, 7, 17–22, 25, 25–27, 235n1

Dungy, Camille T., 74

Easton's Nook, 235

Elia, 1, 13–14, 87–88

enablement, 167, 197, 217, 243n9

Eng, David, 240n4, 241n6

ethnic studies, 5, 7, 15, 34, 94, 120–21, 140, 144, 154–55

Facebook, 118, 150, 205, 246n18

fairness, 97, 115, 118, 122, 153, 161, 173, 208–11, 213, 248n28

feminism, 44; queer of color, 7; queer women of color, 9; women of color, 70, 237n15

feminist studies, 49, 66, 112, 154–56

Ferguson uprising (2014), 128, 156

Fink, Jennifer, 168

Flipgrid, 198

Floyd, George, 156

Fong, Kelly, 244n27

forced intimacy, 214

Ford Foundation, 245n3

Freeman, Elizabeth, 140, 235, 237n13, 246n14